READING ENGLISH POETRY

READING **English Poetry**

JAMES G. TAAFFE

JOHN LINCKS

 THE FREE PRESS, NEW YORK

PR1175
T27

printing number

1   2   3   4   5   6   7   8   9   10

Contents

Introduction

This book is one solution to the problem of dealing adequately in the classroom with some major English poets. Other books now available either slight the poets by including too few poems for an in-depth study, or they include enough poems, but without the study material to help in the reading of the poems. Before compiling the poems in this anthology, we carefully examined the standard English literature anthologies, and our personal impressions were substantiated. The same few poems were anthologized over and over again, as though some divine power had handed down tablets containing the canon of the few poems that students ought to read. Lynch and Evans in their *High School English Textbooks*, 1963, commented on how the major poets were slighted in favor of anthologizing a few well-known poems by a large number of poets, and no textbook either for college or high school has adequately remedied this shortcoming.

The subtitle of this book might appropriately be *For Study in Depth*, for we have included here a rich collection of poems by twelve poets worth examining in depth. The decision as to the twelve poets to be included was influenced both by modern critical opinion and traditional emphasis. Although modern critical opinion was considered, the readability of the selections and their adequacy to represent the best of the period were the final criteria.

One other criterion used in the selection of the poems was the classroom teachability. Short poems are convenient for classroom discussion; to go beyond the simple statement in a poem and appreciate it as a work of art, the reader must be aware of the structure and techniques used to embody the statement. This process takes much time and frequent repetition before a reader can appreciate the form, the meaning, and the appropriateness of the form to the meaning as he reads a poem. Except for Milton's "Lycidas," and poetry by Pope, the poetry discussed in this book is short; a few long poems appear in the additional reading for those who would like such representation. We considered "Lycidas" too great a poem to eliminate because of its length, and it is the only long poem discussed in detail and followed by study questions. Because no excerpts are included, Pope, who wrote little else but long poems, is represented by some long poems. The sonnet, which is a perfect teaching instrument to convey the artistic harmony of form and meaning, is well represented. Any of the twelve poets who wrote sonnets is represented here by some of his best sonnets. Through these sonnets also, the reader can see the continuity of the tradition of English poetry; he can see in this collection how the form is used and modified from Shakespeare to Hopkins.

The richness of seventeenth-century English poetry, slighted in many anthologies, is particularly evident in this collection, and the substantial selections from Alexander Pope and William Blake allow the student to make meaningful generalities about eighteenth-century poetry. From Shakespeare to William Butler Yeats, the periods of English literature are evenly represented by two

Elizabethans, two seventeenth-century poets, two eighteenth-century poets, two early nineteenth-century poets, three late nineteenth-century poets (Hopkins might more appropriately be considered a twentieth-century poet), and one twentieth-century poet.

The spelling and punctuation of the earlier poetry in this collection have been modernized, and many difficult words and allusions have been glossed to facilitate reading without consulting another book for reference. The modernization of the spelling does not alter the basic pronunciation or syllabification; the poetry reads aloud as it would with earlier spelling, which is just another obstacle to the student's getting into the heart of the poem.

The poetry, with the accompanying discussions and questions, has been used in a variety of classes. For their help in the proving of this material we thank Father John Kraker, Eloise Manning, Mildred Montain, Renee Betz, Sam Schulman and Lyn Thomas. And finally, for her help in the preparation of the manuscript, we thank Reggie Lincks.

J. G. T. and J. L.

Cleveland, Ohio, 1967

Using this book

This book offers in depth the work of twelve major English poets arranged for chronological study, but the poetry together with the discussions might be consulted as a guide, or handbook, to the reading of some important English poems. The poetry is arranged chronologically to convey better a sense of the historical context. The discussions which supplement the poetry deal not only with the problems of reading individual poems, but they also trace influences of earlier poets on later ones, and often introduce comparative considerations, such as similar or diverging treatments of a recurring theme.

READING POEMS, NOT POETS

Because the philosophy of this book is that the reader should look at the *poem* rather than the poet, most of the biographical information is found in an appendix. The notes which follow the poems contain information that is essential to the reading of the poem, but not if the background information is only of biographical interest. The "sense of the poet" who produced the poems may best be discovered in the poems themselves; indeed, this may be one of the major reasons to read any literature. Rather than expecting complete essays on Jonson's or Pope's "poetics" and then going to their poems to see how they mirror these attitudes, *the reader should expect to begin with the poem.* For those who want supplementary biographical data, the appendix at the back of the book provides some information related to the literary careers of the twelve poets.

TECHNIQUES OF LITERARY STUDY

In the reading of poems, not poets, the reader must familiarize himself with certain techniques, and these are introduced progressively as one moves chronologically through the book. Particular emphasis is placed on mastering useful literary terminology for a more precise discussion of the techniques of poetry. By the time the reader has reached the modern poets, he should be capable of more complex kinds of understanding. The reader is repeatedly encouraged to look at the poems for what they are in themselves, and to read, understand, and appreciate them, not only for what they say, but for how they say it. Experiencing the poem as a work of art is a different kind of experience from reading paraphrasable prose meaning out of it. To appreciate the poem as a work of art, the reader must be aware of the techniques and the structure as he "reads" the meaning and experiences the feeling. To encourage the reader to aspire to this extra level of experience, the basic techniques are described and the necessary terms are supplied. When a literary term is introduced for the first time, it is italicized as a reminder to the reader that he can find the definition in the glossary at the back of the book. For convenience, all the poems are numbered every four or five lines to help the reader perceive the structure of the poem.

READING ENGLISH POETRY

Sonnet 1

From fairest creatures we desire increase,*   *offspring*
That thereby beauty's rose might never die,
But as* the riper should by time decease,   *For when*
4 His tender heir might bear his memory;
But thou, contracted* to thine own bright eyes,   *engaged*
Feed'st thy light's flame with self-substantial* fuel,   *made of one's*
Making a famine where abundance lies,   *own substance*
8 Thyself thy foe, to thy sweet self too cruel.
Thou that art now the world's fresh ornament
And only herald to the gaudy spring,
Within thine own bud buriest thy content*   *contents*
12 And, tender churl,* mak'st waste in niggarding.   *a miserly boor*
Pity the world, or else this glutton be,
To eat the world's due, by the grave and thee.

UNDERSTANDING SHAKESPEARE'S LANGUAGE—USING THE GLOSS

The marginal *gloss* will help you through your first reading of this sonnet. Closer examination of the *diction*, however, will reveal the richness of Shakespeare's language. The word "increase," for instance, in line 1, means more in context than simply "offspring"; it suggests what the speaker wishes from "fairest creatures"— that is, that they propagate and multiply what they are. The result is a *paradox*; one wishes that "fairest creatures" could become more fair. In line 5 Shakespeare uses the word "contracted," which is glossed as "engaged," but the careful reader will recognize in "contracted" a contrast to "increase." Rather than propagate and enlarge, the one addressed in the sonnet has withdrawn into himself. The suggestion of withdrawal is reintroduced in line 11 where the subject is seen not as a rose but as an immature spring bud. He is entirely contained with the bud, so all his contentment (a *pun* on "content") is found in himself. The speaker has hoped that his subject will provide a "tender" (young) heir to remind the world of his beauty; but the attitude of the one addressed is too "tender" (immature), for he wastes his beauty by keeping it to himself. This brief consideration of the complexity of Shakespeare's language will caution the reader to use the gloss only as a point of departure to a fuller understanding of the poet's language. Definitions of literary terms contained in this discussion and all those that follow may be found on pages 250-254. Analyze the diction by answering the following questions.

1. How are terms like "eat," "famine," "abundance," "niggarding," and "glutton" related?

2. How do terms like "rose," "riper," "fresh," and "bud" describe the subject of the sonnet?

* * *

Sonnet 2

When forty winters shall besiege thy brow
And dig deep trenches in thy beauty's field,
Thy youth's proud livery, so gazed on now,
4 Will be a tattered weed* of small worth held: *shabby garment*
Then being asked where all thy beauty lies,
Where all the treasure of thy lusty days,
To say, within thine own deep-sunken eyes
8 Were an all-eating shame and thriftless* praise.   *wastful*
How much more praise deserved thy beauty's use
If thou couldst answer, "This fair child of mine
Shall sum my count* and make my old excuse,'°   *total my account
12 Proving his beauty by succession thine."   °excuse in old age
This were to be new made when thou art old,
And see thy blood warm when thou feel'st it cold.

RELATING DICTION TO CONTEXT

When you look up "livery" (line 3) in a dictionary, you will find a definition like the following: "An identifying uniform such as was formerly worn by feudal retainers or is now worn by servants or those in some particular group, trade, etc." Relating this definition to context, however, requires that the reader ignore a substantial part of the dictionary definition and recognize Shakespeare's metaphorical use of the term; for in this instance, the literal definition is extended and generalized to suggest that beauty is youth's clothing, clothing which will in time become the "tattered weed" of old age.

QUESTIONS

1. The word "livery" is associated with fuedal aristocracy. What other words in the first quatrain are related to feudal life?

2. How is "succession" (line 12) related to the diction of the first quatrain?

* * *

Sonnet 15

When I consider everything that grows
Holds in perfection but a little moment,
That this huge stage presenteth nought but shows
4 Whereon the stars in secret influence comment;
When I perceive that men as plants increase,
Cheered and checked even by the selfsame sky,
Vaunt* in their youthful sap, at height decrease,   *boast*
8 And wear their brave state out of memory:
Then the conceit* of this inconstant stay   *thought*
Sets you most rich in youth before my sight,
Where wasteful Time debateth with Decay
12 To change your day of youth to sullied night;
   And, all in war with Time for love of you,
   As he takes from you, I engraft* you new.   *graft (as a plant)*

DICTION AND IMAGE

Like Sonnets 1 and 2, this sonnet is concerned with the *theme* of mutability (change). While time is the lover's constant enemy, the poet can try to immortalize his subject in poetry; he can "engraft" (propagate or implant) his beloved in a little song (a sonnet). The word "engraft" is related to the numerous words associated with plants and growth in the poem.

QUESTIONS

   1. What words in the sonnet are related to "engraft"?
   2. How does the diction of the second *quatrain* create a plant image?

* * *

Sonnet 17

Who will believe my verse in time to come,
If it were filled with your most high deserts?
Though yet, heaven knows, it is but as a tomb
4 Which hides your life and shows not half your parts.
If I could write the beauty of your eyes
And in fresh numbers* number all your graces, *verses*
The age to come would say, "This poet lies—
8 Such heavenly touches ne'er touched earthly faces."
So should my papers, yellowed with their age,
Be scorned, like old men of less truth than tongue,
And your true rights be termed a poet's rage
12 And stretched meter* of an antique° song. *exaggerated poetry*
 But were some child of yours alive that time, °fantastic
 You should live twice—in it and in my rime.

QUESTIONS

1. In line 3 the poet refers to his sonnet as a "tomb." How does this word appropriately identify in context the sonnet's relationship to the person addressed?

2. In line 6 what is the effect of a word used as different parts of speech?

3. In line 8 what is the effect of "touches . . . touched"? What effect does this second instance have upon the first ("numbers number")?

4. In lines 11 and 12 what is the cumulative effect of the words "rage," "stretched meter," and "antique"?

5. What is the appropriateness of "rime" (associated with "verse," "numbers," "papers," and "song") as the last word in the sonnet?

* * *

Sonnet 60

Like as the waves make towards the pebbled shore,
So do our minutes hasten to their end;
Each changing place with that which goes before;
4 In sequent toil all forwards do contend.
Nativity, once in the main* of light,   *sea; center*
Crawls to maturity, wherewith being crowned,
Crooked* eclipses 'gainst his glory fight,   *malignant*
8 And time that gave doth now his gift confound.*   *destroy*
Time doth transfix* the flourish set on youth   *pierce*
And delves the parallels in beauty's brow,
Feeds on the rarities of nature's truth,
12 And nothing stands but for his scythe to mow:
     And yet to times* in hope° my verse shall stand,   *in the future
     Praising thy worth, despite his cruel hand.   °hopefully*

IMAGE PATTERNS

Shakespeare's Sonnet 60 opens with a generalized and relatively impersonal *image* of the natural movement of waves towards the shore. Their incessant action is likened to the constant passage of time to emphasize the mutability theme. In a matter-of-fact tone, the speaker states a truth we all accept. The imagery in the second quatrain deals more specifically with man's struggle, and the diction begins to suggest an attitude towards time's passage. Time can be man's malignant enemy ("crooked eclipses"), fighting against his best efforts, and, seemingly indulgent, time can also destroy his gift of life. The reader begins to recognize the speaker's deepening involvement in the subject and his increasingly human and emotional reaction. The third quatrain becomes more specific as the image suggests how time "feeds on" the wonders of youth. The speaker envisions time as increasingly voracious; it becomes the eternal reaper, cutting down the beauty we cherish. While the *argument* remains a logical one, the poem has become increasingly emotional. Yet, ironically, the *couplet* presents what appears to be an illogical statement. The speaker appears to be saying that poems will outlive time: in spite of what he knows is true, he wants to believe the *cliche* that "my verse shall stand." The paradox is an emotionally charged one, and the poem seems to be saying that only through an irrational outburst that we know is not true can we try to fool ourselves that it is true. The poet has argued logically in lines 1–12 and, without rejecting his logic or the truth of his statements, hopes that somehow his verse, in spite of all he knows, will prove an exception to time's conquest.

1. Each successive quatrain is organized around a separate image: sea, sun, and earth. How is each image developed within its quatrain?
2. How are the image patterns of the first 12 lines interrelated?

* * *

Sonnet 65

Since brass, nor stone, nor earth, nor boundless sea,
But sad mortality o'er-sways their power,
How with this rage shall beauty hold a plea,
4 Whose action is no stronger than a flower?
O, how shall summer's honey breath hold out
Against the wreckful* siege of batt'ring days,   *destructive*
When rocks impregnable are not so stout,
8 Nor gates of steel so strong but Time decays?
O fearful meditation! where, alack,
Shall Time's best jewel from Time's chest* lie hid?   *jewel box*
Or what strong hand can hold his swift foot back,
12 Or who his spoil of beauty can forbid?
    O, none, unless this miracle have might,
    That in black ink my love may still shine bright.

QUESTIONS

1. What is the effect of the progression of the nouns in line 1?
2. What is the source of the *metaphor* in lines 3 and 4? (Consider the specialized vocabulary which uses words like "plea" and "action.")
3. How do the images in lines 1–2 and 3–4 establish the basic contrast of the first quatrain?
4. The poem's basic metaphor is that of a siege. How is this metaphor established in each quatrain?
5. How is the primary contrast in the first quatrain intensified in the second?
6. What other meaning is appropriate to the context for the word "chest" in line 10?
7. The "miracle" in line 13 is the paradox of line 14. What is the paradox?

* * *

Sonnet 33

Full many a glorious morning have I seen
Flatter the mountain tops with sovereign eye,
Kissing with golden face the meadows green,
4 Gilding pale streams with heavenly alchemy;
Anon permit the basest clouds to ride
With ugly rack* on his celestial face,   *clouds*
And from the forlorn world his visage hide,
8 Stealing unseen to west with his disgrace:
Even so my sun one early morn did shine
With all-triumphant splendor on my brow;
But, out alack, he was but one hour mine,
12 The region* cloud hath masked him from me now.   *of the upper air*
    Yet him for this my love no whit disdaineth;
    Suns of the world may stain when heaven's sun
      staineth.

THE STRUCTURE OF SHAKESPEARE'S SONNETS

By now it should be obvious that the Shakespearian sonnet is composed of three quatrains and a rhyming couplet. The *open quatrains* rhyme *abad, cdcd, efef.* One watches for emotional or intellectual progressions among them or for the movements from the impersonal to the personal, from the rational to the irrational, from the abstract to the concrete. Shakespeare may develop one central metaphor in detail from quatrain to quatrain, unifying the entire sonnet, or he may introduce three different, but related, image groups. Usually the couplet functions as a resolution of the preceding lines. This is not to say that the couplet summarizes what has preceded, for it seldom does that; however, it may appear to contradict everything that has gone before, it may suggest an emotional response as opposed to a rational one, or it may suddenly turn the sonnet from the impersonal to the personal. There are as many patterns as there are sonnets.

In Sonnet 33, for instance, the opening quatrain begins with an impersonal observation of the sunrise. The quatrain's imagery suggests the regal nature of the sun and its beams as they move upon mountaintop, meadow and stream. Although the speaker has yet to introduce a personal note into the sonnet, he has personified the sun to prepare us for his later analogy. The second quatrain continues the natural image as the speaker relates how high, windswept clouds often obscure the face of the sun, hiding it from the earth. The behaviour of the clouds somehow disgraces the sun, but the comet suffers silently. The third quatrain personalizes the *analogy* by extending it into the realm of human behaviour. Once the poet's friend (his "sun") shone upon him and transformed him also, but now the "sun" has disappeared. A "cloud" has passed between them. While the first two quatrains have extended the natural observation, the third offers the human analogy. Without alarm and regally aloof, the speaker maintains his love for his friend regardless of the temporary eclipse in their relationship. The speaker's calm acceptance of the present situation resolves the situation by stoical resignation; the final result is our impression that such eclipses are only momentary and always in the nature of things.

* * *

Sonnet 129

Th' expense* of spirit° in a waste of shame   *extravagant loss*
Is lust in action; and till action, lust   °*vital power*
Is perjured, murderous, bloody, full of blame,
4 Savage, extreme, rude, cruel, not to trust;
Enjoyed no sooner but despised straight;
Past reason hunted, and no sooner had,
Past reason hated as a swallowed bait
8 On purpose laid to make the taker mad:
Mad in pursuit, and in possession so;
Had, having, and in quest to have, extreme;
A bliss in proof, and proved, a very woe;
12 Before, a joy proposed; behind, a dream.*   *nightmare*
   All this the world well knows; yet none knows well
   To shun the heaven that leads men to this hell.

QUESTIONS

1. The first line states the topic of Sonnet 129; the extreme emotion of lust. *Paraphrase* the poet's definition of lust in line 1.

2. How does the series in lines 3–4 characterize the speaker's tone?

3. Quatrain 2 describes man after he acts lustfully. What is the effect upon him of his indulgence?

3. What is the *tone* of quatrain 3 compared to that of quatrains 1 and 2?

5. How does quatrain 3 recapitulate the attitudes towards lust in quatrains 1 and 2?

6. What is the relationship of the couplet to the first 12 lines?

* * *

Spring

When daisies pied and violets blue
And lady-smocks all silver-white
And cuckoo-buds of yellow hue
4   Do paint the meadows with delight,
The cuckoo then, on every tree,
Mocks married men; for thus sings he, "Cuckoo;
Cuckoo, cuckoo!"* O, word of fear,   *a homophone for cuckold*
8   Unpleasing to a married ear!

When shepherds pipe on oaten straws,
And merry larks are ploughmen's clocks,
When turtles* tread, and rooks, and daws,   *turtle doves*
4   And maidens bleach their summer smocks,
The cuckoo then, on every tree,
Mocks married men; for thus sings he, "Cuckoo;
Cuckoo, cuckoo!" O, word of fear,
8   Unpleasing to a married ear!

Winter

When icicles hang by the wall,
And Dick the shepherd blows his nail,
And Tom bears logs into the hall,
4   And milk comes frozen home in pail,
When blood is nipped, and ways be foul,
Then nightly sings the staring owl, "Tu-whit,
Tu-who!" a merry note,
8   While greasy Joan doth keel* the pot.   *cool*

When all aloud the wind doth blow,
And coughing drowns the parson's saw,
And birds sit brooding in the snow,
4   And Marian's nose looks red and raw,
When roasted crabs* hiss in the bowl,   *crab apples*
Then nightly sings the staring owl, "Tu-whit,
Tu-who!" a merry note,
8   While greasy Joan doth keel the pot.

TWO SONGS OF SHAKESPEARE

At the conclusion of Shakespeare's *Love's Labor's Lost* are two songs, one in praise of spring, one of winter. The pleasures of spring are the obvious ones of the outdoors; spring is the time of natural renewal. Of course, it is also the season of youth and love, and the song tells us, it is a likely time when wives may make cuckolds of their husbands.

As in a debate, the second speaker presents the claims for the winter season. He is willing to concede the disadvantages of winter—its cold, its muddy roads, its wind, the throat and nasal discomforts we all endure—but his plea for winter is a subtle one. He arranges each stanza to move us indoors, for there we experience the pleasures of his season. Roasted crab apples sizzling in hot cider, steaming soup tended by a perspiring maid, a warm room: these are pleasures all the keener for the cold we know is just outside.

QUESTIONS

1. What is the tone of the refrain which begins, "The cuckoo then, on every tree"? What detail helps establish the tone of the refrain?

2. Compare the tone of the refrain beginning, "Then nightly sings the staring owl," with the tone of the refrain in the spring song.

WHAT TO LOOK FOR IN THE ADDITIONAL READING

The following sonnets treat themes already presented: the immortality of poetry, mutability, the trials of love, and the problems of friendship. Each is glossed for an easier first reading, but, as the discussion has illustrated, the gloss is only a limited aid. You will wish to consider diction in context, various image patterns as they are created by the poet's diction, the relationships between image patterns, various progressions made by successive quatrains, the relationship of the couplet to the quatrains, and the tone. As you read, have a standard desk dictionary readily available, and be sure to check through all the various definitions of a hard word. To begin your readings, paraphrase each quatrain before you attempt any further analysis. While paraphrasing (which is only a means and not an end in itself) you will probably become aware of subtleties of language which previously escaped you. See the discussion following Sonnet 60 (page 5) as an example of how a poet's language can be rephrased in a prose statement.

Sonnet 27

Weary with toil, I haste me to my bed,
The dear repose for limbs with travel tired,
But then begins a journey in my head
4 To work my mind when body's work expired;
For then my thoughts, from far where I abide,
Intend* a zealous pilgrimage to thee,   *make*
And keep my drooping eyelids open wide,
8 Looking on darkness which the blind do see;
Save that my soul's imaginary* sight   *imaginative*
Presents thy shadow to my sightless view,
Which, like a jewel hung in ghastly night,
12 Makes black night beauteous and her old face new.
    Lo thus, by day my limbs, by night my mind,
    For thee and for myself no quiet find.

Sonnet 32

If thou survive my well-contented day
When that churl Death my bones with dust shall cover,
And shalt by fortune once more resurvey
4 These poor rude lines of thy deceased lover,
Compare them with the bett'ring of the time,
And though they be outstripped by every pen,
Reserve them for my love, not for their rime,
8 Exceeded by the height of happier* men.   *fortunate*
O, then vouchsafe me but this loving thought:
"Had my friend's Muse grown with this growing age,
A dearer birth than this his love had brought
12 To march in ranks of better equipage;
    But since he died, and poets better prove,
    Theirs for their style I'll read, his for his love."

Sonnet 34

Why didst thou promise such a beauteous day
And make me travel forth without my cloak,
To let base clouds o'ertake me in my way,
4 Hiding thy bravery in their rotten smoke?
'Tis not enough that through the cloud thou break
To dry the rain on my storm-beaten face,
For no man well of such a salve can speak
8 That heals the wound, and cures not the disgrace:
Nor can thy shame give physic to my grief;
Though thou repent, yet I have still the loss:
Th' offender's sorrow lends but weak relief
12 To him that bears the strong offence's cross.
    Ah, but those tears are pearl which thy love sheeds,*   *sheds*
    And they are rich and ransom all ill deeds.

Sonnet 38

How can my Muse want* subject to invent   *lack*
While thou dost breathe, that pour'st into my verse
Thine own sweet argument,* too excellent   *theme*
4 For every vulgar paper to rehearse?
O, give thyself the thanks if aught in me
Worthy perusal stand against thy sight,
For who's so dumb that cannot write to thee
8 When thou thyself dost give invention light?
Be thou the tenth Muse, ten times more in worth
Than those old nine which rimers invocate,*   *invoke*
And he that calls on thee, let him bring forth
12 Eternal numbers to outlive long date.
    If my slight Muse do please these curious days,
    The pain be mine, but thine shall be the praise.

Sonnet 117

Accuse me thus, that I have scanted* all   *neglected*
Wherein I should your great deserts repay;
Forgot upon your dearest love to call,
4 Whereto all bonds do tie me day by day;
That I have frequent been with unknown minds
And given to time your own dear-purchased right;
That I have hoisted sail to all the winds
8 Which should transport me farthest from your sight.
Book* both my wilfulness and errors down,   *record*
And on just proof surmise accumulate;
Bring me within the level of your frown,
12 But shoot not at me in your wakened hate:
    Since my appeal says I did strive to prove
    The constancy and virtue of your love.

Sonnet 130

My mistress' eyes are nothing like the sun;
Coral is far more red than her lips' red;
If snow be white, why then her breasts are dun;*   *brown*
4 If hairs be wires, black wires grow on her head.
I have seen roses damasked, red and white,
But no such roses see I in her cheeks;
And in some perfumes is there more delight
8 Than in the breath that from my mistress reeks.
I love to hear her speak; yet well I know
That music hath a far more pleasing sound:
I grant I never saw a goddess go;
12 My mistress, when she walks, treads on the ground.
    And yet, by heaven, I think my love as rare
    As any she belied with false compare.

Sonnet 144

Two loves I have, of comfort and despair,
Which like two spirits do suggest* me still: *tempt*
The better angel is a man right fair,
4   The worser spirit a woman colored ill.*   *dark complected*
To win me soon to hell, my female evil
Tempteth my better angel from my side,
And would corrupt my saint to be a devil,
8   Wooing his purity with her foul pride.
And whether that my angel be turned fiend
Suspect I may, yet not directly tell;
But being both from me, both to each friend,
12   I guess one angel in another's hell.
        Yet this shall I ne'er know, but live in doubt,
        Till my bad angel fire my good one out.

Sonnet 146

Poor soul, the center of my sinful earth,*   *body*
[Fooled by] these rebel pow'rs that thee array,*   *dress*
Why dost thou pine within and suffer dearth,
4   Painting thy outward walls so costly gay?
Why so large cost, having so short a lease,
Dost thou upon thy fading mansion spend?
Shall worms, inheritors of this excess,
8   Eat up thy charge?* Is this thy body's end?   *expenditure*
Then, soul, live thou upon thy servant's loss,
And let that pine to aggravate* thy store;   *increase*
Buy terms divine in selling hours of dross;
12   Within be fed, without be rich no more:
        So shalt thou feed on Death, that feeds on men,
        And Death once dead, there's no more dying then.

Sonnet 151

Love is too young to know what conscience is;
Yet who knows not conscience is born of love?
Then, gentle cheater, urge not my amiss,*   *sin*
4 Lest guilty of my faults thy sweet self prove.
For, thou betraying me, I do betray
My nobler part to my gross body's treason;
My soul doth tell my body that he may
8 Triumph in love; flesh stays no farther reason,
But, rising at thy name, doth point out thee
As his triumphant prize. Proud of this pride,
He is contented thy poor drudge to be,
12 To stand in thy affairs, fall by thy side.
   No want of conscience hold it that I call
   Her "love," for whose dear love I rise and fall.

TOPICS FOR WRITING AND DISCUSSION

FOR WRITING IN CLASS

1. Describe the development of the journey metaphor in Sonnet 27.
2. Describe the organization of Sonnet 27. (How are the quatrains related, and how is the couplet related to the rest of the sonnet?)
3. Trace the relationships among the quatrains and the couplet of Sonnet 34.
4. Describe how Shakespeare develops the theme of Sonnet 130.
5. Trace the development of the underlying siege metaphor in Sonnet 146.

FOR WRITING OUTSIDE OF CLASS

1. Compare the attitudes towards poetry in Sonnet 33 and Sonnet 38.
2. Describe how Sonnets 33 and 34 are related in diction and imagery.
3. Describe how the diction and imagery of Sonnet 130 determine its tone.
4. Choose two sonnets among those for additional reading which treat a similar theme, and compare the treatment of the theme.

To William Camden

Camden, most reverend head, to whom I owe
 All that I am in arts, all that I know,
(How nothing's that?) to whom my country owes
 The great renown, and name wherewith she goes.

5 Than thee the age sees not that thing more grave,
 More high, more holy, that she more would crave.
What name, what skill, what faith hast thou in things!

What sight in searching the most antique springs!
What weight, and what authority in thy speech!
10 Man scarce can make that doubt, but thou canst teach.

Pardon free truth, and let thy modesty,
 Which conquers all, be once overcome by thee:
Many of thine this better could, than I,
 But for their powers, accept my piety.

NOTE William Camden (1551–1623) was Ben Jonson's teacher and the headmaster of Westminster School. As the author of the topographical and historical *Britannia* (1586), Camden was one of England's leading historians and antiquarians.

JONSON'S STYLE

Ben Jonson's language, unlike Shakespeare's, gains strength from its plainness, its insistence upon *denotation*, and the frequent sparseness of *connotative* richness. Jonson believed a poem ought to be an "honest" thing, that is, without clever ambiguity or equivocation. Twisted or complex metaphors suggested, on the other hand, a poetic personality which was untutored and asymmetrical, one without the Jonsonian virtues of balance, restraint, and proportion. The directness and openness of his poems reflected the social values of honesty and sincerity which he held most dearly. Jonson's professional views, however, did not prevent him from admiring the very different work of his two friends, Shakespeare and Donne.

QUESTIONS

1. What qualities does Jonson most admire in Camden?
2. Find as many examples of metaphorical language as you can in this poem. What is the effect of the sparseness of metaphor?
3. In lines 8–10 what particular virtues does Jonson praise in Camden?
4. What poetic effect is achieved by lines of ten monosyllables?
5. Describe the structure of this *epigram*. (Note that although the poem is written in *heroic couplets*, the couplets of lines 5–10 are divided.)

To John Donne

Donne, the delight of Phoebus* and each muse,   *a deity associated with poetry
   Who, to thy one, all other brains refuse;*   *reject
Whose every work, of thy most early wit,*   *intelligence
   Came forth example, and remains so yet:
5 Longer a knowing, than most wits do live.
   And which no affection praise enough can give!
*To it, thy language, letters, arts, best life,   *add
   Which might with half mankind maintain a strife.
All which I meant to praise, and, yet, I would;
10   But leave, because I cannot as I should!

QUESTIONS

1. Where in the poem does Jonson use metaphorical language? From what category of human experience is this metaphor drawn? Describe the compliment the metaphor conveys.

2. In lines 3–4, what does Jonson mean when he says that Donne's "every work . . . came forth example"?

3. How is the final couplet *hyperbolic* praise?

4. How does the last line intensify the adulation given to Donne in the preceding lines?

* * *

To Sir Henry Goodyere

Goodyere, I'm glad and grateful to report
   Myself a witness of thy few days sport:
Where I both learned why wise men hawking follow,
   And why that bird was sacred to Apollo,
5 She doth instruct men by her gallant flight,
   That they to knowledge so should tower upright,
And never stoop, but to strike ignorance:
   Which if they miss, they yet should readvance
To former height, and there in circle tarry,
10   Till they be sure to make the fool their quarry.
Now, in whose pleasures I have this discerned,
   What would his serious actions me have learned?

NOTE   Sir Henry Goodyere, a minor poet, was a friend of Ben Jonson and John Donne.

AN ANALOGY

Unlike the complimentary epigrams to Camden and Donne, the epigram to Goodyere employs elaborate figurative language. Goodyere's penchant for hawking supplied Jonson with an analogy; watching the bird slowly circle in flight before he attacks suggested to Jonson the educated man carefully accumulating knowledge so that he would eventually be in a position to strike at ignorance. Each time the hawk missed his target he reascended and extended the circle of observation. Similarly, the intelligent man who strikes inconclusively at first should return to his studies to prepare for the next attempt.

QUESTIONS

1. Describe the movement of the language from the literal to the figurative in this poem.

2. What does the analogy tell us of Sir Henry Goodyere? Can we see Goodyere's characteristics as clearly as we can Camden's and Donne's?

3. Describe the relationship of the final couplet to the rest of the poem.

On My First Son

Farewell, thou child of my right hand, and joy;
  My sin was too much hope of thee, loved boy;
Seven years tho'wert lent to me, and I thee pay,
  Exacted by thy fate, on the just day.
5 O, could I lose all father now. For why
  Will man lament the state he should envy?
To have so soon scaped world's, and flesh's rage,
  And, if no other misery, yet age?
Rest in soft peace, and, asked, say here doth lie
10 Ben Jonson his best piece of poetry.
For whose sake, henceforth, all his vows be such,
  As what he loves may never like too much.

NOTES Jonson's son, Benjamin, died in 1603; in Hebrew his name means "child of the right hand."

In line 10, "his" is an outmoded use of the pronoun in place of the possessive form, Jonson's.

In the same line Jonson puns on the classical meaning of "poetry"; he uses it in the sense of "the thing made," that is, his best creation.

This poem is an example of the Jonsonian *epitaph* (literally "upon the stone"). Usually epitaphs are devoted to praising the qualities and virtues of the deceased in catalogue fashion. Here, however, we learn more about the father than we do about the son.

1. What do we learn of the father's relationship to his son in lines 1–4?
2. What does Jonson mean when he says in line 5, "O, could I lose all father now."?
3. What is the difference between "loves" and "like" in line 12? Paraphrase line 12.

Epitaph on Elizabeth, L. H.

Would'st thou hear what man can say
   In a little? Reader, stay.
Underneath this stone doth lie
   As much beauty as could die:
5 Which in life did harbour give
   To more virtue than doth live.
If, at all, she had a fault,
   Leave it buried in this vault.
One name was Elizabeth,
10   Th'other, let it sleep with death:
Fitter, where it died, to tell,
   Than that it lived at all. Farewell.

NOTE "L.H." has not been identified.

QUESTIONS

1. Count the number of multisyllabic words in this poem. What effect is achieved in the poem by the predominance of monosyllables?
2. What instances of metaphoric diction do you find here? What is the effect of metaphoric sparseness in the poem?
3. In lines 3–6 what two compliments does the poet pay his subject? What is the effect of the hyperbole?
4. What is the effect of introducing the conditional statement about a possible "fault"?
5. Paraphrase lines 11–12. What is the antecedent of "it" in line 11?

Epitaph on S. P.: A Child of Queen Elizabeth's Chapel

Weep with me all you that read
   This little story:
And know for whom a tear you shed,
4   Death's self is sorry.
'Twas a child that so did thrive
   In grace and feature,
As Heaven and Nature seemed to strive
8   Which owned the creature.
Years he numbred scarce thirteen
   When Fates turned cruel,
Yet three filled Zodiacs had he been
12   The stage's jewel;
And did act (what now we moan)
   Old men so duly,
As, sooth, the Parcae* thought him one,   *the Fates*
16   He played so truly.
So, by error, to his fate
   They all consented;
But viewing him since (alas, too late)
20   They have repented
And have sought (to give new birth)
   In baths to steep him;
But being so much too good for earth,
24   Heaven vows to keep him.

NOTE Salathiel Pavy (S.P.) was a boy actor; Jonson wrote plays for his company (Children of Queen Elizabeth's Chapel).

QUESTIONS

1. This epitaph is divided into three parts: lines 1–4, lines 5–16, and lines 17–24. What is the relationship among the three parts?
2. Why did the Fates make a mistake with Salathiel Pavy?
3. Paraphrase Jonson's "little story."
4. Compare this epitaph with Jonson's "On my First Son." What are some of the differences between the two?

To Penshurst

Thou art not, Penshurst, built to envious show,
    Of touch or marble; nor canst boast a row
Of polished pillars or a roof of gold:
    Thou hast no lanthorn,* whereof tales are told,   *a glassed-in room*
5 Or stair, or courts, but stand'st an ancient pile,
    And these grudged* at, art reverenced the while.   *envied*
Thou joy'st in better marks, of soil, of air,
    Of wood, of water: therein thou art fair.
Thou hast thy walks for health, as well as sport:
10   Thy mount to which the Dryads do resort,
Where Pan and Bacchus their high feasts have made,
    Beneath the broad beech and the chestnut shade;
That taller tree, which of a nut was set,
    At his* great birth, where all the Muses met.   *Sir Philip Sidney*
15 There, in the writhed bark, are cut the names
    Of many a sylvan,* taken with his flames.   *country person*
And thence, the ruddy satyrs oft provoke
    The lighter fauns, to reach thy lady's oak.
Thy copse, too, named of Gamage, thou hast there,
20   That never fails to serve thee seasoned deer,
When thou would'st feast, or exercise thy friends.
    The lower land that to the river bends,
Thy sheep, thy bullocks, kine, and calves do feed:
    The middle grounds thy mares and horses breed.
25 Each bank doth yield thee coveys; and the tops   *two neighboring*
    Fertile of wood, Ashore and Sidney's* copse,   *fields*
To crown thy open table, doth provide
    The purpled pheasant, with the speckled side:
The painted partridge lies in every field,
30   And, for thy mess, is willing to be killed.
And if the high swolne Medway* fail thy dish,   *a local river*
    Thou hast thy ponds, that pay thee tribute fish,
Fat, aged carps, that run into thy net.
    And pikes, now weary their own kind to eat,
35 As loth, the second draught, or cast to stay,
    Officiously, at first, themselves betray.
Bright eels, that emulate them, and leap on land,
    Before the fisher, or into his hand.
Then hath thy orchard fruit, thy garden flowers,
40   Fresh as the air, and new as are the hours.

The early cherry, with the later plum,
    Fig, grape, and quince, each in his time doth come:
The blushing apricot, and wooly peach
    Hang on thy walls, that every child may reach.
45 And though thy walls be of the country stone,
    They're reared with no man's ruin, no man's groan,
There's none, that dwell about them, wish them down;
    But all come in, the farmer and the clown,
And no one empty-handed, to salute
50   Thy lord, and lady, though they have no suit.*   *petition*
Some bring a capon, some a rural cake,
    Some nuts, some apples, some that think they make
The better cheeses, bring 'em, or else send
    By their ripe daughters, whom they would commend
55 This way to husbands; and whose baskets bear
    An emblem of themselves, in plum, or pear.
But what can this (more than express their love)
    Add to thy free provisions, far above
The need of such? whose liberal board doth flow
60   With all that hospitality doth know!
Where comes no guest, but is allowed to eat,
    Without his fear, and of thy lord's own meat:
Where the same beer, and bread, and self-same wine,
    That is his lordship's shall be also mine.
65 And I not fain to sit (as some, this day,
    At great men's tables) and yet dine away.
Here no man tells* my cups; nor, standing by,   *counts*
    A waiter, doth my gluttony envy:
But gives me what I call, and lets me eat,
70   He knows, below, he shall find plenty of meat,
Thy tables hoard not up for the next day,
    Nor when I take my lodging, need I pray
For fire, or lights, or livery: all is there;
    As if thou, then, wert mine, or I reigned here:
75 There's nothing I can wish, for which I stay.
    That found King James when hunting late, this way,
With his brave son, the Prince, they saw thy fires
    Shine bright on every hearth as the desires
Of thy Penates* had been set on flame   *household gods*
80   To entertain them; or the country came,
With all their zeal to warm their welcome here.
    What (great, I will not say, but) sudden cheer

Did'st thou, then, make 'em! and what praise was heaped
On thy good lady, then! who, therein, reaped
85 The just reward of her high housewifery;
To have her linen, plate, and all things nigh,
When she was far; and not a room, but dressed,
As if it had expected such a guest!
These, Penshurst, are thy praise, and yet not all.
90 Thy lady's noble, fruitful, chaste withal.
His children thy great lord may call his own:
A fortune, in this age, but rarely known.
They are, and have been taught, religion: thence
Their gentler spirits have sucked innocence.
95 Each morn, and even, they are taught to pray,
With the whole household, and may, everyday,
Read in their virtuous parents' noble parts,
The mysteries of manners, arms, and arts.
Now, Penshurst, they that will proportion thee
100 With other edifices, when they see
Those proud, ambitious heaps, and nothing else,
May say, their lords have built, but thy lord dwells.

NOTES   Penshurst was the country home of the famous English poet, Sir Philip Sidney.
Jonson's tribute to the Sidney family centers upon the famous estate, Penshurst. To
indicate the idyllic nature of the country estate and to associate it with the Golden Age of
innocence and fruitfulness, Jonson employs numerous *allusions* to classical mythology: the
Dryads, Pan, Bacchus, Satyrs, Fauns, and Panates. These allusions provide Penshurst with an
ideal mythological past.

QUESTIONS

1. Look up each of the classical allusions. To what does each refer, how does
each (in context) suggest a different aspect of Penshurst's history, and what is the
cumulative effect of these allusions?

2. Characterize the natural environment of Penshurst. What details of imagery
and diction create the scene of order and fertility?

3. What is the relationship between the Sidney family and the peasants who
live and work on the estate?

4. The relationship between the human beings at Penshurst and the natural
environment is a happy reciprocal one. What evidence do you find of this relationship in the poem?

5. How does Jonson characterize Lady Sidney?

6. In the last few lines what is Jonson's distinction between Penshurst and other
country houses?

7. In this poem what are the social values Jonson cherishes?

A Fit of Rhyme Against Rhyme

Rhyme, the rack of finest wits,
That expresseth but by fits,*   *fitfully*
    True conceit.
Spoiling senses of their treasure,
5 Cozening* judgement with a measure,°   *cheating;* °*meter*
    But false weight.
Wresting words, from their true calling;
Propping verse, for fear of falling
    To the ground.
10 Jointing* syllabes°, drowning letters,   *disjointing*
Fast'ning vowels, as with fetters   °*syllables*
    They were bound!
Soon as lazy thou wert known,
All good poetry hence was flown,
15   And art banished.
For a thousand years together,
All Parnassus'* green did wither,   *mount sacred to the*
    And wit vanished.   *Muses*
Pegasus* did fly away,   *the winged horse*
20 At the wells* no Muse did stay,   *sacred founts of*
    But bewailed,   *inspiration*
So to see the fountain dry,
And Apollo's music die,
    All light failed!
25 Starveling rhymes did fill the stage,
Not a poet in an age,
    Worth crowning.
Not a work deserving bays,*   *reward*
Nor a line deserving praise,
30   Pallas frowning;
Greek was free from rhyme's infection,
Happy Greek by this protection
    Was not spoiled!
Whilst the Latin, queen of tongues,
35 Is not yet free from rhyme's wrongs,
    But rests foiled.
Scarce the hill* again doth flourish,   *Parnassus*
Scarce the world a wit doth nourish,
    To restore
40 Phoebus to his crown again;
And the Muses to their brain;
    As before.

Vulgar* languages that want   *non-classical*
Words and sweetness, and be scant
45   Of true measure,
Tyrant rhyme hath so abused,
That they long since have refused
          Other ceasure.*   *pause or break in a
He that first invented thee,   line*
50 May his joints tormented be,
          Cramped forever;
Still may syllabes jar with time,
Still may reason war with rhyme,
          Resting never.
55 May his sense, when it would meet,
The cold tumor in his feet,
          Grow unsounder.
And his title be long fool,
That in rearing such a school,
60   Was the founder.

NOTE In this poem Jonson used *rhyme* while condemning it. He deliberately cramped his
manner of expression to illustrate his point.

QUESTIONS

1. How does the poet use rhyme with comic, or satiric, effect?

2. The allusions to Parnassus, Pegasus, Apollo, Pallas, Phoebus and the muses
suggest classical purity (Greek and Roman classics employed no rhyme). In "To
Penshurst" Jonson identified the present with the past. What is the relation of
the present to the past in this poem?

Inviting a Friend to Supper

Tonight, grave sir, both my poor house, and I
  Do equally desire your company;
Not that we think us worthy such a guest,
  But that your worth will dignify our feast,
5 With those that come, whose grace may make that seem
  Something, which else, could hope for no esteem.
It is the fair acceptance, Sir, creates
  The entertainment perfect: not the cates.*   *delicacies*
Yet shall you have, to rectify your palate,
10   An olive, capers, or some better salad
Ush'ring the mutton; with a short-leg'd hen,
  If we can get her, full of eggs, and then,
Lemons, and wine for sauce; to these, a coney*   *rabbit*
  Is not to be despaired of, for our money;
15 And, though fowl, now, be scarce,* yet there are   *expensive*
    clarks,*   *poor scholars*
  The sky not falling, think we may have larks.
I'll tell you of more, and lie, so you will come:
  Of partridge, pheasant, woodcock, of which some
May yet be there; and godwit,* if we can:
20   Knat,* raile,* and ruffe* too. How so ere, my man   *edible birds*
Shall read a piece of Virgil, Tacitus,
  Livy, or of some better book to us,
Of which we'll speak our minds, amidst our meat;
  And I'll profess no verses to repeat:
25 To this, if ought appear which I know not of,
  That will the pastry, not my paper, show of.
Digestive cheese and fruit there sure will be;
  But that which most doth take my Muse and me
Is a pure cup of rich Canary wine
30   Which is the Mermaid's now, but shall be mine:
Of which had Horace or Anacreon tasted,
  Their lives, as do their lines, till now had lasted.
Tobacco, nectar, or the Thespian spring,
  Are all but Luther's* beer, to this I sing.   *German*
35 Of this we will sup free, but moderately,
  And we will have no Pooly or Parrot* by;   *informers*
Nor shall our cups make any guilty men:
  But at our parting, we will be as when
We innocently met. No simple word,
40   That shall be uttered at our mirthful board,
Shall make us sad next morning or affright
  The liberty, that we'll enjoy tonight.

JONSON'S SOCIAL VALUES

For Jonson the dinner party was a decorous occasion of natural formality. It was an ideal ceremony where, traditionally, guests treated one another with cordiality and familiarity, never going beyond the bounds of decorum. The entertainment was simple: good talk about good books, easy humor, palatable wine, pleasant banter. Expensive, ostentatious entertainments, exotic delicacies, drunken guests—all these Jonson indirectly condemns, for they bespeak disproportion and lack of restraint. The poem's key words are "moderately" (line 35), "innocently" (line 39), "simple" (line 39), "mirthful" (line 40), and "liberty" (line 42). For Jonson the supper was honored by the guests; it did not do honor to them. The attitude, in short, is urbane, erudite, and sophisticated. It honors human beings, not things, and gives highest regard to human relationships.

QUESTIONS

1. Compare Jonson's attitude towards hospitality with that of the Sidneys in "To Penshurst," What kinds of details are used here to convey his attitude?

2. What place in a supper party does Jonson give to classical authors (Virgil, Tacitus, Livy, Horace and Anacreon)?

3. What techniques does Jonson use to achieve the relaxed informality of the *verses?* How is this tone appropriate to the subject matter?

WHAT TO LOOK FOR IN THE ADDITIONAL READING

Because of the directness of his language, Jonson's poems do not pose the same problems as those of his contemporaries, Shakespeare and Donne. One will not often find complexity of metaphor or ambiguity, but he will find sincere, well-balanced statements of feelings and ideas. The reader must pay attention to the sense of Jonson's verse, observing how Jonson structures a poetic line: that is, observing the relationship between the *syntax* of the sentence itself and the demands of the *metered* line. For a variety of effects Jonson may choose to end a thought in the second *foot* of the line, in the exact middle of the line, or at the end of a line. His sentences, in other words, do not always conclude at the end of a line. Determining Jonson's particular and unique *cadences* is one of the reader's primary tasks, for only after he has done this can he say that he is reading poetry. Then he is able to give the poetic reasons why Jonson ends and begins where he does on the page. Verse, unlike prose, does not go continually to the end of the page; that it does not is what makes it verse. The relative simplicity of Jonson's verse makes it imperative that the reader emphasize the cadences of his sentences.

Jonson was a significant classical scholar, and what he and his literate contemporaries memorized as school boys most modern readers have never learned. Consequently to read poetry packed with classical allusions, the modern reader may need a reference work to help him. The reader must go beyond simple identification to consider how the allusion functions in context. He will find in these additional poems, however, themes, attitudes, and techniques already considered in the preceding selections.

To Henry Goodyere

When I would know thee Goodyere, my thought looks
    Upon thy well-made choice of friends, and books;
Then do I love thee, and behold thy ends
    In making thy friends books, and thy books friends:
5 Now, I must give thy life, and deed, the voice
    Attending such a study, such a choice.
Where, though't be love that to thy praise doth move.
It was a knowledge that begat that love.

To John Donne

Who shall doubt, Donne, where* I a poet be,   *whether*
    When I dare send my Epigrams* to thee?   *Jonson's volume*
That so alone canst judge, so alone dost* make: *whatever you*
    And in thy censures, evenly, dost take
5 As free simplicity* to disavow,   *artlessness*
    As thou hast best authority, t'allow.
Read all I send: and, if I find but one
    Marked by thy hand, and with the better stone,*   *a mark of happiness*
My title's sealed. Those that for claps* do write,   *applause*
10   Let pui'nees,* porters, players praise delight,   *inferiors*
    And till they burst their backs like asses load:
A man should seek great glory, and not broad.

To William Roe

Roe* (and my joy to name) th'art now to go,   *friend of Jonson's*
    Countries and climes, manners, and men to know,
T'extract and choose the best of all these known,
    And those to turn to blood and make thine own.
5 May winds as soft as breath of kissing friends
    Attend thee hence; and there, may all thy ends,
As the beginnings here, prove purely sweet
    And perfect in a circle always meet.
So, when we, blest with thy return, shall see
10   Thy self, with thy first thoughts, brought home by thee,
We each to other may this voice inspire:
    This is that good Aeneas,* past through fire,   *Virgil's travelling hero*
Through seas, storms, tempests; and embarked for hell,
    Came back untouched. This man hath travailed* *a pun on travel*
    well.

28 BEN JONSON [1572–1637]

On Lucy, Countess of Bedford

This morning, timely* rapt with holy fire,   *happily*
    I thought to form unto my zealous muse,
What kind of creature I could most desire,
4   To honor, serve, and love, as poets use.*   *do*
I meant to make her fair and free and wise,
    Of greatest blood,* and yet more good than great;   *nobility of birth*
I meant the daystar should not brighter rise,
8   Nor lend like influence from his lucent seat.
I meant she should be courteous, facile, sweet,
    Hating that solemn vice of greatness, pride;
I meant each softest virtue there should meet,
12   Fit in that softer bosom to reside.
Only a learned and a manly soul
    I proposed her, that should, with even powers,
The rock, the spindle, and the shears* control   *symbols of the three fates*
16   Of destiny, and spin her own free hours.
Such when I meant to feign, and wished to see,
    My muse bade, Bedford write, and that was she.

NOTE   The Countess of Bedford (1581–1627) was a famous patron and friend of Jonson and Donne.

On My First Daughter

Here lies to each her parents' ruth,*   *sorrow*
Mary, the daughter of their youth:
Yet, all heaven's gifts being heaven's due,
It makes the father less to rue.
5   At six month's end, she parted hence
With safety of her innocence;
Whose soul, heaven's queen (whose name she bears),
In comfort of her mother's tears,
Hath placed amongst her virgin train:
10   Where, while that severed* doth remain,   *body from soul*
This grave partakes the fleshly birth.
Which cover lightly, gentle earth.

On English Monsieur

Would you believe, when this monsieur see,
   That his whole body should speak French, not he?
That so much scarf of France, and hat, and feather,
   And shoe, and tie, and garter should come hither,
5 And land on one, whose face durst never be
   Toward the sea, farther than half-way tree?*   *a landmark to
That he, untravelled, should be French so much,   Dover(?)
   As Frenchmen in his company should seem Dutch?
Or had his father, when he did him get,
10   The French disease, with which he labours yet?
Or hung some monsieur's picture on the wall,
   By which his dame conceived him clothes and all?
Or is it some French statue? No: 't doth move,
   And stoop, and cringe. O then, it needs must prove
15 The new French tailors' motion, monthly made,
   Daily to turn* in Paul's° and help the trade.   *walk; °St. Paul's
                                                        Churchyard, a
NOTE In this poem Jonson makes fun of the English fad of imitating   popular place
things French.   for a walk

Why I Write Not of Love

Some act of Love's bound to rehearse,
I thought to bind him, in my verse:
Which when he felt, "Away" (quoth he)
"Can poets hope to fetter me?
5 It is enough they once did get
Mars and my Mother in their net:
I wear not these my wings in vain."
With which he fled me; and again,
Into my rhymes could ne'er be got
10 By any art. Then wonder not,
That since,* my numbers are so cold   afterwards
When Love is fled, and I grow old.

My Picture Left in Scotland

I now think Love is rather deaf than blind,
  For else it could not be,
       That she,
Whom I adore so much, should so slight me
5   And cast my love behind:
I'm sure my language to her was as sweet,
       And every close* did meet   *conclusion, as a*
     In sentence, of as subtle feet,   *musical phrase*
       As hath the youngest he
10 That sits in shadow of* Apollo's tree.   *i.e., inspired by*
Oh, but my conscious fears,
     That fly my thoughts between,
     Tell me that she hath seen
    My hundreds of gray hairs,
15   Told* seven and forty years.   *the total of*
Read so much waist,* as she cannot embrace   *a pun on waste*
My mountain belly, and my rocky face,
And all these through her eyes, have stopt her ears.

TOPICS FOR WRITING AND DISCUSSION

FOR USE IN CLASS

1. Jonson is justly famous for the way in which he handles concluding couplets. Describe the effectiveness, or appropriateness, of the couplets which end the two epigrams to Henry Goodyere.

2. Paraphrase Jonson's second epigram on John Donne ("Who shall doubt...").

3. Describe the particular virtues of William Roe which Jonson prizes.

4. Paraphrase Jonson's epigram to "Lucy, Countess of Bedford."

5. How does Jonson satirize the Englishman who pretends to be French ("On English Monsieur")?

FOR PREPARATION OUTSIDE OF CLASS

1. Based on your reading of the epigrams in the collection, discuss "Jonson and the Art of the Epigram." (Remember, epigrams are short, usually straightforward, often witty poems; epitaphs are funeral epigrams.)

2. Compare Jonson's two complimentary epigrams: "To William Roe" and "On Lucy, Countess of Bedford." (Note that a *circle metaphor* dominates the epigram to Roe. Is there a controlling metaphor in the other epigram, or is the progression in a straight line?)

3. Compare the emotional intensity in the epitaphs ("On My First Son" and "On My First Daughter").

4. Compare the attitude towards love in Jonson's "Why I Write Not of Love" and "My Picture Left in Scotland."

The Good Morrow

I wonder by my troth, what thou, and I
Did, till we loved? Were we not weaned till then?
But sucked on country pleasures, childishly?
Or snorted* we in the Seven Sleepers' den?   *snored*
5 T'was so; but* this, all pleasures fancies be.   *except*
If ever any beauty I did see,
Which I desired, and got, t'was but a dream of thee.

And now good morrow to our waking souls,
Which watch not one another out of fear;
10 For love, all love of other sights controls,
And makes one little room an everywhere.
Let sea-discoverers to new worlds have gone,
Let maps to other, worlds on worlds have shown,
Let us possess one world, each hath one, and is one.

15 My face in thine eyes, thine in mine appears,
And true plain hearts do in the faces rest,
Where can we find two better hemispheres
Without sharp North, without declining West?
Whatever dies, was not mixt equally;
20 If our two loves be one, or, thou and I
Love so alike, that none do slacken, none can die.

NOTE Legend tells us of seven young men—the Seven Sleepers— who took refuge in a cave
to escape religious persecution. There they slept for two centuries, though it seemed to them
like one night.

DRAMATIC SITUATION

Donne's poems (he called them "songs") are extremely dramatic; the reader is
always aware of the speaker's tensions, anxieties, and pressures. In *Songs and
Sonnets* (Donne's collection of love poems) the speaker is usually a man addressing
his beloved in most of the standard love situations: lovers' parting, infidelity,
on love tokens, on the possibility of death, or debating over platonic and sexual
love. Often a direct outburst in the opening line indicates the occasion for the
poem; it may tell us the time of day, where the lovers are (if they are together),
and something of the speaker's present attitude. Determining this context is important, for then the reader can follow more easily the often devious argument
and anticipate what the beloved's reactions might be to her lover's attitude.

"The Good Morrow" presents an optimistic lover, ecstatic over the possibility of requited love. He feels he has, as it were, been "reborn" in love, and he extends the metaphor and bids "good morrow" (good morning) to his "new soul," one now joined equally with the soul of the beloved. (It has a new substance and a new immortality.) Donne's poems imply that lovers create their own world, the only one of any validity and worth; when one proved unfaithful, the other faced death and desolation alone. In Donne's view, the world which lovers create is holy and sanctified, and that "little" world of love is magically greater than any of the secular "worlds" we know separately. The speaker continues the metaphor concerned with geographical terms, indicating how his love will suffer neither cold nor decline (line 18).

A Lecture Upon the Shadow

Stand still, and I will read to thee
A lecture, love, in love's philosophy.
    These three hours that we have spent,
    Walking here, two shadows went
5 Along with us, which we our selves produced;
But, now the sun is just above our head,
    We do those shadows tread;
    And to brave* clearness all things are reduced.   *fine*
    So whilst our infant love did grow,
10   Disguises did, and shadows, flow,
From us, and our cares; but now 'tis not so.

That love hath not attained the high'st degree,
Which is still diligent lest others see.

    Except* our love at this noon stay,   *unless*
15 We shall new shadows make the other way.
    As the first were made to blind
    Others, these which come behind
Will work upon our selves, and blind our eyes.
If our love faint, and westwardly decline,
20   To me thou, falsely, thine,
    And I to thee mine actions shall disguise.
    The morning shadows wear away,
    But these grow longer all the day,
But oh, love's day is short, if love decay.

25 Love is a growing, or full constant light;
And his first minute, after noon, is night.

METAPHYSICAL CONCEIT

Donne is famous for what some critics refer to as the *metaphysical conceit;* that is, a figure of speech in which two dissimilars are compared at length with one another. We are always aware of how unlike the two are and amazed at the wit and ingenuity of a speaker who can point out likenesses we never expected. Often the conceit, a variety of metaphor, is extended detail by detail throughout the *lyric,* and it becomes the figure around which the poem is organized. In "A Lecture upon the Shadow," Donne's speaker chooses the shadows thrown by the sun in morning and afternoon as conceits for disguises used by lovers. In the morning (that is, in the beginning of the love affair) lovers employ disguises to fool their friends, and the couple are mutually aware of the pretense. In the afternoon (that is, later in the course of the love affair) lovers use disguises to fool one another after the romance has declined. Perfect love, we are told, can exist only at noon when there are no "shadows," but we all know that compared to morning and afternoon, noon is but a short moment. The lover here both celebrates and bemoans the shortness of perfect love. Although love is subject to mutability, he wishes it were not so and probably would like to take refuge in a Shakespearian cliché, but Donne's lover is always too much a realist to admit false consolation.

QUESTIONS

1. Explain the relationship of the poem's primary conceit to the final couplet.
2. What comment do lines 12 and 13 make upon lines 1 through 10?
3. Describe the tone of this poem. Is the speaker bitter about his discovery or resigned to it?

The Triple Fool

I am two fools, I know,
For loving, and for saying so
   In whining poetry;
But where's that wise man, that would not be I,
5   If she would not deny?
Then, as th'earth's inward narrow crooked lanes
Do purge sea water's fretful salt away,
   I thought, if I could draw my pains,
Through rhyme's vexation, I should them allay.
10 Grief brought to numbers cannot be so fierce,
   For, he tames it, that fetters it in verse.

But when I have done so,
Some man, his art and voice to show,
Doth set* and sing my pain,   *set to music*
15 And, by delighting many, frees again
Grief, which verse did restrain.
To love and grief tribute of verse belongs,
But not of such as pleases when 'tis read,
Both are increased by such songs:
20 For both their triumphs so are published,
And I, which was two fools, do so grow three;
Who are a little wise, the best fools be.

QUESTIONS

1. What effect does the speaker achieve by characterizing poetry as "whining" in line 3?
2. What value does the speaker attribute to poetry in lines 8 to 11?
3. Discuss the effectiveness of the simile in lines 6 and 7.
4. Paraphrase the poem's final couplet.
5. What three kinds of fool is the speaker?
6. Describe the speaker's attitude towards his assumption that he is a "triple fool."

A Valediction: Forbidding Mourning

As virtuous men pass mildly away,
And whisper to their souls, to go,
Whilst some of their sad friends do say,
4   The breath goes now, and some say, "No":

So let us melt, and make no noise,
No tear-floods, nor sigh-tempests move;
T'were profanation of our joys
8   To tell the laity our love.

Moving of th'earth* brings harms and fears,   *earthquakes*
Men reckon what it did and meant;
But trepidation* of the spheres,°   *movement;* °*planets*
12   Though greater far, is innocent.*   *harmless*

Dull sublunary* lovers' love   *earthly*
(Whose soul is sense) cannot admit
Absence, because it doth remove
16   Those things which elemented it.

But we, by a love so much refined
    That our selves know not what it is,
Inter-assured of the mind,
20   Care less, eyes, lips, and hands to miss.

Our two souls, therefore, which are one,
    Though I must go, endure not yet
A breach, but an expansion,
24   Like gold to airy thinness beat.

If they be two, they are two so
    As stiff twin compasses* are two;
Thy soul, the fixt foot, makes no show
28   To move, but doth, if th'other do;

*an instrument for
drawing circles*

And though it in the center sit,
    Yet when the other far doth roam
It leans, and hearkens after it,
32   And grows erect, as that comes home.

Such wilt thou be to me, who must
    Like th' other foot, obliquely run;
Thy firmness draws my circle just,
36   And makes me end where I begun.

NOTE Sir Isaac Walton's *Life of Donne* tells us that the poet gave these lines to his wife as he was about to leave for an extended journey to France in 1611.

QUESTIONS

  1. Paraphrase the simile in the opening stanzas. What effect is gained by beginning with this comparison?
  2. Explain the *ellipsis* in line 6.
  3. What elements of diction in the second stanza indicate the sanctity of true love?
  4. What is the place of stanza 3 in the lover's argument that his beloved not mourn his leaving?
  5. What does the lover say is the difference between his love and that of earthly lovers? (Note the pun on "Absence" in line 15; Donne plays on the Latin prefix "ab" in "absence," that is, from the senses. Earthly lovers cannot endure separation because their love is based only on the senses and needs physical presence to be fulfilled.)
  6. What is the sense of "refined" in line 17?
  7. How does the simile in stanza 6 describe the nature of the lovers' separation?
  8. Paraphrase the last 3 stanzas. Comment on the effectiveness of the extended compass conceit.

A Nocturnal Upon St. Lucy's Day

'Tis the year's midnight, and it is the day's,
Lucy's who scarce seven hours herself unmasks;
   The sun is spent, and now his flasks*   *powder horns*
   Send forth light squibs,* no constant rays;   *charges*
5   The world's whole sap is sunk:
The general balm th' hydroptic* earth hath drunk,   *thirsty*
Whither, as to the bed's-feet, life is shrunk,
Dead and interred; yet all these seem to laugh,
Compared with me, who am their epitaph.

10 Study me then, you who shall lovers be
At the next world, that is, at the next spring:
   For I am every dead thing,
   In whom Love wrought new alchemy.
     For his art did express
15 A quintessence* even from nothingness,   *distillation*
From dull privations, and lean emptiness:
He ruined* me, and I am re-begot   *destroyed*
Of absence, darkness, death: things which are not.

All others, from all things, draw all that's good,
20 Life, soul, form, spirit, whence they being have;
   I, by Love's limbeck,* am the grave   *a still*
   Of all that's nothing. Oft a flood
     Have we two wept, and so
Drowned the whole world, us two; oft did we grow
25 To be two chaoses, when we did show
Care to ought else; and often absences
Withdrew our souls, and made us carcasses.

But I am by her death (which word wrongs her),
Of the first nothing, the elixir* grown;   *distillation*
30   Were I a man, that I were one.
   I needs must know; I should prefer,
     If I were any beast.
Some ends, some means; yea plants, yea stones detest,
And love; all, all some properties invest;
35 If I an ordinary nothing were,
As shadow, a light and body must be here.

But I am none; nor will my sun renew.
You lovers, for whose sake the lesser sun
    At this time to the Goat is run
40 To fetch new lust, and give it you,
        Enjoy your summer all;
Since she enjoys her long night's festival,
Let me prepare towards her, and let me call
This hour her vigil, and her eve, since this
45 Both the year's, and the day's deep midnight is.

NOTES Donne believed St. Lucy's day (December 13, Julian calendar) was the shortest day of
the year. We do not know to whom the poem is addressed, but it may be to the celebrated
Lucy, Countess of Bedford.
    In line 6, Donne has in mind certain terminal illnesses where life seems to pass progress-
ively from the body: from the head, through the trunk, to the feet (of the person and the bed).
    In lines 39 and 40 the speaker refers to "the Goat," which is the symbol in the zodiac for
the Tropic of Capricorn, identified with the month of December. The Goat is also the
medieval sign for lust. The allusion implies that the cycle of the year with its love and lust
begins again after this day.

A BEREAVED LOVER

    In this difficult poem the lover maintains his "vigil" in honor of the deceased
as he tries to make sense of his existence now that she is gone. The poem is not
so much about his beloved's death (that is not mentioned until line 28) as it is
about the lover's reaction to her death. He has chosen midnight of the longest
night of the year as the time of his vigil because when his grief is most intense
he is also at the moment when relief is imminent. Midnight is the ideal setting
for his reverie, for it is paradoxically that moment which is the end of all things
past and the beginning of all things to come.
    When his beloved died, the world they made together dissolved; deprived of
her, he feels as if he has been reborn as the elixir of nothingness. This rebirth, however, is ironically rebirth into death or into this life (Donne's lovers think when
they are together, that their world is the only reality, that it is timeless, immortal,
and boundless). The lover knows nonetheless that his exaggerated and extravagant
reaction to the lady's death must appear somewhat strange to future lovers, and he
knows, too, that time will pass and years will succeed years, and in time he may
find his consolation. Paradoxically, then, the source of his sorrow and salvation
is identical.

QUESTIONS

    1. List examples of diction associated with alchemy. What is the cumulative
effect of this diction?
    2. How does the religious diction in lines 42–45 characterize the speaker's love?
    3. Find some instances of *hyperbole* in the poem. What is the effect of the

lover's hyperbolic statements? (Does hyperbole suggest a certain distance on the lover's part, and, perhaps, then some insincerity which makes the intensity of the poem suspect?)

4. What is the speaker's opinion of love in stanza 2?

5. Describe the effect of the diction and imagery of lines 22–27.

6. To what does "my sun" refer in line 37? How is it related to the "lesser sun" in line 38?

Sonnet

Oh my black soul! now thou art summoned
By sickness, death's herald, and champion;
Thou art like a pilgrim, which abroad hath done
4 Treason, and durst not turn to whence he is fled,
Or like a thief, which till death's doom be read,
Wisheth himself delivered from prison,
But damned and haled to execution,
8 Wisheth that still he might be imprisoned.
Yet grace, if thou repent, thou canst not lack;
But who shall give thee that grace to begin?
Oh, make thy self with holy mourning black,
12 And red with blushing, as thou art with sin;
Or wash thee in Christ's blood, which hath this might,
That being red, it dyes red souls to white.

DONNE'S SONNETS

In addition to his secular poetry, John Donne produced a substantial body of religious poems. Among the most famous are his nineteen Holy Sonnets. He chose to work in the *Italian* form, more confining than the Shakespearian form, and made up of two large divisions: an octave (lines 1 through 8) and a sestet (lines 9 through 14). The octave is composed of two quatrains and only two rhymes, rhyming *abba, abba;* the sestet may follow numerous rhyme variations, but the most common for Donne is *cdcd ee.* A widely held concept about the Italian sonnet maintains that at line 9 the sonnet takes a "turn," or a reverse. The speaker's attitude, or his argument, may or may not change or reverse at line 9, and the speaker may even choose to ignore these tight divisions and end the octave in the middle or end of line 9. Likewise, he may ignore the complete stop at line 4, deciding instead to conclude his first major syntactic unit at line 5, or line 4½. Regardless of how he handles the cadences, the poet always has rhyme as a control to help him structure the sonnet. He may choose to counterpoint his syntax against the rhyme, extending his first sentence for five lines rather than four, resulting in an initial five line unit rhyming *abbaa.*

Many of Donne's sonnets are meditations on death and last things—the agonies of the sinful soul, judgment, and resurrection. The sonnet, "Oh my black soul," anticipates the prospect of death and the plight of the doomed soul. The opening quatrain establishes that context and in a simile compares the soul to a traveller whose excursion into the body has so tainted it that it cannot return to heaven when summoned. The simile dramatizes the abstract situation by characterizing the traveller as a treasonous "pilgrim." Usually a pilgrimage is taken to cleanse or purge oneself of impurities; here the pilgrimage has been to sin rather than away from it. The second quatrain presents another simile as it considers the soul in the body's prison. Pure souls always wish to be relieved of the body's burden; sinful souls, however, dread the day of release. For them that day means death rather then eternal life, but neither can escape punishment; inevitably all undergo final judgment.

The sonnet proceeds logically with the argument in the sestet. The answer to the soul's predicament is simple; repentance is never too late and must precede grace. Let the soul prepare itself by indicating it knows it is sinful. Let it turn to Christ, let it remember His sacrifice and love, let it partake of His spirit, for His blood has the strength to cleanse the shame of sinful souls. Through love of Christ that which is black can be made white.

The speaker has moved from "black" (line 1) to "white" (line 14), from ignorance in sin to the knowledge that will be his salvation. The mediator here is another color, red, the color of Christ's blood and the metaphor of His love for man. Actually the sonnet has a three-part argumentative structure. The speaker first imagines a context, then comes to an understanding of his sinfulness, and finally reveals that now he knows how to change his ways to achieve salvation. As in most of Donne's sonnets, the speaker presents an argument and arrives at an intellectual and spiritual enlightenment.

Sonnet

This is my play's last scene; here heavens appoint
My pilgrimage's last mile, and my race
Idly, yet quickly run, hath this last pace,
4 My span's last inch, my minute's latest point,
And gluttonous death will instantly unjoint
My body and soul, and I shall sleep a space,
But my'ever-waking part shall see that face,
8 Whose fear already shakes my every joint:
Then, as my soul, to'heaven her first seat, takes flight,
And earth-born body, in the earth shall dwell,
So, fall my sins, that all may have their right,
12 To where they're bred, and would press me, to hell.
Impute* me righteous, thus purged of evil,   *consider*
For thus I leave the world, the flesh, the devil.

1. What is the effect in the first quatrain of the progression from "scene" to "mile" to "inch" to "point"?
2. What adjective is used several times in the opening quatrain? Why?
3. What is the "ever-waking part" in line 7?
4. What is the "right" (line 11) due the earth?
5. Describe how the sonnet is organized around "the world, the flesh, the devil" (line 14).
6. What is the function of the *apostrophe* in the final couplet?
7. How similar is the pattern in this sonnet to the pattern observed in "Oh my black soul"?

WHAT TO LOOK FOR IN THE ADDITIONAL READING

Here are three more Holy Sonnets for you to read. Remember that Donne frequently follows a three-part intellectual progression in the sonnets, and that the sestet, often introduced with words like "yet" or "but," contains the intellectual resolution to the problem posed in the octave. A good way to begin is to paraphrase each sonnet, following the logic of the argument. Remember, too, that these arguments are made by a speaker passionately involved in his religious problems, and a passionate argument always shifts rapidly from subject to subject.

In each of these additional poems, religious or secular, establish the dramatic context, investigate the diction and imagery (especially that concerned with the metaphysical conceit), and determine the tone of the poem. Donne's speaker in the love poems is a witty, urbane, audacious, coaxing, and outrageous suitor prone to exaggerating his attitudes and to proving the truth of proposals we might not otherwise believe. Nowhere, he tells us, will we ever find a woman who is both beautiful and true; and without reluctance, in the context of his poems, we often believe him.

Sonnet

At the round earth's imagined corners, blow
Your trumpets, angels, and arise, arise
From death, you numberless infinities
4 Of souls, and to your scattered bodies go,
All whom the flood did, and fire shall o'erthrow,
All whom war, dearth, age, agues,* tyrannies,   *pestilences*
Despair, law, chance hath slain, and you whose eyes
8 Shall behold God, and never taste death's woe.
But let them sleep, Lord, and me mourn a space,
For, if above all these, my sins abound,
'Tis late to ask abundance of thy grace
12 When we are there; here on this lowly ground
Teach me how to repent; for that's as good
As if thou'hadst sealed my pardon, with thy blood.

Sonnet

What if this present were the world's last night?
Mark in my heart, O soul, where thou dost dwell,
The picture of Christ crucified, and tell
4   Whether that countenance can thee affright:
Tears in his eyes quench the amazing light,
Blood fills his frowns, which from his pierced head fell.
And can that tongue adjudge thee unto hell,
8   Which prayed forgiveness for his foes' fierce spite?
No, no; but as in my idolatry
I said to all my profane* mistresses,   *earthly*
Beauty, of pity, foulness only is
12 A sign of rigor: so I say to thee,
To wicked spirits are horrid shapes assigned,
This beauteous form assures a piteous mind.

NOTES In line 6 in *What if this present* Donne uses the verb "to frown" as a noun to indicate the furrows apparent in Christ's frowning.

    The ellipsis in lines 11–12 may be paraphrased as follows: "Beauty and pity are associated; the beautiful person is the pitiful one (beauty is a "sign" of pity). He who is "foul" is therefore rigorous (strict or severe).

Sonnet

Batter my heart, three personed* God; for you   *Father, Son, Holy Ghost*
As yet but knock, breathe, shine, and seek to mend;
That I may rise, and stand, o'erthrow me,'and
4   Your force, to break, blow, burn and make me new.
I, like an usurpt town, to'another due,
Labour to'admit you, but Oh, to no end;
Reason, your viceroy* in me, me should defend,   *deputy*
8   But is captived, and proves weak or untrue.
Yet dearly I love you, and would be loved fain,*   *willingly*
But am betrothed unto your enemy:
Divorce me,'untie, or break that knot again,
12 Take me to you, imprison me, for I
Except you'enthrall me, never shall be free,
Nor ever chaste, except you ravish me.

NOTE In lines 3, 5, 6, 11, and 13 Donne indicates a metrical elision by use of an apostrophe. In these instances readers are meant to jam two syllables together to act as one in the *scansion*.

The Bait

Come live with me, and be my love,
And we will some new pleasures prove*   *try*
Of golden sands, and crystal brooks,
4 With silken lines, and silver hooks.

There will the river whispering run
Warmed by thy eyes, more than the sun.
And there the enamored fish will stay,
8 Begging themselves they may betray.

When thou wilt swim in that live bath,
Each fish, which every channel hath,
Will amorously to thee swim,
12 Gladder to catch thee, than thou him.

If thou, to be so seen, be'st loath,
By sun, or moon, thou darknest both,
And if my self have leave to see,
16 I need not their light, having thee.

Let others freeze with angling reeds,*   *rods*
And cut their legs with shells and weeds,
Or treacherously poor fish beset,
20 With strangling snare, or windowy net:

Let coarse bold hands from slimy nest
The bedded fish in banks out-wrest,
Or curious traitors, sleave-silk* flies,   *a fine silk thread*
24 Bewitch poor fishes wand'ring eyes.

For thee, thou needst no such deceit,
For thou thy self art thine own bait;
That fish, that is not catched thereby,
28 Alas, is wiser far than I.

NOTE Donne's poem is a *parody* of the popular song by Christopher Marlowe (1564–1593),
"The Passionate Shepherd to His Love," which follows:

The Passionate Shepherd to His Love

Come live with me and be my love,
And we will all the pleasures prove
That valleys, groves, hills, and fields,
4 Woods, or steepy mountain yields.

And we will sit upon the rocks,
Seeing the shepherds feed their flocks,
By shallow rivers to whose falls
8 Melodious birds sing madrigals.

And I will make thee beds of roses
And a thousand fragrant posies,
A cap of flowers, and a kirtle
12 Embroidered all with leaves of myrtle;

A gown made of the finest wool
Which from our pretty lambs we pull;
Fair lined slippers for the cold,
16 With buckles of the purest gold;

A belt of straw and ivy buds,
With coral clasps and amber studs:
And if these pleasures may thee move,
20 Come live with me, and be my love.

The shepherds' swains shall dance and sing
For thy delight each May morning:
If these delights thy mind may move,
24 Then live with me and be my love.

Song

Go and catch a falling star,
   Get with child a mandrake* root,
Tell me where all past years are,
   Or who cleft the devil's foot,
5 Teach me to hear mermaids singing,
   Or to keep off envy's stinging,
       And find
       What wind
Serves to advance an honest mind.

the root resembles the human form

10 If thou be'st born to strange sights,
   Things invisible to see,
Ride ten thousand days and nights,
   Till age snow white hairs on thee;
Thou, when thou return'st, wilt tell me
15 All strange wonders that befell thee,
       And swear
       No where
Lives a woman true, and fair.

If thou find'st one, let me know,
20   Such a pilgrimage were sweet;
Yet do not, I would not go,
   Though at next door we might meet,
Though she were true, when you met her,
And last, till you write your letter,
25   Yet she
       Will be
False, ere I come, to two, or three.

Love's Deity

I long to talk with some old lover's ghost,
 Who died before the God of Love was born:
I cannot think that he who then loved most
 Sunk so low as to love one which did scorn.
5 But since this god produced a destiny*,   *declared a fate
 And that vice-nature*, custom, lets it be,   *second nature
 I must love her, that loves not me.

Sure, they which made him god, meant not so much
 Nor he, in his young godhead, practised it.
10 But when an even flame two hearts did touch,
 His office was indulgently to fit
Actives to passives. Correspondency
 Only his subject was; it cannot be
 Love, till I love her that loves me.

15 But every modern god will* now extend   *wants to
 His vast prerogative, as far as Jove.
To rage, to lust, to write to, to commend,
 All is the purlieu* of the God of Love.   *prerogative
Oh, were we wak'ned by this tyranny
20 To ungod this child again, it could not be
 I should love her, who loves not me.

Rebel and atheist too, why murmur I,
 As though I felt the worst that love could do?
Love might make me leave loving, or might try
25 A deeper plague, to make her love me too,
 Which, since she loves before*, I'm loth to see;   *already has a lover
Falsehood is worse than hate, and that must be,
 If she whom I love, should love me.

The Autumnal

No spring, nor summer beauty hath such grace,
    As I have seen in one autumnal face.
Young beauties force our love, and that's a rape,
5 If 'twere a shame to love, here 'twere no shame,
    Affection here takes reverence's name.
Were her first years the golden age, that's true,
    But now she's gold oft tried, and ever new.
That was her torrid and inflaming time,
10   This is her tolerable tropic clime.
Fair eyes, who asks more heat than comes from hence,
    He in a fever wishes pestilence.
Call not these wrinkles, graves; if graves they were,
    They were Love's graves, for else he is nowhere.
15 Yet lies not Love dead here, but here doth sit
    Vowed to this trench, like an anchorite*.   *hermit*
And here, till hers, which must be his death, come,
    He doth not dig a grave, but build a tomb.
Here dwells he, though he sojourn everywhere,
20   In progress, yet his standing house is here.
Here, where still evening is; not noon, nor night;
    Where no voluptuousness, yet all delight.
In all her words, unto all hearers fit,
    You may at revels, you at counsel, sit.
25 This is love's timber, youth his under-wood*;   *shrubbery*
    There he, as wine in June, enrages blood,
Which then comes seasonabliest, when our taste,
    And appetite to other things, is past.
Xerxes' strange Lydian love, the platane tree,
30   Was loved for age, none being so large as she,
Or else because, being young, nature did bless
    Her youth with age's glory, barrenness.
If we love things long sought, age is a thing
    Which we are fifty years in compassing.
35 If transitory things, which soon decay,
    Age must be loveliest at the latest day.
But name no winter faces, whose skin's slack,
    Lank as an unthrift's* purse, but a soul's sack,   *spendthrift*
Whose eyes seek light within, for all here's shade,
40   Whose mouths are holes, rather worn out, than made,
Whose every tooth to a several place is gone,
    To vex their souls at resurrection;

Name not these living death's heads unto me,
For these, not ancient, but antique be.
45 I hate extremes; yet I had rather stay
With tombs than cradles, to wear out* a day.   *spend*
Since such love's natural lation* is, may still   *movement*
My love descend, and journey down the hill;
Not panting after growing beauties, so,
50 I shall ebb out with them, who homeward go.

NOTE Xerxes, according to legend, decorated a great plane tree he discovered in Lydia.

TOPICS FOR WRITING AND DISCUSSION

FOR USE IN CLASS

1. In the sonnet, "At the round earth's imagined corners", discuss the relationship of the octave and the sestet.

2. Describe the tone of "Song: Go and catch a falling star." In your description discuss whether the tone changes within stanzas as well as from stanza to stanza.

3. Describe the tone of Donne's "The Bait."

4. Trace the intellectual progression of Donne's sonnet, "What if this present were the world's last night."

5. Write a paraphrase of Donne's "The Autumnal."

FOR PREPARATION OUTSIDE OF CLASS

1. Discuss the relationship of Donne's parody, "The Bait," to Marlowe's poem.

2. Compare Donne's attitude towards love in "Song: Go and catch a falling star" with that in "A Lecture upon the Shadow."

3. Describe those mature qualities Donne admires in "The Autumnal."

4. Discuss the range of Donne's attitudes towards love in the poems collected here.

5. Describe in detail the dominant metaphor in "Batter my heart," and discuss how it functions in the sonnet. Describe also the metaphor introduced in the sestet. How are the two metaphors related?

On The University Carrier

Here lies old Hobson, death hath broke his girt,*   *hold*
And here, alas hath laid him in the dirt,
Or else the ways being foul, twenty to one,
He's here stuck in a slough,* and overthrown,   *ditch*
5 'Twas such a shifter,* that if truth were known,   *skillful driver*
Death was half glad when he had got him down;
For he had any time this ten years full,
Dodged with him, betwixt Cambridge and the Bull.*   *London tavern*
And surely, death could never have prevailed,
10 Had not his weekly course of carriage failed;
But lately finding him so long at home,
And thinking now his journey's end was come,
And that he had ta'en up his latest inn,
In the kind office of a chamberlain*   *an attendant*
15 Showed him his room where he must lodge that night,
Pulled off his boots, and took away the light:
If any ask for him, it shall be said,
"Hobson has supt, and's newly gone to bed."

NOTE   Thomas Hobson was the coachman whose route lay between Cambridge and London; he made weekly trips carrying the students back and forth, and when he was forced to discontinue the journey because of the plague, he died in 1631. Old Hobson inspired the expression, "Hobson's Choice," meaning no choice at all; when a student wished to rent a horse from Hobson's stable, he was always told he could have any animal he wished, as long as he took the one closest to the door.

MILTON'S HUMOR

Milton's sense of humor, often completely ignored by those readers who think of him only as the stern, serious Puritan propagandist, reveals itself in his first of three poems on the passing of the University Carrier, another of which is in the additional reading. Milton develops his poem economically, using Hobson's daily journey as a *metonymy* for Hobson's life. Like all men's lives, Hobson's was a race with death, but Hobson literally raced with death on every journey, for he was known as the fastest, most adroit coach driver in Cambridge. On every trip he defeated the death that awaited him in the bad roads and adverse weather. Only after he stopped because travel in and out of London was forbidden during the plague year did death have a chance; and in a compact metaphor of death as the attendant at the inn, Milton describes Hobson quietly laid to rest by his enemy. One's impression is that although death is the ultimate victor, when Hobson awakes from that "sleep," death may have more than he bargained for.

1. How does the poem, despite its comic tone, reveal the speaker's affection for his subject?

2. How does "girt" (line 1) function metaphorically and how is it related to the extended metaphor of the poem?

3. What is the effect of the inn metaphor which concludes the poem?

* * *

An Epitaph on the Marchioness of Winchester

This rich marble doth inter
The honored wife of Winchester,
A viscount's daughter, an earl's heir,
Besides what her virtues fair
5 Added to her noble birth,
More than she could own from earth.
Summers three times eight save one
She had told;* alas too soon,   *counted*
After so short time of breath,
10 To house with darkness, and with death,
Yet had the number of her days
Been as complete as was her praise,
Nature and fate had had no strife
In giving limit to her life.
15 Her high birth, and her graces sweet,
Quickly found a lover meet;*   *appropriate*
The virgin choir for her request
The God* that sits at marriage feast;   *Hymen, god of marriage*
He at their invoking came
20 But with a scarce-well-lighted* flame;   *foreshadowing a short marriage*
And in his garland as he stood,
Yet might discern a cypress bud.*   *a sign of death*
Once had the early matrons run
To greet her of a lovely son,
25 And now with second hope she goes,
And calls Lucina* to her throes;   *goddess of childbirth*
But whether by mischance or blame
Atropos* for Lucina came,   *the Fate who cuts the thread of life*
And with remorseless cruelty,
30 Spoiled at once both fruit and tree:
The hapless babe before his birth
Had burial, yet not laid in earth,
And the languisht mother's womb
Was not long a living tomb.

35 So have I seen some tender slip
Saved with care from winter's nip,
The pride of her carnation train,
Pluckt up by some unheedy swain,
Who only thought to crop the flow'r
40 New shot up from vernal show'r
But the fair blossom hangs the head
Sideways as on a dying bed,
And those pearls of dew she wears,
Prove to be presaging tears
45 Which the sad morn had let fall
On her hast'ning funeral.
Gentle Lady, may thy grave
Peace and quiet ever have:
After this thy travail sore
50 Sweet rest seize thee evermore,
That to give the world increase,
Short'ned hast thy own life's lease;
Here, besides the sorrowing
That thy noble house doth bring,
55 Here be tears of perfect moan
Wept for thee in Helicon,*   *sacred mount of
And some flowers and some bays   Muses
For thy hearse to strew the ways,
Sent thee from the banks of Came,*   *the river at
60 Devoted to thy virtuous name;   Cambridge
Whilst thou, bright saint, high sitt'st in glory,
Next her much like to thee in story,
That fair Syrian shepherdess,*   *Rachel
Who after years of barrenness
65 The highly favored Joseph bore
To him that served for her before,
And at her next birth, much like thee,
Through pangs fled to felicity,
Far within the bosom bright
70 Of blazing majesty and light;
There with thee, new welcome saint,
Like fortunes may her soul acquaint,
With thee there clad in radiant sheen,
No Marchioness, but now a Queen.

NOTE Jane Paulet, the Marchioness of Winchester, died along with her newborn child
on April 15, 1631. It was standard practice for university students to be assigned such subjects
to commemorate important patrons and their families. (Ben Jonson also wrote an epitaph for
her.)

AN EARLY EPITAPH

This epitaph reveals the more serious, less personal, tone usually associated with Milton. The poem was obviously an assigned exercise, and the affection and sentiment appear conventional and impersonal. Milton included in orthodox fashion information about the subject's age, family, the number of her children, and the circumstances of her death. The poem could have been embellished anywhere with additional similes from nature or classical mythology. The comic epitaph "On the University Carrier" Milton could handle in his university days perhaps better than the serious epitaph. This *genre* would require more practice and a more tenacious adherence to organization before he would be able to reach the level of "Lycidas."

QUESTIONS

1. What facts can you glean from the poem about life of the Marchioness of Winchester?
2. What is the effect of the extended simile in lines 35–46?
3. Look up the story of Rachel (Genesis, XXIX, 35). What parallels does the allusion suggest?
4. What is the function of the classical and Biblical allusions in this epitaph?

On Shakespeare

What needs my Shakespeare for his honored bones
The labor of an age in piled stones,
Or that his hallowed relics* should be hid   *remains*
Under a star-ypointing pyramid!
5 Dear son of memory, great heir of fame,
What need'st thou such weak witness of thy name?
Thou in our wonder and astonishment
Hast built thyself a livelong monument.
For whilst to th'shame of slow-endeavoring art,
10 Thy easy numbers flow, and that each heart
Hath from the leaves of thy unvalued* book   *priceless*
Those Delphic* lines with deep impression took,   *inspired by the Greek oracle*
Then thou our fancy of itself bereaving,
Dost make us marble with too much conceiving;
15 And so sepulchered in such pomp dost lie,
That kings for such a tomb would wish to die.

NOTE "Astonishment" (line 7) literally means "turn to stone." Shakespeare's "astonished" readers are his appropriate "monument." In lines 13 and 14, Milton's hyperbole implies that our imaginations, confronted with the wealth of Shakespeare's poetry, are, as it were, confounded and lost in themselves and stand as if they were marble.

Milton's early verse contains an example of almost each poetic *genre:* there are serious and witty epitaphs, epigrams, translations, a spring song, sonnets, *pastoral elegies,* and *odes.* His epigram "On Shakespeare" might be compared with Ben Jonson's complimentary epigrams to Donne and Camden. Milton was purposely preparing himself for the writing of the *epic poem, Paradise Lost,* and he followed a rigorous program, practicing on the less difficult, shorter poems before he tried the extended argument.

QUESTION

Describe how Milton develops the poem's basic conceit.

Lycidas

  Yet once more, O ye laurels, and once more
Ye myrtles brown, with ivy never sere,
I come to pluck your berries harsh and crude,*   *unripe*
And with forc't fingers rude
5 Shatter your leaves before the mellowing year.
Bitter constraint, and sad occasion dear
Compels me to disturb your season due:
For Lycidas is dead ere his prime,
Young Lycidas, and hath not left his peer:
10 Who would not sing for Lycidas? he well knew
Himself to sing, and build the lofty rhyme.
He must not float upon his wat'ry bier
Unwept, and welter to the parching wind
Without the meed* of some melodious tear.   *gift*
15 Begin then, Sisters* of the sacred well   *the Muses*
That from beneath the seat of Jove doth spring,
Begin, and somewhat loudly sweep the string.*   *play the lyre*
Hence with denial vain, and coy excuse,
So may some gentle muse
20 With lucky words favour my destined urn,
 And as he passes, turn
And bid fair peace be to my sable shroud.
 For we were nurst upon the self-same hill,
 Fed the same flock by fountain, shade, and rill.
25 Together both ere the high lawns appeared
 Under the opening eyelids of the morn,
 We drove afield, and both together heard

What time the gray fly* winds her sultry horn,   *an insect: trumpet fly*
Batning* our flocks with the fresh dews of night,   *feeding*
30 Oft till the star that rose at evening bright
Toward heaven's descent had sloped his west'ring wheel.
Meanwhile the rural ditties were not mute,
Tempered to th' oaten flute:
Rough satyrs danct, and fauns with clov'n heel
35 From the glad sound would not be absent long,
And old Damætas* loved to hear our song.   *a Cambridge tutor(?)*
    But O the heavy change now thou art gone,
Now thou art gone, and never must return!
Thee shepherd, thee the woods and desert caves
40 With wild thyme, and the gadding vine o'regrown,
And all their echoes mourn.
The willows, and the hazel copses green
Shall now no more be seen,
Fanning their joyous leaves to thy soft lays.
45 As killing as the canker to the rose,
Or taint-worm to the weanling herds that graze,
Or frost to flow'rs that their gay wardrobe wear,
When first the white thorn blows;
Such, Lycidas, thy loss to shepherd's ear.
50 Where were ye nymphs when the remorseless deep
Closed o'er the head of your loved Lycidas?
For neither were ye playing on the steep,
Where your old bards the famous Drüids lie,
Nor on the shaggy top of Mona* high,   *Isle of Anglesey*
55 Nor yet where Deva* spreads her wizard stream: *River Dee*
Ay me, I fondly* dream!   *foolishly*
Had ye been there, for what could that have done?
What could the Muse* herself that Orpheus bore,   *Calliope*
The Muse herself for her enchanting son
60 Whom universal nature did lament,
When by the rout that made the hideous roar
His gory visage down the stream was sent,
Down the swift Hebrus* to the Lesbian shore.   *the stream*
    Alas! What boots it* with incessant care   *what advantage is it*
65 To tend the homely slighted shepherd's trade
And strictly meditate the thankless muse?
Were it not better done as others use,*   *do*
To sport with Amaryllis in the shade,
Or with the tangles of Neæra's hair?
70 Fame is the spur that the clear spirit doth raise

(That last infirmity of noble mind)
To scorn delights, and live laborious days;
But the fair guerdon* when we hope to find   *reward*
And think to burst out into sudden blaze,
75 Comes the blind Fury* with th' abhorred shears   *Atropos*
And slits the thin-spun life. "But not the praise,"
Phoebus replied, and toucht my trembling ears;
"Fame is no plant that grows on mortal soil,
Nor in the glistering* foil   *glittering*
80 Set off to th' world, nor in broad rumor lies,
But lives and spreads aloft by those pure eyes
And perfect witness of all-judging Jove
As he pronounces lastly on each deed,
Of so much fame in Heav'n expect thy meed."
85   O Fountain Arethuse* and thou honoured flood,   *a Sicilian fountain*
Smooth-sliding Minicius,* crowned with vocal reeds,   *a river in Italy*
That strain I heard was of a higher mood:
But now my oat* proceeds   *reed pipe*
And listens to the Herald of the Sea*   *Triton*
90 That came in Neptune's plea,
He askt the waves, and askt the felon winds,
What hard mishap hath doomed this gentle swain?
And questioned every gust of rugged wings
That blows from off each beaked promontory,
95 They knew not of his story,
And sage Hippotades* their answer brings   *Aeolus, god of wind*
That not a blast was from his dungeon strayed,
The air was calm, and on the level brine
Sleek Panope* with all her sisters played.   *sea nymph*
100 It was that fatal and perfidious bark
Built in th' eclipse*, and rigged with curses dark,   *i.e. accursed*
That sunk so low that sacred head of thine.
     Next Camus*, reverend Sire, went footing slow,   *the River Cam*
His mantle hairy, and his bonnet sedge,
105 Inwrought with figures dim, and on the edge
Like to that sanguine flow'r* inscribed with woe.   *hyacinth*
"Ah! who hath reft," quoth he, "my dearest pledge?"
Last came and last did go
The Pilot* of the Galilean lake,   *St. Peter*
110 Two massy keys he bore of metals twain
(The golden opes, the iron shuts amain).
He shook his mitred locks and stern bespake,
"How well could I have spared for thee, young swain,

Enow* of such as for their bellies' sake   *enough*
115 Creep and intrude, and climb into the fold?
Of other care they little reck'ning make
Than how to scramble at the shearers' feast
And shove away the worthy bidden guest.
Blind mouths! that scarce themselves know how to hold
120 A sheephook, or have learned ought else the least
That to the faithful herdman's art belongs!
What recks it* them? What need they? They are sped;°   *means it; °prosperous*
And when they list,* their lean and flashy songs   *like*
Grate on their scrannel* pipes of wretched straw,   *thin*
125 The hungry sheep look up and are not fed,
But swoln with wind, and the rank mist they draw,
Rot inwardly, and foul contagion spread:
Besides what the grim wolf with privy paw*   *with secrecy*
Daily devours apace, and little said,
130 But that two-handed engine* at the door   *sword*
Stands ready to smite once and smite no more."
    Return Alpheus, the dread voice is past
That shrunk thy streams; return Sicilian Muse,
And call the vales and bid them hither cast
135 Their bells, and flowrets of a thousand hues.
Ye valleys low where the mild whispers use,
Of shades and wanton winds, and gushing brooks,
On whose fresh lap the swart star* sparely looks,   *summer dog star*
Throw hither all your quaint enameled eyes
140 That on the green turf suck the honeyed show'rs
And purple all the ground with vernal flow'rs.
Bring the rathe* primrose that forsaken dies,   *early*
The rufted crowtoe and pale jessamine,
The white pink, and the pansy freakt* with jet,   *spotted*
145 The glowing violet,
The musk rose and the well-attired woodbine,
With cowslips wan that hang the pensive head,
And every flower that sad embroidery wears:
Bid amaranthus all his beauties shed
150 And daffadillies fill their cups with tears
To strew the laureate hearse where Lycid' lies.
For so to interpose a little ease,
Let our frail thoughts dally with false surmise;
Ay me! Whilst thee the shores and sounding seas
155 Wash far away, where're thy bones are hurled,
Whether beyond the stormy Hebrides

Where thou perhaps under the whelming tide
Visit'st the bottom of the monstrous world;
Or whether thou to our moist vows denied
160 Sleep'st by the fable of Bellerus* old   *a mythical Cornish giant*
Where the great vision of the guarded mount*   *Large rock off Cornwall*
Looks toward Namancos,* and Bayona's* hold: *cities in Spain*
Look homeward Angel now and melt with ruth
And O ye dolphins, waft the hapless youth.
165 Weep no more, woeful shepherds, weep no more,
For Lycidas your sorrow is not dead,
Sunk through he be beneath the watery floor,
So sinks the day star in the ocean bed
And yet anon repairs his drooping head
170 And tricks his beams, and with newspangled ore
Flames in the forehead of the morning sky:
So Lycidas sunk low but mounted high
Through the dear might of him that walkt the waves:
Where other groves and other streams along
175 With nectar pure his oozy locks he laves*   *washes*
And hears the unexpressive nuptial song
In the blest kingdoms meek of joy and love.
There entertain him all the saints above
In solemn troops, and sweet societies
180 That sing, and singing in their glory move
And wipe the tears forever from his eyes.
Now Lycidas, the shepherds weep no more;
Henceforth thou art the Genius* of the shore   *spirit*
In thy large recompense, and shalt be good
185 To all that wander in that perilous flood.
Thus sang the uncouth* swain to th' oaks and rills,   *unsophisticated*
While the still morn went out with sandals gray;
He toucht the tender stops of various quills,
With eager thought warbling his Doric lay:
190 And now the sun had stretch out all the hills,
And now was dropt into the western bay;
At last he rose and twitcht his mantle blue:
Tomorrow to fresh woods and pastures new.

NOTES "Lycidas" honors Edward King, drowned in the Irish Sea on August 10, 1637. A
student at Christ's College, Cambridge, King planned eventually to enter the clergy. Milton's
poem, one of many in memory of King, is the last poem in a little volume of elegies published
by Cambridge students to honor their lost friend.
   Milton's "Lycidas" is the most difficult poem you have read so far, and it may be the most
difficult poem in this book. It is, however, a poem which repays constant study, and which
rewards the reader in proportion to the skill and knowledge he brings to the poem.

THE PASTORAL ELEGY

Milton chose to honor his fellow student with the highly artificial conventions of the pastoral elegy: the genre was firmly established in the seventeenth century (and continues today). Pastoral poetry originated in Sicily and is remembered in the laments of Theocritus for Thrysis (215 B.C.) and later Moschus (100 B.C.) for Bion. For Milton, however, the great pastoral poet was Virgil, and after him the practitioners of the mode were legion. Traditionally the speaker assumes the guise of a shepherd (pastor), and the friend lamented is portrayed as another shepherd. Since shepherds' lives are usually passed out of doors, pastoral poetry is an occasion for all sorts of natural description and catalogues of trees, flowers, rivers, and mountains. Shepherds, also according to tradition, had time to sing and philosophize and lived in a kind of Eden while they watched their flocks graze peacefully on green hillsides. Milton and Edward King, of course, were not sheperds, but King was training for the ministry; soon he was to have been a pastor with his own flock (congregation) protecting it against the greatest wolf known: Lucifer himself. So when Milton chose to call his friend "Lycidas" he was immediately committed to a tradition and a genre which he could exploit in two ways. King is honored by his position among the great shepherd-poet-priest figures of history and mythology. Secondly, the many pastoral allusions which modern readers find mystifying accumulate significance as they metaphorize an almost perfect world, stunned by the death of a young man whose life could have returned the world to perfection.

An unknown shepherd, then, bemoans the death of a fellow. In his *monody* he tell us something of his thoughts and something of his attitudes towards the world in general. Like the speaker in Donne's "A Nocturnal upon St. Lucy's Day," the shepherd reassesses the meaning of his own life after he has been confronted with death. Naturally he is concerned with what appears to be a meaningless and futile existence, if when death comes it takes with it the immature and the unfulfilled. He wonders why he should lead a good life if the good are taken early and the wicked seem to prosper. He wonders why life ends in a seemingly pointless way.

When one looks at the poem, he can see that it is divided into three large blocks of action. The first subject concerns the value of the ascetic life when the future is always uncertain. Some assurance is given by Phoebus, whose "strain . . . was of a higher mood." After this *modulation*, the pastoral proceeds, and later the terrible figure of St. Peter resolves the next question: why are the faithful taken early while the unfaithful seem to thrive? St. Peter assures us that justice will eventually triumph in the world. We are convinced that a poet's way of life is not folly and that evil will not ultimately prosper. The third part of the elegy confirms the *apotheosis* of the poet-priest-shepherd, an apotheosis as "genius of the shore." The elegy exemplifies the classical movement from sorrow to joy.

QUESTIONS

1. In what sense are the "berries" (line 3) appropriate tributes for Lycidas?
2. What do laurels, myrtles, and ivy have in common?
3. In what lines does the speaker wish to have his own passing celebrated as Lycidas' is?
4. What is the effect of the pastoral imagery (lines 23–36) which characterizes the relationship between the speaker and Lycidas?
5. Describe the effect upon that ideal world enjoyed together, now that Lycidas is dead (lines 37–49).
6. Paraphrase the question the speaker asks in lines 50–55.
7. Look up in a reference book the story of Orpheus. What is the effect or function of the allusion to Orpheus' death in lines 58–63?
8. Paraphrase Phoebus' answer to the speaker's argument about the uselessness of the ascetic life.
9. What do lines 90–102 tell us of nature's responsibility in the death of Lycidas?
10. What consolation is offered the speaker by St. Peter?
11. Describe nature's tribute to Lycidas (lines 133–151). What is the function of the long catalogue of flowers?
12. Describe the vision of Lycidas at the conclusion of the poem (lines 165–185).
13. Twice the speaker refers to his song as a "tear." Discuss how the water imagery functions in the poem.
14. Divide the poem into its three major sections. Give your reasons for making such divisions.
15. Describe how the first 14 lines of "Lycidas" are a variation on the sonnet form.
16. What is the effect of the short lines of the poem?
17. What effect is gained from lines that do not rhyme?
18. Name the stanza form with which "Lycidas" concludes (lines 186–193). Speculate on the relationship of this to the version of a sonnet which opens the poem.

Sonnet VIII

Captain or colonel, or knight in arms,
  Whose chance on these defenseless doors may seize,
  If ever deed of honor did thee please,
4   Guard them, and him within protect from harms;
He can requite thee, for he knows the charms
  That call fame on such gentle acts as these,
  And he can spread thy name o'er lands and seas,
8   Whatever clime the sun's bright circle warms.
Lift not thy spear against the muses' bow'r:
  The great Emathian conqueror* bid spare   *Alexander*
  The house of Pindarus,* when temple and tow'r   *Greek poet, 522-443 B.C.*
12 Went to the ground; and the repeated air
  Of sad Electra's poet* had the pow'r   *Euripides*
  To save th'Athenian walls from ruin bare.

NOTES   This sonnet was written in November, 1642, while England was engaged in civil war, and when Milton, in London, expected the city to be assaulted.

    Milton's allusion to Pindar's house (line 11) reminds the reader that Alexander the Great spared that house when the rest of the city was razed.

    Tradition has it that the opening chorus of the play *Electra* convinced the Spartans not to destroy Athens (lines 12–14).

MILTON'S SONNETS

    Milton wrote only 23 sonnets; seventeen are in English, and all are in the Italian form. Obviously he regarded the sonnet as a significant form for the *occasional poem*, returning to it time and again from 1630 to 1657. With their variety and skill, these sonnets provide excellent examples in miniature of Milton's syntactical patterns, of his use of metrical inversions and rhyme variations, his colloquial vigor, and his subtle tonal manipulations. For students who think of the Italian sonnet as a tight grammatical unit with clear breaks at lines 4 and 8 and another at 11 to divide the sestet, Milton's sonnets may come as a surprise. Many do not observe these strictures, and some break at line 9, or after $8\frac{1}{2}$ lines, or at line 6 instead of line 4, and some look very much like Shakespearian sonnets concluding in a rhymed couplet. Milton's divisions are those required by thought rather than by model; pauses occur anywhere in the lines, and clauses often continue on into the *tercet*.

QUESTIONS

    1. What is the full range of meaning suggested by the word "gentle" in line 6?
    2. What is the "muses' bow'r" (line 9)?
    3. Describe the claim that Milton makes for the power of poetry.
    4. What is the relationship of the sestet to the octave?

Sonnet XVIII

Avenge, O Lord, thy slaughtered saints, whose bones
  Lie scattered on the Alpine mountains cold,
  Ev'n them who kept thy truth so pure of old
4   When all our fathers worshipt stocks* and stones,   *idols*
Forget not: in thy book record their groans
  Who were thy sheep and in their ancient fold
  Slain by the bloody Piemontese that rolled
8   Mother with infant down the rocks. Their moans
The vales redoubled to the hills, and they
  To heav'n. Their martyred blood and ashes sow
  O'er all th'Italian fields where still doth sway
12   The triple tyrant:* that from these may grow   *the Pope*
  A hundredfold, who having learnt thy way
  Early may fly the Babylonian woe.*   *captivity*

NOTE Milton's impassioned sonnet is in reaction to the massacre of a group called the Vaudois who lived in the Alps and who, in the 12th century, broke with the papacy. To gather favor with the Pope, the Duke of Savoy led a brutal attack upon the Vaudois, and the Protestant world reacted violently to the massacre.

QUESTIONS

1. Most of the words in the sonnet are monosyllabic. What is the effect of the simplicity of language here?

2. Milton's plea is not that God slaughter those responsible for the massacre. What form does he wish God's vengeance to take?

3. Lines 10–13 allude to the myth of Cadmus and the dragon's teeth. Look up the myth in a reference book and describe the effect of the allusion.

4. Milton does not follow the standard practice of breaking at lines 4, 8, and 11. Where does he break in this sonnet, and what is the effect of the variation?

WHAT TO LOOK FOR IN THE ADDITIONAL READING

Here are six additional sonnets, including an example (Sonnet XVII) of the "heroic" sonnet: that is, one commemorative of a great man after the manner of Tasso. The earliest of the sonnets, on the nightingale, presents a young Milton ready to dedicate himself to love lyrics in the accepted tradition; he never wrote another love sonnet. Here is sufficient opportunity to compare a perhaps less successful, more exuberantly undergraduate, epitaph on old Hobson, and here also is a fine verse paragraph praising music as the emblem of heavenly harmony. Soon, Milton hopes, fallen man will raise himself up again and sing, as he once did, in harmony with the heavenly choir.

As you read, you will wish to compare Milton's tributes and the effect of those tributes with Ben Jonson's *encomiastic* epigrams. Perhaps you may even wish to imitate what you think is the typical tone of a Miltonic, or Jonsonian, poem by attempting to write one in their manner.

Sonnet I

O nightingale, that on yon bloomy spray
    Warbl'st at eve, when all the woods are still,
    Thou with fresh hope the lover's heart dost fill,
4 While the jolly hours lead on propitious May;
Thy liquid notes that close the eye of day,
    First heard before the shallow cuckoo's bill,
    Portend success in love; O, if Jove's will
8 Have linkt that amorous power to thy soft lay,
Now timely sing, ere the rude Bird of Hate*   *cuckoo*
    Foretell my hopeless doom in some grove nigh:
    As thou from year to year hast sung too late
12 For my relief, yet hadst no reason why.
    Whether the muse, or love call thee his mate,
    Both them I serve, and of their train am I.

Sonnet IX

Lady, that in the prime of earliest youth,
    Wisely hast shunned the broad way and the green,
    And with those few art eminently seen
4 That labor up the hill of heav'nly truth,
The better part with Mary and with Ruth
    Chosen thou hast; and they that overween,
    And at thy growing virtues fret their spleen,
8 No anger find in thee, but pity and ruth*.   *compassion*
Thy *care* is fixt and zealously attends
    To fill thy odorous lamp with deeds of light,
    And hope that reaps not shame. Therefore be sure
12 Thou, when the bridegroom with his feastful friends
    Passes to bliss at the mid-hour of night,
    Hast gained thy entrance, virgin wise and pure.

NOTES Mary and Ruth (line 5) are *symbols* of feminine perfection (See Luke, x, 42, and Ruth I, 14).
    The predicate verb of the first sentence is the first word of line 6; the subject is "Lady" (line 1).
    Notice also that the predicate verb whose subject is "thou" (line 12) is "Hast gained" (line 14).
    The allusion in lines 10–14 is found in the Parable of the Ten Virgins (Matthew, xxv, 6).

Sonnet XIII

Harry, whose tuneful and well measured song
  First taught our English music how to span
  Words with just note and accent, not to scan
4   With Midas'* ears, committing° short and long,   *insensitive;
Thy worth and skill exempts thee from the throng,   °setting in conflict
  With praise enough for envy to look wan;
  To after age thou shalt be writ the man
8   That with smooth air couldst humor best our tongue.
Thou honor'st verse, and verse must lend her wing
  To honor thee, the priest of Phoebus' choir,
  That tun'st their happiest lines in hymn, or story.
12 Dante shall give fame leave to set thee higher
  Than his Casella, whom he* wooed to sing,   *Dante*
  Met in the milder shades of Purgatory.

NOTES   The sonnet is dedicated to Henry Lawes, a famous musician who collaborated with Milton in producing the poet's *mask, Comus.*
    The allusion to Dante (lines 12–14) refers to Dante's encounter with his friend, the musician Casella. When Dante imagined their meeting in purgatory, Casella's voice was still able to charm him.

Sonnet XVII

Vane, young in years, but in sage counsel old,
  Than whom a better seantor ne'er held
  The helm of Rome, when gowns not arms repelled
4   The fierce Epirot* and the African bold,   *Pyrrhus, ancient Greek king*
Whether to settle peace, or to unfold
  The drift of hollow* states hard to be spelled°,   *literally, Holland; metaphorically, devious;*
  Then to advise how war may best, upheld,   °discovered
8   Move by her two main nerves, iron and gold,
In all her equipage; besides to know
  Both spiritual power and civil, what each means,
  What severs each, thou hast learnt, which few have done.
12 The bounds of either sword to thee we owe.
  Therefore on thy firm hand religion leans
  In peace, and reck'ns thee her eldest son.

NOTE   Sir Henry Vane was a famous English statesman and a strong English moderate in politics. He was four years younger than Milton. In 1652 Vane was in charge of English attempts to ally with Holland, but when he discovered the Dutch duplicity, he severed negotiations.

Sonnet XX

Lawrence, of virtuous father virtuous son,
 Now that the fields are dank and ways are mire,
 Where shall we sometimes meet and by the fire
4 Help waste a sullen day, what may be won
From the hard season gaining? Time will run
 On smoother till Favonius* re-inspire   *the west wind*
 The frozen earth, and clothe in fresh attire
8 The lily and rose, that neither sowed nor spun.
What neat repast shall feast us, light and choice,
 Of Attic* taste, with wine, whence we may rise *Athenian (modest)*
 To hear the lute well toucht, or artful voice
12 Warble immortal notes and Tuscan* air?   *Italian*
 He who of those delights can judge and spare
 To interpose them oft, is not unwise.

NOTE Edward Lawrence (1633–1656) was 22 when Milton addressed the sonnet to him.

Sonnet XXII

Cyriack, this three years' day these eyes, though clear
 To outward view of blemish or of spot,
 Bereft of light their seeing have forgot;
4 Nor to their idle orbs doth sight appear
Of sun or moon or star throughout the year,
 Or man or woman. Yet I argue not
 Against heav'n's hand or will, nor bate* a jot *surrender*
8 Of heart or hope; but still bear up and steer
Right onward. What supports me, dost thou ask?
 The conscience, friend, to have lost them overplied
 In liberty's defense, my noble task,
12 Of which all Europe talks from side to side.
 This thought might lead me through the world's vain mask,
 Content though blind, had I no better guide.

NOTE Cyriack Skinner was a friend of Milton's. In lines 10–11, Milton claims to have lost his eyesight while engaged as Cromwell's Secretary of Foreign Tongues, defending English policies to the rest of the world.

Another on the Same

Here lieth one who did most truly prove
That he could never die while he could move,
So hung his destiny never to rot
While he might still jog on and keep his trot,
5 Made of sphere*-metal, never to decay   *heavenly*
Until his revolution was at stay.
Time numbers* motion, yet (without a crime   *measures*
'Gainst old truth) motion numbered out his time;
And like an engine moved with wheel and weight,
10 His principles* being ceast, he ended straight.°   *bodily faculties;*
Rest that gives all men life, gave him his death,   °*immediately*
And too much breathing put him out of breath;
Nor were it contradiction to affirm
Too long vacation hastened on his term.
15 Merely to drive the time away he sick'ned,
Fainted, and died, nor would with ale be quick'ned;
"Nay," quoth he, on his swooning bed outstretched,
"If I may not carry, sure I'll ne'er be fetched,
But vow, though the cross doctors all stood bearers,
20 For one carrier put down to make six bearers."
Ease was his chief disease, and to judge right,
He died for heaviness that his cart went light.
His leisure told him that his time was come,
And lack of load made his life burdensome,
25 That even to his last breath (there be that say't)
As he were prest to death, he cried, "more weight";
But had his doings lasted as they were,
He had been an immortal carrier.
Obedient to the moon he spent his date
30 In course reciprocal, and had his fate
Linkt to the mutual flowing of the seas,   *pun on wain*
Yet (strange to think) his wain* was his increase: *(wagon)*
His letters are delivered all and gone,   *and wane*
Only remains this superscription.   *(diminish)*

NOTE This poem is also about Hobson; see the earlier discussion.

At a Solemn Music*   *a concert*

Blest pair of Sirens, pledges of heav'n's joy,
Sphere-born* harmonious sisters, voice and verse,   *earthly*
Wed your divine sounds, and mixt power employ,
Dead things with inbreathed sense able to pierce,
5 And to our high-raised fantasy* present   *imagination*
That undisturbed song of pure concent*   *harmony*
Aye, sung before the sapphire-colored throne
To him that sits thereon,
With saintly shout and solemn jubilee,
10 Where the bright seraphim in burning row
Their loud uplifted angel-trumpets blow,
And the cherubic host in thousand choirs
Touch their immortal harps of golden wires,
With those just spirits that wear victorious palms,
15 Hymns devout and holy psalms
Singing everlastingly;
That we on earth with undiscording voice
May rightly answer that melodious noise;
As once we did, till disproportioned sin
20 Jarred against nature's chime, and with harsh din
Broke the fair music that all creatures made
To their great Lord, whose love their motion swayed
In perfect diapason*, whilst they stood   *harmony*
In first obedience and their state of good.
25 O may we soon again renew that song,
And keep in tune with heav'n, till God ere long
To his celestial consort us unite,
To live with him, and sing in endless morn of light.

TOPICS FOR WRITING AND DISCUSSION

FOR USE IN CLASS

1. Describe the specific abilities Milton praises in his friend Henry Lawes, and discuss how the tone of Sonnet XIII is established.

2. Describe the tone of Sonnet XXII. What aspects of diction and syntax contribute significantly to the tone?

3. Paraphrase Sonnet XVII.

4. Describe the effect of *enjambment* in Sonnet XX.

1. Describe how Milton, in a series of witty contrasts, develops the second epitaph on Hobson.

2. Compare the attitudes towards the classical tradition of the dinner party in Jonson's "On Inviting a Friend to Dinner" and in Milton's Sonnet XX.

3. Write an essay on Milton's use of classical and Biblical allusions. (You may wish to limit yourself only to the sonnets.)

4. Write an essay comparing Milton's handling of the sonnet form with that of Shakespeare.

Winter

LYCIDAS

Thyrsis, the music of that murmuring spring
Is not so mournful as the strains you sing,
Nor rivers winding through the vales below,
So sweet by warble, or so smoothly flow.
5 Now sleeping flocks on their soft fleeces lie,
The moon, serene in glory, mounts the sky,
While silent birds forget their tuneful lays,
Oh sing of Daphne's fate, and Daphne's praise!

THYRSIS

Behold the groves that shine with silver frost,
10 Their beauty withered, and their verdure lost.
Here shall I try the sweet Alexis' strain,
That called the listening Dryads to the plain?
Thames heard the numbers as he flowed along,
And bade his willows learn the moving song.

LYCIDAS

15 So may kind rains their vital moisture yield,
And swell the future harvest of the field!
Begin; this charge the dying Daphne gave,
And said; "Ye shepherds, sing around my grave!"
Sing, while beside the shaded tomb I mourn,
20 And with fresh bays her rural shrine adorn.

THYRSIS

Ye gentle muses leave your crystal spring,
Let nymphs and sylvans cypress garlands bring;
Ye weeping loves, the stream with myrtles hide,
And break your bows, as when Adonis died;
25 And with your golden darts, now useless grown,
Inscribe a verse on this relenting stone:
"Let nature change, let heaven and earth deplore,
Fair Daphne's dead, and love is now no more!"
'Tis done, and nature's various charms decay;

30 See gloomy clouds obscure the cheerful day!
Now hung with pearls the dropping trees appear,
Their faded honours scattered on her bier.
See, where on earth the flowery glories lie,
With her they flourished, and with her they die.
35 Ah what avail the beauties nature wore?
Fair Daphne's dead, and beauty is no more!
For her, the flocks refuse their verdant food,
The thirsty heifers shun the gliding flood.
The silver swans her hapless fate bemoan,
40 In notes more sad than when they sing their own.
In hollow caves sweet Echo silent lies,
Silent, or only to her name replies,
Her name with pleasure once she taught the shore,
Now Daphne's dead, and pleasure is no more!
45 No grateful dews descend from evening skies,
Nor morning odours from the flowers arise.
No rich perfumes refresh the fruitful field,
No fragrant herbs their native incense yield.
The balmy zephyrs, silent since her death,
50 Lament the ceasing of a sweeter breath.
The industrious bees neglect their golden store;
Fair Daphne's dead, and sweetness is no more!
No more the mounting larks, while Daphne sings,
Shall listening in mid air suspend their wings;
55 No more the birds shall imitate her lays,
Or hushed with wonder, hearken from the sprays:
No more the streams their murmurs shall forbear,
A sweeter music than their own to hear,
But tell the reeds, and tell the vocal shore,
60 Fair Daphne's dead, and music is no more!
Her fate is whispered by the gentle breeze,
And told in sighs to all the trembling trees;
The trembling trees, in every plain and wood,
Her fate remurmur to the silver flood;
65 The silver flood, so lately calm, appears
Swelled with new passion, and o'erflows with tears;
The winds and trees and floods her death deplore,
Daphne, our grief! our glory now no more!
But see! where Daphne wandering mounts on high,
70 Above the clouds, above the starry sky.
Eternal beauties grace the shining scene,
Fields ever fresh, and groves forever green!

There, while you rest in Amaranthine* bowers   *unfading*
Or from those meads select unfading flowers,
75 Behold us kindly who your name implore,
Daphne, our goddess, and our grief no more!

LYCIDAS

How all things listen, while thy muse complains!
Such silence waits on Philomela's* strains,   *the nightingale*
In some still evening, when the whispering breeze
80 Pants on the leaves, and dies upon the trees.
To thee, bright goddess, oft a lamb shall bleed,
If teeming ewes increase my fleecy breed.
While plants their shade, or flowers their odours give,
Thy name, thy honour, and thy praise shall live!

THYRSIS

85 But see, Orion* sheds unwholesome dews,   *constellation*
Arise, the pines a noxious* shade diffuse;   *presaging storm*
Sharp Boreas* blows, and nature feels decay,   *north wind*
Time conquers all, and we must time obey.
Adieu ye vales, ye mountains, streams and groves,
90 Adieu ye shepherd's rural lays and loves,
Adieu my flocks, farewell ye sylvan crew,
Daphne farewell, and all the world adieu!

NOTE The names Lycidas, Thyrsis, and Daphne are traditional in pastoral poetry.

A PASTORAL

Among Alexander Pope's earliest poems are four pastorals—"Spring," "Summer," "Autumn," and "Winter"—patterned after numerous classical models. "Winter" is a pastoral elegy echoing Theocritus' and Virgil's laments (also in dialogue form) for Daphne; you will also notice specific parallels in Milton's lament for Lycidas. Traditionally, Daphne was considered the sylvan originator of pastoral poetry, and her passing was celebrated by generations of poets.

In contrast to Shakespeare's song on winter, which describes graphically the discomforts of the weather and the pleasures of indoor life, Pope's pastoral uses the season in a metaphorical sense: since winter is identified with the bleakness and sterility of the earth now that Daphne is dead, it is the symbol for death. After the title, Pope never once mentions the literal name of the season; he works by indirection, describing for us, not what winter is like, but what winter is not like. Thus he can describe the pleasures we have lost, mentioning them once more as he catalogues, negatively, what we have lost at the passing of Daphne. It is as if the world and the poet never experienced death before; their trust in song had been so great they thought it should confer immortality at least.

QUESTIONS

1. How do the refrain lines structure the progression of Thyrsis' lament (lines 21–76)?
2. How are the classical allusions to Adonis, Echo, and Philomela appropriate to the desolation of the dramatic situation?
3. Describe the effect gained by the use of sound images in the poem.
4. Compare the attitude of Thyrsis' resolution (lines 69–76) with the tone of his final speech. How do you reconcile the apparent optimism of the one with the pessimism of the other?
5. Explain the unity of the imagery in lines 13–14, 21–24, 31–32, and 65–67.
6. The poem is extremely rich in sound patterns. What patterns of alliteration or assonance can you observe, and what is their effect upon you? (Look especially at lines 1, 2, 5, 7, 11, 47, 81, and 82.)

* * *

Epistle to a Lady: Of the Characters of Women

Nothing so true as what you once let fall,
"Most women have no characters at all."
Matter too soft a lasting mark to bear,
And best distinguished by black, brown, or fair.
5 How many pictures of one nymph* we view, *lady*
All how unlike each other, all how true!
Arcadia's countess, here, in ermined pride,
Is there, Pastora by a fountain side.
Here Fannia, leering on her own good man,
10 And there, a naked Leda with a swan.
Let then the fair one beautifully cry,
In Magdalen's loose hair and lifted eye,
Or drest in smiles of sweet Cecilia shine,
With simpering angels, palms, and harps divine;
15 Whether the charmer sinner it, or saint it,
If folly grows romantic,* I must paint it. *extravagant*
  Come then, the colours and the ground prepare!
Dip in the rainbow, trick her off* in air, *imagine her*
Choose a firm cloud, before it falls, and in it

20 Catch, ere she change, the Cynthia of this minute.
  Rufa, whose eye quick-glancing o'er the park,
  Attracts each light gay meteor of a spark,*   *fashionable young man*
  Agrees as ill with Rufa studying Locke,*   *British philosopher*
  As Sappho's diamonds with her dirty smock,
25 Or Sappho at her toilet's greasy task
  With Sappho fragrant at an evening mask:
  So morning insects that in muck begun,
  Shine, buzz, and fly-blow* in the setting sun.   *flit*
  How soft is Silia! fearful to offend,
30 The frail one's advocate, the weak one's friend:
  To her, Calista* proved her conduct nice,   *a fallen woman*
  And good simplicius* asks of her advice.   *a simpleton*
  Sudden, she storms! she raves! You tip the wink,*   *raise eyebrows*
  But spare your censure; Silia does not drink.
35 All eyes may see from what the change arose,
  All eyes may see—a pimple on her nose.
  Papilla, wedded to her doting spark,
  Sighs for the shades—"How charming is a Park!"
  A park is purchased, but the fair he sees
40 All bathed in tears—"Oh odious, odious trees!"
  Ladies, like variegated tulips, show,
  'Tis to their changes half their charms we owe;
  Their happy spots the nice admirer take,
  Fine by defect, and delicately weak.
45 'Twas thus Calypso* once each heart alarmed,   *a famous nymph*
  Awed without virtue, without beauty charmed;
  Her tongue bewitched as oddly as her eyes,
  Less wit than mimic, more a wit than wise:
  Strange graces still, and stranger flights she had,
50 Was just not ugly, and was just not mad;
  Yet ne'er so sure our passion to create,
  As when she touched the brink of all we hate.
  Narcissa's nature, tolerably mild,
  To make a wash,* would hardly stew a child;   *a hair rinse*
55 Has even been proved to grant a lover's prayer,
  And paid a tradesman once to make him stare,
  Gave alms at Easter, in a Christian trim,*   *manner*
  And made a widow happy, for a whim.
  Why then declare good-nature is her scorn,
60 When 'tis by that alone she can be born?
  Why pique all mortals, yet affect a name?
  A fool to pleasure, yet a slave to fame:

Now deep in Taylor* and the Book of Martyrs,*   *religious literature*
    Now drinking citron* with his grace and Chartres.   *brandy and lemon*
65 Now conscience chills her, and now passion burns:
    And atheism and religion take their turns;
    A very heathen in the carnal part,
    Yet still a sad, good Christian at her heart.
    See Sin in state, majestically drunk,
70 Proud as a peeress, prouder as a punk,*   *a prostitute*
    Chaste to her husband, frank to all beside,
    A teeming mistress, but a barren bride.
    What then? let blood and body bear the fault,
    Her head's untouched, that noble seat of thought:
75 Such this day's doctrine—in another fit
    She sins with poets through pure love of wit.
    What has not fired her bosom or her brain?
    Caesar and tall-boy,* Charles° and Charlemagne.   *a booby; °a footman
    As Helluo,* late dictator of the feast,   glutton
80 The nose of hautgout,* and the tip of taste,   strong-smelling food
    Criticked your wine, and analyzed your meat,
    Yet on plain pudding deigned at home to eat;
    So Philomede, lect'ring all mankind
    On the soft passion, and the taste refined,
85 The address, the delicacy—stoops at once,
    And makes her hearty meal upon a dunce.
        Flavia's a wit, has too much sense to pray,
    To toast our wants and wishes, is her way;
    Nor asks of God, but of her stars to give
90 The mighty blessing, "While we live, to live."
    Then all for death, that opiate of the soul!
    Lucretia's dagger, Rosamonda's bowl.
    Say, what can cause such impotence of mind?
    A spark too fickle, or a spouse too kind.
95 Wise wretch! with pleasures too refined to please,
    With too much spirit to be e'er at ease,
    With too much quickness ever to be taught,
    With too much thinking to have common thought:
    You purchase pain with all that joy can give,
100 And die of nothing but a rage to live.
        Turn then from wits; and look on Simo's mate,
    No ass so meek, no ass so obstinate:
    Or her, that owns her faults, but never mends,
    Because she's honest, and the best of friends:
105 Or her, whose life the church and scandal share,

Forever in a passion, or a prayer:
Or her, who laughs at Hell, but (like her grace)
Cries, "Ah! how charming if there's no such place!"
Or who in sweet vicissitude appears
110 Of mirth and opium, ratafie* and tears, *cherry brandy*
The daily anodyne, and nightly draught,
To kill those foes to fair ones, time and thought.
Woman and fool are two hard things to hit,
For true no-meaning* puzzles more than wit. *enigma*
115 But what are these to great Atossa's mind?
Scarce once herself, by turns all womankind!
Who, with herself, or others, from her birth
Finds all her life one warfare upon earth:
Shines, in exposing knaves, and painting fools,
120 Yet is, whate'er she hates and ridicules.
No thought advances, but her eddy brain
Whisks* it about, and down it goes again. *whirls*
Full sixty years the world has been her trade,
The wisest fool much time has ever made.
125 From loveless youth to unrespected age,
No passion gratified except her rage.
So much the fury still outran the wit,
The pleasure missed her, and the scandal hit.
Who breaks with her, provokes revenge from Hell,
130 But he's a bolder man who dares be well:
Her every turn with violence pursued,
Nor more a storm her hate than gratitude.
To that each passion turns, or soon or late;
Love, if it makes her yield, must make her hate:
135 Superiors? death! and equals? what a curse!
But an inferior not dependant? worse.
Offend her, and she knows not to forgive;
Oblige her, and she'll hate you while you live:
But die, and she'll adore you—then the bust
140 And temple rise—then fall again to dust.
Last night, her Lord was all that's good and great,
A knave this morning, and his will a cheat.
Strange! by the means defeated of the ends,
By spirit robbed of power, by warmth of friends,
145 By wealth of followers! without one distress
Sick of herself through very selfishness!
Atossa, cursed with every tranted* prayer, *hypocritical*
Childless with all her children, wants an heir.

To heirs unknown descends the unguarded store
150 Or wanders, heaven-directed, to the poor.
     Pictures like these, dear Madam, to design,
Asks no firm hand, no unerring line;
Some wandering touches, some reflected light,
Some flying stroke alone can hit them right:
155 For how should equal colours do the knack?
Chameleons who can paint in white and black?
     "Yet Cloe sure was formed without a spot—"
Nature in her then erred not, but forgot.
"With every pleasing, every prudent part,
160 Say, what can Cloe want?"—she wants a heart.
She speaks, behaves, and acts just as she ought;
But never, never, reached one generous thought.
Virtue she finds too painful an endeavour,
Content to dwell in decencies forever.
165 So very reasonable, so unmoved,
As never yet to love, or to be loved.
She, while her lover pants upon her breast,
Can mark the figures on an Indian chest;
And when she sees her friend in deep despair,
170 Observes how much a chintz exceeds mohair.
Forbid it heaven, a favour or a debt
She e'er should cancel—but she may forget.
Safe in your secret still in Cloe's ear;
But none of Cloe's shall you ever hear.
175 Of all her dears she never slandered one,
But cares not if a thousand are undone.
Would Cloe know if you're alive or dead?
She bids her footman put it in her head.
Cloe is prudent—would you too be wise?
180 Then never break your heart when Cloe dies.
     One certain portrait may (I grant) be seen,
Which heaven has varnished out, and made a queen:*   *Queen Caroline
The same forever! and described by all   (1683–1737)
With truth and goodness, as with crown and ball:
185 Poets heap virtues, painters gems at will,
And show their zeal, and hide their want of skill.
'Tis well—but artists! who can paint or write,
To draw the naked is your true delight.
That robe of quality so struts and swells,
190 None see what parts of nature it conceals.
The exactest traits of body or of mind,

We own to models of an humble kind.
If Queensbury to strip there's no compelling,
'Tis from a handmaid we must take a Helen,
195 From peer or bishop 'tis no easy thing
To draw the man who loves his God, or king:
Alas! I copy (or my draught would fail)
From honest Mah'met,* or plain Parson Hale.   *a servant*
But grant, in public men sometimes are shown,
200 A woman's seen in private life alone:
Our bolder talents in full light displayed;
Your virtues open fairest in the shade.
Bred to disguise, in public 'tis you hide;
There, none distinguish 'twixt your shame or pride,
205 Weakness or delicacy; all so nice,
That each may seem a virtue, or a vice.
In man, we various ruling passions find,
In women, two almost divide the kind;
Those, only fixed, they first or last obey,
210 The love of pleasure, and the love of sway.
That, nature gives; and when the lesson taught
Is but to please, can pleasure seem a fault?
Experience, this, by man's oppression cursed,
They seek the second not to lose the first.
215 Men, some to business, some to pleasure take;
But every woman is at heart a rake;
Men, some to quiet, some to public strife;
But every lady would be queen for life.
Yet mark the fate of a whole sex of queens!
220 Power all their end, but beauty all the means.
In youth they conquer with so wild a rage,
As leaves them scarce a subject in their age:
For foreign glory, foreign joy, they roam;
No thought of peace of happiness at home.
225 But wisdom's triumph is well-timed retreat,
As hard a science to the fair as great!
Beauties, like tyrants, old and friendless grown,
Yet hate repose, and dread to be alone,
Worn out in public, weary every eye,
230 Nor leave one sigh behind them when they die.
Pleasures the sex, as children birds, pursue,
Still out of reach, yet never out of view,
Sure, if they catch, to spoil the toy at most,
To covet flying, and regret when lost:

235 At least, to follies youth could scarce defend,
It grows their age's prudence to pretend;
Ashamed to own they gave delight before,
Reduced to feign it, when they give no more:
As hags* hold sabbaths, less for joy than spite,   *witches*
240 So these their merry, miserable night;
Still round and round the ghosts of beauty glide,
And haunt the places where their honors died.
See how the world its veterans rewards!
A youth in frolics, and old age of cards,
245 Fair to no purpose, artful to no end,
Young without lovers, old without a friend,
A fop their passion, but their prize a sot,
Alive, ridiculous, and dead, forgot!
Ah friend! to dazzle let the vain design,
250 To raise the thought and touch the heart, be thine!
That charm shall grow, while what fatigues the ring
Flaunts and goes down, an unregarded thing.
So when the sun's broad beam has tired the sight,
All mild ascends the moon's more sober light,
255 Serene in virgin modesty she shines,
And unobserved the glaring orb declines.
Oh! blest with temper, whose unclouded ray
Can make tomorrow cheerful as today;
She, who can love a sister's charms, or hear
260 Sighs for a daughter with unwounded ear;
She, who ne'er answers till a husband cools,
Or, if she rules him, never shows she rules;
Charms by accepting, by submitting sways,
Yet has her humour most, when she obeys;
265 Let fops or fortune fly which way they will;   *lottery tickets*
Disdains all loss of tickets,* or codille;°   °*term in card*
Spleen, vapours, or smallpox, above them all,   *playing*
And mistress of herself, though China fall.
And yet believe me, good as well as ill,
270 Woman's at best a contradiction still.
Heaven, when it strives to polish all it can
Its last best work, but forms a softer man;
Picks from each sex, to make the favourite blest,
Your love of pleasure, our desire of rest,
275 Blends, in exception to all general rules,
Your taste of follies, with our scorn of fools,
Reserve with frankness, art with truth allied,

Courage with softness, modesty with pride,
Fixed principles, with fancy ever new;
280 Shakes all together, and produces—you.
   Be this a woman's fame: with this unblest,
Toasts live a scorn, and queens may die a jest.
This Phoebus promised (I forget the year)
When those blue eyes* first opened on the sphere;   *probably Martha Blount's
285 Ascendant Phoebus watched that hour with care,
Averted half your parents' simple prayer,
And gave you beauty, but denied the pelf*   *money
That buys your sex a tyrant o'er itself.
The generous God, who wit and gold refines,
290 And ripens spirits as he ripens mines,
Kept dross for duchesses, the world shall know it,
To you gave sense, good-humor, and a poet.

NOTES This letter in verse was probably addressed to a particular lady—Martha Blount, a close friend of Pope.
   In lines 7–13, Pope alludes to some ways in which artists had depicted some fashionable women—as a shepherdess (Pastora), a classical beauty (Leda), a Biblical fallen woman (Magdalen), and a saint (Cecilia).
   Although Pope's contemporaries recognized, or guessed at the identities of the women given the fictional names in this poem, the modern reader can appreciate the general satire of the poem without associating a particular woman with each name.

POPE'S SATIRE

   In this epistle Pope satirizes especially the contrariness and the fickleness of women. Ladies, Pope writes, owe their charms to the fact that they are contrary, and their contradictory natures are likened to spotted flowers. Their "variegated" beauty, admired by discerning men, is not only their characteristic trait, but beauty found in "spots" is extended to imply beauty found in defects. Men love ladies then because of what turns out to be a paradoxical situation. Ladies are loved and attractive for what they are (i.e., contrary) and what they are is the source of their major shortcoming (lines 41–44). Pope's harsh view of women is mitigated a little in the conclusion as he describes the perfection of the woman to whom the poem is addressed. Among the women anatomized are the hypocritical flirt (Rufa), the self-centered simpleton (Silia), the contrary bride (Papilla), the fickle hedonist (Flavia), the self-indulgent atheist (Simo), the domineering old wit (Atossa), and the cold-hearted lover (Chloe). In the service of his satire, Pope time and again employs irony in his reversals from the beginning to the end of a line or a couplet. The result is a devastating catalogue of the faults of women as Pope knew them in fashionable society.

Almost without exception, Pope's favorite form was the heroic couplet; perhaps his success with the couplet form for satiric effect is unparalleled in English poetry. Through clever juxtaposition he could render the sublime ridiculous, or the ridiculous sublime; with a pair of *feminine rhymes* (lines 15 and 16) he could ridicule his own subject, or through what might be called the "tailed effect," he could quickly reverse in the latter half of the line the sense of the first half (lines 71–72). Pope's couplets tend to act as contained units within which he is free to explode as many sound and syntactic patterns as possible, always depending upon the couplet rhyme to hold the unit together. Consider, for instance, the comic effects in the passage about soft-natured ladies (lines 29–36). Pope is eager to exploit elements within such ladies which are contrary to their basic natures, thus "soft Silia" (her name itself suggests she is both weak and silly), "storms" and "raves" when she discovers—in a comic anti-climax—a cosmetic blemish, "a pimple on her nose." Usually such excess comes either from the shrew, the drunkard, or the lady who has been undone; Silia's raving is disproportionate to its object, and thus Pope has illustrated her ridiculous behavior. Silia's weaknesses are catalogued bluntly as if they were strengths; only simpletons seek her advice, and fallen ladies easily convince her that their behavior had always been virtuous and delicate. Simple Silia has been anatomized for all to see, and Pope concludes his portrait with the devastating revelation. The second half of the couplet succeeds in its comic effect by reversing our expectation, and that simple reversal is one of Pope's most often employed devices.

QUESTIONS

1. What instances of contrariety does Pope attribute to the women he anatomizes?

2. Explain the verbal irony in line 74.

3. Paraphrase the couplet in lines 113–114.

4. Explain some techniques Pope employs in his famous portrait of Atossa (lines 115–150).

5. Describe the development of the painting metaphor Pope uses in the poem.

6. Describe the tone of Pope's satire. (Consider the strength of Pope's language—*passion, fury, hate*—and the grotesque creatures he creates.)

7. What do lines 181–198 tell of Pope's social attitudes?

8. Explain how each of the portraits illustrates Pope's theme: that women are dominated by two ruling passions—"The love of pleasure, and the love of sway."

9. Explain how the first 20 lines introduce Pope's subject.

10. Describe Pope's attitude in lines 243–248 as he characterizes the older woman. What devices achieve the particular effect in these lines?

11. How does he characterize Martha Blount?

12. Describe the effect of the final couplet. Look especially at the feminine rhyme.

Epitaph on Mr. Gay: In Westminster Abbey, 1732

Of manners gentle, of affections mild;
In wit, a man; simplicity, a child;
With native humor tempering virtuous rage,
Formed to delight at once and lash the age;
5 Above temptation, in a low estate,
And uncorrupted, even among the great;
A safe companion, and an easy friend,
Unblamed through life, lamented in thy end.
These are thy honours! not that here thy bust
10 Is mixed with heroes, or with kings thy dust.
But that the worthy and the good shall say,
Striking their pensive bosoms—*Here* lies Gay.

NOTE Famous for his descriptive poem on the pleasures of London, *Trivia*, John Gay (1685–1732), Pope's friend, is the celebrated author of *The Beggars' Opera*.

Epitaph: On John, Lord Caryll

A manly form; a bold, yet modest mind;
Sincere, though prudent; constant, yet resigned;
Honour unchanged; a principle profest;
Fixed to one side, but moderate to the rest;
5 An honest courtier, and a patriot too;
Just to his prince, and to his country true:
All these were joined in one, yet failed to save
The wise, the learned, the virtuous, and the brave;
Lost, like the common plunder of the grave!
10 Ye few, whom better genius does inspire,
Exalted souls, informed with purer fire!
Go now, learn all vast science can impart;
Go fathom nature, take the heights of art!
Rise higher yet: learn even yourselves to know;
15 Nay, to yourselves alone that knowledge owe.
Then, when you seem above mankind to soar,
Look on this marble, and be vain no more!

NOTE Pope's friend died in 1711.

QUESTIONS

1. Describe how the virtues of moderation and balance (the mean between extremes) admired in these two men are reflected in the balance and proportion of the couplets and individual lines.
2. What is the purpose of the final three words of Gay's epitaph?

Epistle to Miss Blount:
On Her Leaving the Town After the Coronation

As some fond* virgin, whom her mother's care   *foolish*
Drags from the town to wholesome country air,
Just when she learns to roll a melting eye,
And hear a spark, yet think no danger nigh;
5 From the dear man unwilling she must sever,
Yet takes one kiss before she parts forever:
Thus from the world fair Zephalinda* flew,   *Teresa Blount*
Saw others happy, and with sighs withdrew;
Not that their pleasures caused her discontent,
10 She sighed not that they stayed, but that she went.
   She went, to plain work, and to purling* brooks,   *rippling*
Old-fashioned halls, dull aunts, and croaking rooks,
She went from opera, park, assembly, play,
To morning walks, and prayers three hours a day;
15 To pass her time 'twixt reading and Bohea,*   *tea*
To muse, and spill her solitary tea,
Or o'er cold coffee trifle with the spoon,
   Count the slow clock, and dine exact at noon;
Divert her eyes with pictures in the fire,
20 Hum half a tune, tell stories to the squire;
Up to her godly garret after seven,
There starve and pray, for that's the way to heaven.
   Some squire, perhaps, you take delight to rack;*   *ruin*
Whose game is whisk, whose treat a toast in sack,*   *sherry*
25 Who visits with a gun, presents you birds,
Then gives a smacking buss, and cries—No words!
Or with his hound comes hollowing from the stable,
Makes love with nods, and knees beneath a table;
Whose laughs are hearty, though his jests are coarse,
30 And loves you best of all things—but his horse.
   In some fair evening, on your elbow laid,
You dream of triumphs in the rural shade;
In pensive thought recall the fancied scene,
See coronations rise on every green;
35 Before you pass the imaginary sights
Of lords, and earls, and dukes, and gartered knights;
While the spread fan o'ershades your closing eyes;
Then give one flirt,* and all the vision flies.   *nod*
Thus vanish sceptres, coronets, and balls,
40 And leave you in lone woods, or empty walls.

So when your slave,* at some dear idle time,   *Pope*
(Not plagued with headaches, or the want of rhyme)
Stands in the streets, abstracted from the crew,
And while he seems to study, thinks of you:
45 Just when his fancy points* your sprightly eyes,   *imagines*
Or sees the blush of soft Parthenia* rise,   *Martha Blount*
Gay* pats my shoulder, and you vanish quite;   *John Gay*
Streets, chairs, and coxcombs rush upon my sight;
Vext to be still in town, I knit my brow,
50 Look sour, and hum a tune—as you may now.

NOTE The poem is addressed to Miss Teresa Blount, Pope's good friend, on the occasion of
the coronation of George I.

POPE'S EPISTLE

Pope's epistle to Miss Blount celebrates as much the sophistication of the
city as it satirizes rusticity. Although one could observe sham and affectation
in the city, there worldly men were able to pursue pleasures both amorous and
intellectual, sometimes with restraint. London was an exciting city of coffee houses,
great celebrations, expensive parties, and successive flirtations. Most literary men
knew each other, frequented the same taverns and inns, and sought patronage from
the same titled families. They attacked each other in print for individual foibles,
political idiosyncracies, ridiculous excesses—or because one of them had stolen
someone's mistress. About all these subjects Pope could be witty and devastating
in his satire, but he could also write a personal epistle with some sincerity. One
stands in wonder at the balanced stateliness and restraint characteristic of these
lines, accomplished by a man who spent few days without suffering intense
physical pain, and who was himself a cripple.

QUESTIONS

1. Describe Pope's attitude towards life in the country.
2. How does Pope satirize Zephalinda's country spark? (Be sure to consider
the special effect of line 30.)
3. Describe the tone of lines 41–50. What is the particular effect of the four
words which conclude the poem?

WHAT TO LOOK FOR IN THE ADDITIONAL READING

The additional reading suggests the variety of genres in which Pope was
accomplished; here is another pastoral, a translation, a verse prologue, and two
little poems on the content of *Gulliver's Travels*. One of the most skillful trans-
lators in English, Pope also published many moral epistles and verse essays. Here
you will find sufficient examples of Pope's use of the heroic couplet as an epigram-

matic unit, for he often depends upon it to express terse, pointed, and often witty observations. For instance, consider the following epigrams:

> "Shall we like reptiles, glory in conceit?
> Humility's the virtue of the great."

> "Thus honey combs seem palaces to bees:
> And mites imagine all the world a cheese."

> "In pitying love we but our weakness show,
> And wild ambition well deserves its woe."

Here also you will find him concerned with subjects and attitudes you have seen in the previous poems.

Summer

A shepherd's boy (he seeks no better name)
Led forth his flocks along the silver Thame,*   *Thames*
Where dancing sunbeams on the waters played,
And verdant alders formed a quiv'ring shade.
5 Soft as he mourned, the streams forgot to flow,
The flocks around a dumb compassion show,
The Naiads* wept in every wat'ry bower,   *water nymphs*
And Jove consented in a silent shower.
    Accept, O Garth,* the muse's early lays,   *the poet's friend*
10 That adds this wreath of ivy to thy bays;
Hear what from love unpractised hearts endure,
From love, the sole disease thou canst not cure!
    "Ye shady beeches, and ye cooling streams,
Defence from Phoebus', not from Cupid's beams;
15 To you I mourn; nor to the deaf I sing,
The woods shall answer, and their echo ring.
The hills and rocks attend my doleful lay,
Why art thou prouder and more hard than they?
The bleating sheep with my complaints agree,
20 They parched with heat, and I inflamed by thee.
The sultry Sirius* burns the thirsty plains,   *the Dog-Star of Summer*
While in thy heart eternal winter reigns.
    Where stray ye muses, in what lawn or grove,
While your Alexis pines in hopeless love?
25 In those fair fields where sacred Isis* glides,   *Thames*
Or else where Cam his winding values divides?
As in the crystal spring I view my face,
Fresh rising blushes paint the watery glass;
But since those graces please thy eyes no more,

30 I shun the fountains which I sought before.
Once I was skilled in every herb that grew,
And every plant that drinks the morning dew;
Ah, wretched shepherd, what avails thy art,
To cure thy lambs, but not to heal thy heart!
35   Let other swains attend the rural care,
Feed fairer flocks, or richer fleeces share;
But nigh yon mountain let me tune my lays,
Embrace my love, and bind my brows with bays.
That flute is mine which Colin's* tuneful breath   *a pastoral name*
40 Inspired when living, and bequeathed in Death;
He said; "Alexis, take this pipe, the same
That taught the groves my Rosalinda's name—"
But now the reeds shall hang on yonder tree,
For ever silent, since despised by thee.
45 O were I made by some transforming power,
The captive bird that sings within thy bower!
Then might my voice thy listening ears employ,
And I those kisses he receives, enjoy.
   And yet my numbers please the rural throng,
50 Rough satyrs* dance, and Pan° applauds the song: *sylvan deities*
The Nymphs forsaking every cave and spring,
Their early fruit, and milk-white turtles bring;
Each amorous nymph prefers her gifts in vain,
On you their gifts are all bestowed again!
55 For you the swains the fairest flowers design,
And in one garland all their beauties join;
Accept the wreath which you deserve alone,
In whom all beauties are comprised in one.
   See what delights in sylvan scenes appear!
60 Descending gods have found Elysium* here.   *Paradise*
In woods bright Venus with Adonis strayed,
And chaste Diana haunts the forest shade.
Come, lovely nymph, and bless the silent hours,
When swains from shearing seek their nightly bowers;
65 When weary reapers quit the sultry field,
And crowned with corn* their thanks to Ceres yield.   *grain*
This harmless grove no lurking viper hides,
But in my breast the serpent love abides.
Here bees from blossoms sip the rosy dew,
70 But your Alexis knows no sweets but you.
Oh deign to visit our forsaken seats,
   The mossy fountains, and the green retreats!
Where'er you walk, cool gales shall fan the glade,

Trees, where you sit shall crowd into a shade,
75 Where'er you tread, the blushing flowers shall rise,
And all things flourish where you turn your eyes.
Oh! how I long with you to pass my days,
Invoke the muses, and resound your praise;
Your praise the birds shall chant in every grove,
80 And winds shall waft it to the powers above.
But would you sing, and rival Orpheus' strain,
The wondering forests soon should dance again,
The moving mountains hear the powerful call,
And headlong streams hang listening in their fall!
85   But see, the shepherds shun the noonday heat,
The lowing herds to murmuring brooks retreat,
To closer shades the panting flocks remove,
Ye gods! and is there no relief for love?
But soon the sun with milder ray descends
90 To the cool ocean, where his journey ends;
On me love's fiercer flames for ever prey,
By night he scorches, as he burns by day."

Argus

When wise Ulysses, from his native coast
Long kept by wars, and long by tempests tost,
Arrived at last, poor, old, disguised, alone,
To all his friends, and even his queen, unknown,
5 Changed as he was, with age, and toils, and cares,
Furrowed his reverend face, and white his hairs,
In his own palace forced to ask his bread,
Scorned by those slaves his former bounty fed,
Forgot of all his own domestic crew;
10 The faithful dog alone his rightful master knew!
Unfed, unhoused, neglected, on the clay,
Like an old servant now cashiered, he lay;
Touched with resentment of ungrateful man,
And longing to behold his ancient lord again.
15 Him when he saw—he rose, and crawled to meet,
('Twas all he could) and fawned, and licked his feet,
Seized with dumb joy—then falling by his side,
Owned his returning lord, looked up, and died!

NOTE   Pope made the following comment about this poem in a letter: "Homer's account
of Ulysses' dog, Argus, is the most pathetic imaginable . . . and an excellent proof of the old
bard's good nature. Ulysses had left him at Ithaca when he embarked for Troy, and found him
on his return after 20 years."

The Garden of Alcinous

Close to the gates a spacious garden lies,
From storms defended, and inclement skies:
Four acres was the allotted space of ground,
Fenced with a green enclosure all around.
5 Tall thriving trees confessed the fruitful mold;
The red'ning apple ripens here to gold,
Here the blue fig with luscious juice o'erflows,,
With deeper red the full pomegranate glows,
The branch here bends beneath the weighty pear,
10 And verdant olives flourish round the year.
The balmy spirit of the western gale
Eternal breathes on fruits untaught to fail:
Each dropping pear a following pear supplies,
On apples apples, figs on figs arise:
15 The same mild season gives the blooms to blow,
The buds to harden, and the fruits to grow.
Here ordered vines in equal ranks appear
With all the united labours of the year,
Some to unload the fertile branches run,
20 Some dry the blackening clusters in the sun,
Others to tread the liquid harvest join,
The groaning presses foam with floods of wine.
Here are the vines in early flower descried,
Here grapes discolored on the sunny side,
25 And there in autumn's richest purple dyed.
Beds of all various herbs, forever green,
In beauteous order terminate the scene.
Two plenteous fountains the whole prospect crowned;
This thro' the gardens leads its streams around,
30 Visits each plant, and waters all the ground:
While that in pipes beneath the palace flows,
And thence its current on the town bestows;
To various use their various streams they bring,
The people one, and one supplies the king.

NOTE This passage Pope translated from the seventh book of Homer's *Odyssey*. Although
it forms a part of the larger poem, Pope translated this passage many years before he began
the total translation. At the court of Alcinous, Ulysses weeps over the long tale sung by the
blind bard Demodocus, and it is there that he reveals his identity.

To Quinbus Flestrin, The Man-Mountain
A Lilliputian Ode

In amaze
Lost, I gaze!
Can our eyes
Reach thy size?
5 May my lays
Swell with praise
Worthy thee!
Worthy me!
Muse inspire,
10 All thy fire!
Bards of old
Of him told,
When they said
Atlas' head
15 Propt the skies:
See! and believe your eyes!

See him stride
Valleys wide:
Over woods,
20 Over floods.
When he treads
Mountains' heads
Groan and shake;
Armies quake,
25 Lest his spurn
Overturn
Man and steed:
Troops take heed!
Left and right,
30 Speed your flight!
Lest an host
Beneath his foot be lost.

Turned aside
From his hide,
35 Safe from wound
Darts rebound.
From his nose
Clouds he blows;

When he speaks,
40 Thunder breaks!
When he eats,
Famine threats;
When he drinks,
Neptune shrinks!
45 Nigh thy ear,
In mid air,
On thy hand
Let me stand,
So shall I,
50 Lofty poet! touch the sky!

NOTE "Quinbus Flestrin" was the name given to Gulliver by the Lilliputians in Swift's *Gulliver's Travels*. Like a "man-mountain," Gulliver towered over the little people of that country.

The Words of the King of Brobdinggnag as He Held Captain Gulliver Between His Finger and Thumb for the Inspection of the Sages and Learned Men of the Court

In miniature see nature's power appear;
Which wings the sun-born insects of the air,
Which frames the harvest-bug, too small for sight,
And forms the bones and muscles of the mite!
5 Here view him stretched. The microscope explains,
That the blood, circling, flows in human veins;
See, in the tube* he pants, and sprawling lies,   *seen through the microscope*
Stretches his little hands, and rolls his eyes!

Smit with his country's love, I've heard him prate
10 Of laws and manners in his pigmy state.
By travel, generous souls enlarge the mind,
Which home-bred prepossession had confined;
Yet will he boast of many regions known,
But still, with partial love, extol his own.
15 He talks of senates, and of courtly tribes,
Admires their ardour, but forgets their bribes;
Of hireling lawyers tells the just decrees,
Applauds their eloquence, but sinks* their fees.   *diminishes*
Yet who his country's partial love can blame?
20 'Tis sure some virtue to conceal its shame.

The world's the native city of the wise;
He sees his Britain with a mother's eyes;
Softens defects, and heightens all its charms,
Calls it the seat of empire, arts and arms!
25 Fond of his hillock isle, his narrow mind
Thinks worth, wit, learning, so that spot confined;
Thus ants, who for a grain employ their cares,
Think all the business of the earth is theirs.
Thus honey combs seem palaces to bees;
30 And mites imagine all the world a cheese.

When pride in such contemptuous beings lies,
In beetles, Britons, bugs and butterflies,
Shall we, like reptiles, glory in conceit?
Humility's the virtue of the great.

Prologue To Mr. Addison's Tragedy of Cato

To wake the soul by tender strokes of art,
To raise the genius, and to mend the heart;
To make mankind, in conscious virtue bold,
Live o'er each scene, and by what they behold:
5 For this the tragic muse first trod the stage,
Commanding tears to stream thro' every age;
Tyrants no more their savage nature kept,
And foes to virtue wondered how they wept.
Our author shuns by vulgar springs to move,
10 The hero's glory, or the virgin's love;
In pitying love we but our weakness show,
And wild ambition well deserves its woe.
Here tears shall flow from a more generous cause,
Such tears, as patriots shed for dying laws:
15 He bids your breasts with ancient ardour rise,
And calls forth Roman drops from British eyes.
Virtue confessed in human shape he draws,
What Plato thought, and godlike Cato was:
No common object to your sight displays,
20 But what with pleasure heaven itself surveys;
A brave man struggling in the storms of fate,
And greatly falling with a falling state!
While Cato gives his little senate laws,
What bosom beats not in his country's cause?
25 Who sees him act, but envies every deed?

Who hears him groan, and does not wish to bleed?
Even when proud Caesar 'midst triumphal cars,
The spoils of nations, and the pomp of wars,
Ignobly vain and impotently great,
30 Showed Rome her Cato's figure drawn in state;
As her dead father's reverend image past,
The pomp was darkened, and the day o'ercast,
The triumph ceased—tears gushed from every eye;
The world's great victor passed unheeded by;
35 Her last good man dejected Rome adored,
And honored Caesar's less than Cato's sword.
     Britons attend: Be worth like this approved,
And show, you have the virtue to be moved.
With honest scorn the first famed Cato viewed
40 Rome learning arts from Greece, whom she subdued;
Our scene precariously subsists too long
On French translation, and Italian song.
Dare to have sense your selves; assert the stage,
Be justly warmed with your own native rage.
45 Such plays alone should please a British ear,
As Cato's self had not disdained to hear.

NOTE Joseph Addison's tragedy, *Cato* (1713), was the most popular drama of the early eighteenth century. The play glorified patriotism and those men willing to die for their country's liberty. The play, set in Rome, honored Cato, the consul, as the spirit of Roman liberty.

TOPICS FOR WRITING AND DISCUSSION

FOR USE IN CLASS

1. How do the typography, diction, and rhyme of "Quinbus Flestrin, the Man Mountain" reflect both the subject of the poem and the speaker?

2. Paraphrase Pope's "The Gardens of Alcinous." What moral values are suggested by the garden's orderly nature?

3. What human values does Pope prize in his "Prologue to Addison's *Cato*"?

4. What is the effect of the concluding line of Pope's poem "Argus"? Describe how the effect is achieved.

FOR PREPARATION OUTSIDE OF CLASS

1. Compare Pope's handling of the pastoral with Milton's treatment of the tradition in "Lycidas."

2. Discuss Pope's handling of the epigrammatic couplet.

3. Discuss Pope's techniques of verse satire.

4. Describe the view of the early 18th century one gets from reading this collection of Pope's poetry.

Introduction to *Songs of Innocence*

Piping down the valleys wild,
Piping songs of pleasant glee,
On a cloud I saw a child,
4 And he laughing said to me:

"Pipe a song about a lamb!"
So I piped with merry cheer,
"Piper, pipe that song again;"
8 So I piped: he wept to hear.

"Drop thy pipe, thy happy pipe;
Sing thy songs of happy cheer:"
So I sung the same again,
12 While he wept with joy to hear.

"Piper, sit thee down and write
In a book, that all may read."
So he vanished from my sight,
16 And I plucked a hollow reed,

And I made a rural pen,
And I stained the water clear,
And I wrote my happy songs
20 Every child may joy to hear.

Introduction to *Songs of Experience*

Hear the voice of the bard!
Who present, past and future, sees;
Whose ears have heard
The holy word
5 That walked among the ancient trees,

Calling the lapsed soul,
And weeping in the evening dew;
That might control
The starry pole,
10 And fallen, fallen light renew!

"O earth, O earth, return!
Arise from out the dewy grass;
Night is worn,
And the morn
15 Rises from the slumberous mass

"Turn away no more;
Why wilt thou turn away?
The starry floor,
The watery shore,
20 Is given thee till the break of day."

BLAKE'S THEMES

Among Blake's most famous poems are two little groups of lyrics illustrated by the author and entitled *Songs of Innocence* (1789) and *Songs of Experience* (1794). The songs are frequently paired with their respective counterparts so that we might see the same character or dramatic situation under its two contrary *modes*. Blake believed that there was no wisdom except through the experience of contraries, and the two groups of songs represent not exclusively separate experiences, but two aspects of existence. According to Blake, human beings pass through the stage of innocence to the stage of experience, neither stage to be prized above the other; both are significant corollaries of one another, and both are contained in the adult's experience. In Blake's view of human existence, we pass from one stage to the other, from innocence to experience, and having successfully grown through experiencing these contraries, we mature to a kind of greater innocence. Life is seen by Blake as a series of births, deaths, and rebirths, man always growing by holding the contraries, as it were, of birth and death in suspension. Each contrary has within it the seeds of its complement; so in many of the *Songs of Innocence* Blake implies that innocence is fragile and short lived and without many of the pleasures one attributes to experience. The state of innocence *must* give way, as the day to night, to the state of experience; that is both a new kind of joy and a new kind of tragedy. In turn, the night gives way to a new day.

Blake begins each group with an introductory song. In "Introduction" to *Songs of Innocence* he envisions himself as a simple pastoral singer composing pleasant happy song as he pipes his way through life. His muse is a child, and his manner appropriately childlike. That muse laughingly asks for a song about the traditional symbol of innocence, the lamb, and the piper obliges. The reader should be aware that the lamb also suggests Christ as the Lamb of God who passed through innocence to experience to a greater innocence. He suffered human existence, having descended to that condition, later reascending, having experienced the great contraries of mortality and immortality. This theme, however, barely suggested in the poem, is completely underplayed by Blake. The piper pipes one song to make us happy (a song of innocence) but that song piped again makes us weep.

This is all explicit in the second quatrain. In the third quatrain the child's reaction holds both states in suspension; now he weeps for joy, for he has been educated by the poet's singing. This child's experience is also to be the reader's. So inspired, the piper will write all this down in a book so that each of us who comes to it "as a child" (that is, unaware of what we are to read) will feel joy to hear the songs that will help us mature. The final quatrain suggests that as he begins to write of innocence, that very act itself carries with it the implication of experience to come, for his pen "stained the water clear" as he wrote. One cannot write of one condition without implying its contrary.

QUESTIONS

1. Describe the tone of the introductory song to the *Songs of Experience*. How does this "night" song differ tonally from the "day" song from *Songs of Innocence*?

2. The imagery of night and day acts as an extended metaphor in the "Introduction" to *Songs of Experience*. How is this metaphor developed, and why is such an image appropriate to Blake's theme?

3. Describe how the second introductory song concludes with a contrary.

4. Compare the first two lines of the two introductory songs. Be sure to notice and comment upon the bard's preoccupation with time. Relate also the concreteness and abstractness in these two pairs of lines to their relative states.

* * *

The Blossom from *Songs of Innocence*

Merry, merry sparrow!
Under leaves so green
A happy blossom
Sees you swift as arrow
5 Seek your cradle narrow
Near my bosom.

Pretty, pretty robin!
Under leaves so green
A happy blossom
10 Hears you sobbing, sobbing,
Pretty, pretty robin,
Near my bosom.

The Sick Rose from Songs of Experience

O rose, thou art sick!
The invisible worm
That flies in the night,
4 In the howling storm,

Has found out thy bed
Of crimson joy,
And his dark secret love
8 Does thy life destroy.

CONTRARY BLOSSOMS

"The Blossom," like many of Blake's poems, poses numerous problems because of its extreme simplicity. Consequently the reader must seize upon each detail and capitalize upon his knowledge of the poem's context within Blake's work to help him with his reading. Here, for instance, the first problem is to determine the speaker; the voice here is that of a flowering tree or bush. The tree observes a merry sparrow seeking its nest near its bosom. The image for the nest is the important detail; the "cradle narrow" suggests youthfulness and innocence. The adjective "narrow" suggests the restricted experience of the cradle; it is "narrow" in the ways of the world, and we remember also that the sparrow is "merry" and the blossom "happy." Blake is suggesting in the first stanza a metaphoric equivalent for the phase of existence which he calls "innocence." It appears, then, that the robin, who is "pretty," but also "sobbing," suggests a fuller existence, perhaps the beauty of a maturity which still recognizes the innocence from which it grew. The poem's *symbols* are by no means definite and clear cut, but the images suggest their metaphoric counterparts. The robin and the sparrow are not symbolic in themselves, but only as they suggest contrasts with one another. They cannot stand alone; one cannot say, "The sparrow symbolizes this or that." The symbols achieve significance as they are paired with one another, and Blake subtly suggests the mysterious relationship between innocence (the sparrow) and experience (the robin). Neither condition really exists in and of itself, and consequently neither bird can be a clear cut symbol—each can only *suggest* the condition with which it is associated.

QUESTIONS

1. Why is the worm described as "invisible"?
2. What does the diction in "The Sick Rose" say about the state of experience?
3. Poets frequently employ the rose as a symbol of love and beauty. What does Blake's description of the rose's condition suggest about his attitude toward earthly love and beauty in the state of experience?
4. Describe the effect of the metaphoric language in the second quatrain of "The Sick Rose." Note how the metaphor personifies the rose.

The Chimney Sweeper from Songs of Innocence

When my mother died I was very young,
And my father sold me while yet my tongue
Could scarcely cry "'weep! 'weep! 'weep! 'weep!"
4 So your chimneys I sweep, and in soot I sleep.

There's little Tom Dacre, who cried when his head,
That curled like a lamb's back, was shaved: so I said,
"Hush, Tom! never mind it, for when your head's bare
8 You know that the soot cannot spoil your white hair."

And so he was quiet, and that very night
As Tom was a-sleeping, he had such a sight!
That thousands of sweepers, Dick, Joe, Ned, and Jack,
12 Were all of them locked up in coffins of black.

And by came an angel who had a bright key,
And he opened the coffins and set them all free;
Then down a green plain leaping, laughing, they run,
16 And wash in a river, and shine in the sun.

Then naked and white, all their bags left behind,
They rise upon clouds and sport in the wind;
And the angel told Tom, if he'd be a good boy,
20 He'd have God for his father, and never want joy.

And so Tom awoke; and we rose in the dark,
And got with our bags and our brushes to work.
Though the morning was cold, Tom was happy and warm;
24 So if all do their duty they need not fear harm.

The Chimney Sweeper from Songs of Experience

A little black thing among the snow,
Crying, "'weep! 'weep!" in notes of woe!
"Where are thy father and mother? say?"
4 "They are both gone up to the church to pray.

"Because I was happy upon the heath,
And smiled among the winter's snow,
They clothed me in the clothes of death,
8 And taught me to sing the notes of woe.

"And because I am happy and dance and sing,
They think they have done me no injury,
And are gone to praise God and his priest and king,
12 Who make up a heaven of our misery."

BLAKE'S SOCIAL PROTEST

Blake is one of the most significant English poets of social protest. He was particularly biting in his attacks on the viciousness of child labor and upon the callousness of a country and a religion which would condone such practices. Both poems on "The Chimney Sweeper" are poignant examples of Blake's humanitarian concerns.

QUESTIONS

1. What is the effect of the white-black imagery in both poems?
2. Explain the irony in the last line of "The Chimney Sweeper" song from the *Songs of Innocence*.
3. Which of the two poems expresses the more bitter attitude? Toward what institutions is the bitterness directed and how is the bitterness conveyed?
4. Describe how one of these songs is more sentimentalized than the other.
5. Characterize and then compare the speakers in the two poems. What is revealed about their respective attitudes towards society?

London from *Songs of Experience*

I wander through each chartered street,
Near where the chartered Thames does flow,
And mark in every face I meet
4 Marks of weakness, marks of woe,

In every cry of every man,
In every infant's cry of fear,
In every voice, in every ban,
8 The mind-forged manacles I hear.

How the chimney sweeper's cry
Every blackening church appalls;
And the hapless soldier's sigh
12 Runs in blood down palace walls.

But most through midnight streets I hear
How the youthful harlot's curse
Blasts the new born infant's tear,
16 And blights with plagues the marriage hearse.

MORE SOCIAL PROTEST

This poem tells us that the society man has contrived ("chartered") is an instrument of oppression ("mind-forged manacles"). As in the two chimney sweeper songs, Blake protests against social injustice, but in this poem he sees a variety of social tragedies, including, again, the pathetic plight of the chimney sweeper.

1. What tragic human conditions does Blake touch on in this poem?
2. Explain the ambiguity of the word "chartered" (lines 1-2).
3. Explain the irony of the diction in line 10. (Look up the etymology of *appalls*.)
4. Describe the metaphor of lines 11 and 12. What social tragedy does the imagery convey?
5. Explain the irony of the last word of the poem. How does this irony convey Blake's view of a respectable social institution?
6. Compare Blake's view of London in this poem with Pope's view in his poem on London.

The Divine Image from *Songs of Innocence*

To mercy, pity, peace, and love
All pray in their distress;
And to these virtues of delight
4 Return their thankfulness.

For mercy, pity, peace, and love
Is God, our father dear,
And mercy, pity, peace, and love
8 Is man, his child and care.

For mercy has a human heart,
Pity a human face,
And love, the human form divine,
12 And peace, the human dress.

Then every man, of every clime,
That prays in his distress,
Prays to the human form divine,
16 Love, mercy, pity, peace.

And all must love the human form,
In heathen, Turk, or Jew;
Where mercy, love, and pity dwell
20 There God is dwelling too.

A Divine Image from Songs of Experience

Cruelty has a human heart,
And jealousy a human face;
Terror the human form divine,
4 And secrecy the human dress.

The human dress is forged iron,
The human form a fiery forge,
The human face a furnace sealed,
8 The human heart its hungry gorge.

NOTE   These two songs grow out of the view that in the beginning man was created in the image of a beneficent God, and he reflected the divine attributes of "mercy, pity, peace, and love." In experience, as the generations passed, man reshaped his vision of divinity and was in turn himself reshaped to reflect a new image. Out of the first God of love, man created a new divinity—a God of oppression.

QUESTIONS

1. Describe how the diction in each poem establishes the tone.

2. Describe the appropriateness of the metaphors used as emblems of the human form in the second quatrain of "A Divine Image."

3. Since these two poems represent Blake's contraries, they should be read together and in the context of the other poems. If each state (i.e. of innocence and experience) contains within it some aspect of the other, what evidence is there to support this contention in these two poems? What has happened to the word "divine" in the song of experience?

4. What is the effect of the use of the word "human" in every line of "A Divine Image"?

5. Describe the method of organization in "A Divine Image."

6. Explain Blake's change of title from "The Divine Image" to "A Divine Image."

Nurse's Song from Songs of Innocence

When the voices of children are heard on the green
And laughing is heard on the hill,
My heart is at rest within my breast
4   And everything else is still.

"Then come home, my children, the sun is gone down
And the dews of night arise;
Come, come, leave off play, and let us away
8 Till the morning appears in the skies."

"No, no, let us play, for it is yet day
And we cannot go to sleep;
Besides, in the sky the little birds fly
12 And the hills are all covered with sheep."

"Well, well, go and play till the light fades away
And then go home to bed."
The little ones leaped and shouted and laughed
16   And all the hills echoed.

Nurse's Song from Songs of Experience

When the voices of children are heard on the green
And whisperings are in the dale,
The days of my youth rise fresh in my mind,
4 My face turns green and pale.

Then come home, my children, the sun is gone down,
And the dews of night arise;
Your spring and your day are wasted in play,
8 And your winter and night in disguise.

QUESTIONS

1. What evidence is there in the "Nurse's Song" from *Songs of Innocence* that the child's state is transitory and will soon pass?

2. Is there any evidence that the state in the other "Nurse's Song" is also transitory? (Consider the imagery of the last line.)

3. How is the tone of each song established? Compare the tone of the two poems.

All the poems for additional reading are from *Songs of Innocence* or *Songs of Experience* except the first two. You might begin by relating each of the poems to Blake's concept of innocence and experience before you attend to the matters of diction, imagery, tone, and organization. In each case try to discover how each poem implies the seeds of its complementary state. In the simpler, more appropriately childlike *Songs of Innocence*, the reader must be extremely careful, for often Blake's suggestion is inherent in a single, concrete image or word. Likewise, that word or image will function symbolically only in the context of innocence or experience. Although many of Blake's images, especially those of lamb and rose, have conventional associations, the reader cannot always rely on the tradition to satisfy all his questions. What he must always be interested in is not the convention itself, but the way the convention is used in Blake's poem.

To Spring

O thou with dewy locks, who lookest down
Thro' the clear windows of the morning, turn
Thine angel eyes upon our western isle,
4 Which in full choir hails thy approach, O Spring!

The hills tell each other, and the listening
Valleys hear, all our longing eyes are turned
Up to thy bright pavilions: issue forth,
8 And let thy holy feet visit our clime.

Come o'er the eastern hills, and let our winds
Kiss thy perfumed garments; let us taste
Thy morn and evening breath; scatter thy pearls
12 Upon our love-sick land that mourns for thee.

O deck her forth with thy fair fingers; pour
Thy soft kisses on her bosom; and put
Thy golden crown upon her languished head,
16 Whose modest tresses were bound up for thee!

To Autumn

O autumn, laden with fruit, and stained
With the blood of the grape, pass not, but sit
Beneath my shady roof, there thou may'st rest,
And tune thy jolly voice to my fresh pipe;
5 And all the daughters of the years shall dance!
Sing now the lusty song of fruits and flowers.

"The narrow bud opens her beauties to
The sun, and love runs in her thrilling veins;
Blossoms hang round the brows of morning, and
10 Flourish down the bright cheek of modest eve,
Till clustering summer breaks forth into singing,
And feathered clouds strew flowers round her head.

The spirits of the air live on the smells
Of fruit; and joy, with pinions* light, roves round   *feathers*
15 The gardens, or sits singing in the trees."
Thus sang the jolly autumn as he sat;
Then rose, girded himself, and o'er the bleak
Hills fled from our sight; but left his golden load.

The Little Black Boy from Songs of Innocence

My mother bore me in the southern wild,
And I am black, but O! my soul is white;
White as an angel is the English child,
4 But I am black, as if bereaved of light.

My mother taught me underneath a tree,
And sitting down before the heat of day,
She took me on her lap and kissed me,
8 And pointing to the east, began to say:

"Look on the rising sun: there God does live,
And gives his light, and gives his heat away;
And flowers and trees and beasts and man receive
12 Comfort in morning, joy in the noonday.

"And we are put on earth a little space,
That we may learn to bear the beams of love;
And these black bodies and this sunburnt face
16 Is but a cloud, and like a shady grove.

"For when our souls have learned that heat to bear,
The cloud will vanish; we shall hear his voice,
Saying: 'Come out from the grove, my love & care,
20 And round my golden tent like lambs rejoice.'"

Thus did my mother say, and kissed me;
And thus I say to little English boy:
When I from black and he from white cloud free,
24 And round the tent of God like lambs we joy,

I'll shade him from the heat, till he can bear
To lean in joy upon our father's knee;
And then I'll stand and stroke his silver hair,
28 And be like him, and he will then love me.

Spring from *Songs of Innocence*

Sound the flute!
Now it's mute.
Birds delight
Day and night;
5 Nightingale
In the dale,
Lark in sky,
Merrily,
Merrily, merrily, to welcome in the year.

10 Little boy,
Full of joy;
Little girl,
Sweet and small;
Cock does crow,
15 So do you;
Merry voice,
Infant noise,
Merrily, merrily, to welcome in the year.

Little lamb,
20 Here I am;
Come and lick
My white neck;
Let me pull
Your soft wool;
25 Let me kiss
Your soft face:
Merrily, merrily, we welcome in the year.

The Garden of Love from Songs of Experience

I went to the garden of love,
And saw what I never had seen:
A chapel was built in the midst,
4 Where I used to play on the green.

And the gates of this chapel were shut,
And "Thou shalt not" writ over the door;
So I turned to the garden of love
8 That so many sweet flowers bore;

And I saw it was filled with graves,
And tomb-stones where flowers should be;
And priests in black gowns were walking their rounds,
12 And binding with briars my joys & desires.

The Human Abstract from Songs of Experience

Pity would be no more
If we did not make somebody poor;
And mercy no more could be
4 If all were as happy as we.

And mutual fear brings peace,
Till the selfish loves increase:
Then cruelty knits a snare,
8 And spread his baits with care.

He sits down with holy fears,
And waters the ground with tears;
Then humility takes its root
12 Underneath his foot.

Soon spreads the dismal shade
Of mystery over his head;
And the caterpillar and fly
16 Feed on the mystery.

And it bears the fruit of deceit,
Ruddy and sweet to eat;
And the raven his nest has made
20 In its thickest shade.

The gods of the earth and sea
Sought thro' nature to find this tree;
But their search was all in vain:
24 There grows one in the human brain.

A Poison Tree from Songs of Experience

I was angry with my friend:
I told my wrath, my wrath did end.
I was angry with my foe:
4 I told it not, my wrath did grow.

And I watered it in fears,
Night and morning with my tears;
And I sunned it with smiles,
8 And with soft deceitful wiles.

And it grew both day and night,
Till it bore an apple bright;
And my foe beheld it shine,
12 And he knew that it was mine,

And into my garden stole
When the night had veiled the pole:
In the morning glad I see
16 My foe outstretched beneath the tree.

TOPICS FOR WRITING AND DISCUSSION

FOR USE IN CLASS

1. Describe the development of the basic conceit in "The Human Abstract."

2. Discuss the development of the metaphor of "A Poison Tree." How does Biblical allusion work?

3. Describe what has happened to the Garden of Eden in Blake's "The Garden of Love."

4. Describe the diction and imagery of "Spring." Define the poet's attitude towards that season. (Be sure to notice the lamb imagery of stanza 3.)

FOR PREPARATION OUTSIDE OF CLASS

1. Compare the two songs on spring, "O thou with dewy locks" and "Sound the flute!"

2. Write an essay on Blake as a humanitarian poet. Support your observations with concrete evidence from the poems.

3. Write an essay on Blake's concept of contraries. Support your generalizations.

4. Discuss the various uses of Blake's black-white and night-day image patterns in this collection of his poems.

William Wordsworth
[1770–1850]

Scorn Not the Sonnet

Scorn not the sonnet; critic, you have frowned,
Mindless of its just honours; with this key
Shakespeare unlocked his heart; the melody
4 Of this small lute gave ease to Petrarch's wound;
A thousand times this pipe did Tasso sound;
With it Camöens soothed an exile's grief;
The sonnet glittered a gay myrtle leaf
8 Amid the cypress with which Dante crowned
His visionary brow; a glow-worm lamp,
It cheered mild Spenser, called from Faeryland
To struggle through dark ways; and, when a damp
12 Fell round the path of Milton, in his hand
The thing became a trumpet; whence he blew
Soul-animating strains—alas, too few!

NOTES Wordsworth's sonnet is rich in allusion to other sonneteers: the Italians Petrarch (1304-1374), Tasso (1544-1595), and Dante (1265-1321), the Portugese Camöens (1524-1580), and the English Shakespeare (1564-1616), Spenser (1552-1599), and Milton (1607-1674).
Line 4 "Petrarch's wound": Petrarch popularized the traditional metaphor of a lover's infatuation as a wound caused by cupid's dart.
Line 8 "cypress": Traditionally the tree or sign of death; here, along with "visionary brow," an allusion to Dante's epic poem *The Divine Comedy*, which emphasizes the progress of the soul after it has been liberated from the body through death.
Line 10 "Faeryland": An allusion to Spenser's allegorical epic, *The Faerie Queen*.

WORDSWORTH'S SONNETS

Wordsworth wrote over 500 sonnets in his career, about four times as many as Shakespeare and almost 25 times as many as Milton. The eighteenth-century poets had, for the most part, completely ignored the sonnet form in their infatuation with the longer form they called the ode. Wordsworth hoped to reestablish the sonnet in the position it had held in the time of Shakespeare and Milton. Consequently, several of his sonnets are specifically about the sonnet form itself, a form in which renowned poets sought solace in times of personal distress. In "Scorn Not the Sonnet," directed to critics who ignored the successful examples of the sonnet, Wordsworth catalogues, through various metaphors, the relationship of the sonnet to its famous practitioners. The sonnets provided Shakespeare with a way to ease his grief, and through them we can view the secrets of his life. The sonnet is our little "key" to Shakespeare's heart. What was "a small lute" for Petrarch, "a pipe" for Tasso, "a gay myrtle leaf" for Dante, "a glow-worm lamp" for Spenser, was for Milton a "trumpet." Where others were satisfied to make of the sonnet a personal lyric, Milton ennobled the form, speaking truths for all men.

In "Scorn Not the Sonnet", Wordsworth breaks the usual close divisions of the Italian sonnet, opening with a line and a half directed to the critic, extending his series of metaphors in catalogue form, finally culminating with the example of Milton. Disregarding the usual conventions except those of rhyme and meter, he still has a three-part division: lines 1-2, 3-12, 13-14. The final couplet is rhymed to convey in sound an additional sense of completion.

Unlike this sonnet, "Nun's Fret Not at Their Convent's Narrow Room" which follows, is completely personal and illustrates a more conventional pattern of development. In the sestet Wordsworth describes his own experience with the sonnet. Both poems are pleas for the continuation of the sonnet tradition.

QUESTIONS

1. What evidence is there that some of the poets mentioned suffered some personal misfortune?

2. How are the metaphors, "glittered a gay myrtle leaf" and "a glow-worm lamp", especially effective?

3. What is the effect of the progression in music imagery from "small lute" to "pipe" to "trumpet"?

4. Compare the tone of the opening line with the tone of the concluding words, "alas, too few."

5. Describe the progression in the speaker's attitudes as he catalogues the history of the sonnet. Notice how the poem ends on a personal note.

Nuns Fret Not at Their Convent's Narrow Room

Nuns fret not at their convent's narrow room;
And hermits are contented with their cells;
And students with their pensive citadels;
4 Maids at the wheel, the weaver at his loom,
Sit blithe and happy; bees that soar for bloom,
High as the highest peak of Furness-fells,*   barren cliffs
Will murmur by the hour in foxglove bells:
8 In truth the prison, into which we doom
Ourselves, no prison is: and hence for me,
In sundry moods, 'twas pastime to be bound
Within the sonnet's scanty plot of ground;
12 Pleased if some souls (for such there needs must be)
Who have felt the weight of too much liberty,
Should find brief solace there, as I have found.

1. The middle of line 9 is the structural center of the poem. How does the line function in this sonnet?

2. What examples of diction emphasize the sonnet's restricted nature?

3. What additional relationship is there between nuns, hermits, and students, which Wordsworth suggests but does not mention?

A Poet!—He Hath Put His Heart to School

A poet!—He hath put his heart to school,
Nor dares to move unpropped upon the staff
Which art hath lodged within his hand—must laugh
4   By precept only, and shed tears by rule.
Thy art be nature; the live current quaff,
And let the groveller sip his stagnant pool,
In fear that else, when critics grave and cool
8   Have killed him, scorn should write his epitaph.
How does the meadow-flower its bloom unfold?
Because the lovely little flower is free
Down to its root, and, in that freedom, bold;
12 And so the grandeur of the forest-tree
Comes not by casting in a formal mould,
But from its *own* divine vitality.

WORDSWORTH AND POETIC CREATION

In this sonnet Wordsworth suggests something of the nature of both poet and poem, arguing against many eighteenth-century attitudes. Poets, he thought, must be men who feel intensely, men whose emotional lives are the very heart of their being. Poets, then, ought not learn their trade by precept and rule, or by following traditions slavishly. Of course, Wordsworth did not really mean that a poet had no need of learning a craft; his argument was against those with a prescribed formula for every occasion. Poetry was for him something alive and organic like a tree or flower, and freedom from convention was its first prerequisite. Wordsworth's plea was to allow the poem to grow, or progress, naturally, dictating its imagery, its diction, its structure as it unfolded. His motto might have been "Poetic liberty is its own form."

1. Paraphrase lines 1 through 4. What kind of poet does Wordsworth describe here?
2. Describe how the second quatrain contrasts Wordsworth's view of some traditional poets with his ideal.
3. What is the effect of the nature images of the sestet?
4. What is the effect of the adjective "divine" in line 14?
5. Describe the structure of the sonnet.

There Is a Pleasure in Poetic Pains

There is a pleasure in poetic pains
Which only poets know;—'twas rightly said;
Whom could the muses else allure to tread
4 Their smoothest paths, to wear their lightest chains?
When happiest fancy has inspired the strains,
How oft the malice of one luckless word
Pursues the enthusiast to the social board,*   *dining table*
8 Haunts him belated on the silent plains!
Yet he repines not, if his thought stand clear,
At last, of hindrance and obscurity,
Fresh as the star that crowns the brow of morn;
12 Bright, speckless, as a softly-moulded tear
The moment it has left the virgin's eye,
Or rain-drop lingering on the pointed thorn.

NOTE The opening quotation in the first line and a half comes from the English poet, William Cowper (1731-1800).

MORE ON POETIC CREATION

Here is another sonnet by Wordsworth about poetic creation, in which he describes the paradox of pain and pleasure in writing poetry. The poet's pleasure is in taking pains with his verses, in his attempt to find the right word or image and to get the exactly appropriate metaphor for his poem without being trite or without depending upon the vast traditional stock of materials which are often clichés.

QUESTIONS

1. Describe how the pleasure-pain paradox is continued in lines 11-14.
2. What well-known scene does the imagery in lines 11-14 suggest, and how is that event appropriate to the poem?
3. Describe the relationship between the sestet and the second quatrain.

Though the Bold Wings of Poesy Affect

Though the bold wings of poesy affect
The clouds, and wheel around the mountain tops
Rejoicing, from her loftiest height she drops
4 Well pleased to skim the plain with wild flowers deckt,
Or muse in solemn grove whose shades protect
The lingering dew—there steals along, or stops
Watching the least small bird that round her hops,
8 Or creeping worm, with sensitive respect.
Her functions are they therefore less divine,
Her thoughts less deep, or void of grave intent
Her simplest fancies? Should that fear be thine,
12 Aspiring votary,* ere thy hand present   *apprentice poet*
One offering, kneel before her modest shrine,
With brow in penitential sorrow bent!

STILL MORE ON POETRY

Here Wordsworth describes metaphorically two kinds of poetry: the cere-
monial, traditionally involved and elevated hymn, and the relatively short, personal, simple lyric. The difference between them, he suggests, is like the difference
between the atmosphere of lofty heights and mountain tops and a plain with wild
flowers and little birds

QUESTIONS

1. Describe the development of the basic metaphor in the octave. (Notice especially how the verbs function here.)
2. What is the effect of enjambment in lines 1 through 6?
3. What kind of poetry ought the young poet write, according to Wordsworth?
4. What is the effect of religious imagery in lines 11–14?
5. What is the relationship of sestet to octave here?

I Grieved for Buonaparté

I grieved for Buonaparté, with a vain
And an unthinking grief! The tenderest mood
Of that man's mind—what can it be? what food
4 Fed his first hopes? what knowledge could *he* gain?
'Tis not in battles that from youth we train
The governor who must be wise and good,
And temper with the sternness of the brain
8 Thoughts motherly, and meek as womanhood.
Wisdom doth live with children round her knees:
Books, leisure, perfect freedom, and the talk
Man holds with week-day man in the hourly walk
12 Of the mind's business: these are the degrees
By which true sway doth mount; this is the stalk
True power doth grow on; and her rights are these.

NOTES From the beginning Wordsworth's sympathies were devoted to the French Revolution, the overthrow of monarchy, and the cause of French freedom. Later, following the
Reign of Terror, England's declaration of war on France, and Napoleon's wars of foreign
conquest, Wordsworth, along with others, suffered great disillusionment. His disillusionment,
however, was hastened by Napoleon's practice of restricting constitutional liberties in the
name of freedom. The General was not following what Wordsworth thought was an ideal
course for the perfect leader.

This sonnet was written in 1802 when Napoleon had himself appointed, by plebiscite,
First Consul for life.

QUESTIONS

1. How does Wordsworth react to Napoleon's quest for power?

2. What is the tone of the opening quatrain (notice the effect of the three
questions)?

3. Paraphrase the sestet. How does Wordsworth characterize true wisdom and
power?

4. What are some possible senses of the word "rights" in line 14?

Great Men Have Been Among Us

Great men have been among us; hands that penned
And tongues that uttered wisdom—better none:
The later Sidney, Marvell, Harrington,
4 Young Vane, and others who called Milton friend.
These moralists could act and comprehend:
They knew how genuine glory was put on;
Taught us how rightfully a nation shone
8 In splendour: what strength was, that would not bend
But in magnanimous meekness. France, 'tis strange,
Hath brought forth no such souls as we had then.
Perpetual emptiness! unceasing change!
12 No single volume paramount, no code,
No master spirit, no determined road;
But equally a want of books and men!

NOTE In this sonnet Wordsworth bemoans the fact that the French Revolution, unlike the English Civil War (1641-1652), produced no morally great men in its ranks.

QUESTIONS

1. What does this sonnet tell us about Wordsworth's ideal leader?
2. Point out an example of *oxymoron*. How does the phrase function in context?
3. Point out some examples of metonomy. How do these examples function in context?
4. What are the connotations of "moralists" (line 5)?

Strange Fits of Passion Have I Known

Strange fits of passion have I known:
And I will dare to tell,
But in the lover's ear alone,
4 What once to me befell.

When she I loved looked every day
Fresh as a rose in June,
I to her cottage bent my way,
8 Beneath an evening-moon.

Upon the moon I fixed my eye,
All over the wide lea;
With quickening pace my horse drew nigh
12 Those paths so dear to me.

And now we reached the orchard-plot;
And, as we climbed the hill,
The sinking moon to Lucy's cot*   *cottage*
16 Came near, and nearer still.

In one of those sweet dreams I slept,
Kind Nature's gentlest boon!
And all the while my eyes I kept
20 On the descending moon.

My horse moved on; hoof after hoof
He raised, and never stopped:
When down behind the cottage roof,
24 At once, the bright moon dropped.

What fond* and wayward thoughts will slide   *foolish*
Into a lover's head!
"O mercy!" to myself I cried,
28 "If Lucy should be dead!"

QUESTIONS

1. Why does the lover call his emotion a "strange fit of passion"?
2. How does the image of the moon function in the poem?
3. Point out an example of *understatement*. What is its effect in context?
4. How does the lover's physical movement coincide with the emotional progression in the poem?

She Dwelt Among the Untrodden Ways

She dwelt among the untrodden ways
Beside the springs of Dove,*   *a stream*
A maid whom there were none to praise
4 And very few to love:

A violet by a mossy stone
Half hidden from the eye!
Fair as a star, when only one
8 Is shining in the sky.

She lived unknown, and few could know
When Lucy ceased to be;
But she is in her grave, and, oh,
12 The difference to me!

1. What various meanings can you assign to the concluding line?
2. Describe Wordsworth's characterization of Lucy in this poem.
3. What importance do you attach to the fact of Lucy's solitude?

Three Years She Grew in Sun and Shower

Three years she grew in sun and shower,
Then Nature said, "A lovelier flower
On earth was never sown;
This child I to myself will take;
5   She shall be mine, and I will make
A lady of my own.

"Myself will to my darling be
Both law and impulse: and with me
The girl, in rock and plain,
10 In earth and heaven, in glade and bower,
Shall feel an overseeing power
To kindle or restrain.

"She shall be sportive as the fawn
That wild with glee across the lawn,
15 Or up the mountain springs;
And hers shall be the breathing balm,
And hers the silence and the calm
Of mute insensate things.

"The floating clouds their state shall lend
20 To her; for her the willow bend;
Nor shall she fail to see
Even in the motions of the storm
Grace that shall mould the maiden's form
By silent sympathy.

25 "The stars of midnight shall be dear
To her; and she shall lean her ear
In many a secret place
Where rivulets dance their wayward round,
And beauty born of murmuring sound
30 Shall pass into her face.

"And vital feelings of delight
Shall rear her form to stately height,
Her virgin bosom swell;
Such thoughts to Lucy I will give
35 While she and I together live
Here in this happy dell."

Thus Nature spake—The work was done—
How soon my Lucy's race was run!
She died, and left to me
40 This heath, this calm, and quiet scene;
The memory of what has been,
And never more will be.

QUESTIONS

1. What images in the three preceding lyrics anticipate the way the speaker describes Lucy here?
2. What qualities does Nature give to Lucy?
3. What does Nature mean by the phrase "law and impulse" (line 8)?
4. Why is ballad form not so appropriate for this poem?
5. Describe the tone of the final stanza.

I Travelled Among Unknown Men

I travelled among unknown men,
In lands beyond the sea;
Nor, England! did I know till then
4 What love I bore to thee.

'Tis past, that melancholy dream!
Nor will I quit thy shore
A second time; for still I seem
8 To love thee more and more.

Among thy mountains did I feel
The joy of my desire;
And she I cherished turned her wheel
12 Beside an English fire.

Thy mornings showed, thy nights concealed
The bowers where Lucy played;
And thine too is the last green field
16 That Lucy's eyes surveyed.

QUESTION

In the first poem the speaker referred to his dream as a "strange fit of passion"; here he calls his dream "melancholy." Describe the differences between the two attitudes.

A Slumber Did My Spirit Seal

A slumber did my spirit seal;
I had no human fears:
She seemed a thing that could not feel
4 The touch of earthly years.

No motion has she now, no force;
She neither hears nor sees;
Rolled round in earth's diurnal course,
8 With rocks, and stones, and trees.

QUESTIONS

1. Explain the relationship between the two stanzas.
2. What significance do you attach to the speaker's progression from "a strange fit of passion" to "a melancholy dream" to a "slumber"?
3. What is the effect of the alliteration in line 1?

THE LUCY POEMS

These five *lyrics* are called the "Lucy poems," for they elegize the death of a young girl named Lucy. The name was an eighteenth-century elegiac commonplace, and whether Lucy has a real counterpart is a literary irrelevancy. The group is presented here in the order Wordsworth possibly intended, and in this order they form a significant lyric progression. The lover's nightmare, his "strange fit of passion," in the first lyric has come true in the second ("She dwelt among the untrodden ways"). There, we discover, Lucy has died (we assume some time lapses between the two poems). In the third lyric the lover goes on to establish what seems to him, at least temporarily, a satisfactory way of facing the world without Lucy. He reorders his vision of life and estimates the value of his experience in quite conventional terms; his life, his England, his countryside have been made all the dearer for his association with Lucy. The statements about Lucy in natural terms made in the first three poems are amplified and expanded in "Three years she grew." There the lover realizes how appropriate it is for one who is as frail and beautiful as a violet, but who is, after all, a violet, to exist immortally as part of the natural cycle. This is the first of the five lyrics to consider Lucy's death as a rightful unification with a beneficent natural world, but the terms of such a realization are present in the preceding lyrics. In the last lyric the lover considers his whole experience. Once he had dreamed that his Lucy could never die. Ironically, now in death, she is exactly as he had hoped she would be; she does not "feel the touch of earthly years." The lover has learned a bitter but necessary lesson; he has learned to confront and accept mortality as a condition of life.

All the lyrics except the third are written in *ballad* measure: a four line stanza of alternating iambic *tetrameter* and iambic *trimeter* rhyming *abab* (most traditional ballads rhyme *abcd*). Wordsworth probably chose the ballad stanza because the ballad is generally associated with narrative poetry concerned with love and death. For although he is interested in tracing the lover's intellectual enlightenment, he is also telling a story. Consequently, the poems assume several of the characteristics of a parable.

At Vallombrosa

Thick as autumnal leaves that strew the brooks
In Vallombrosa, where Etrurian shades
Hie over-arched embower.*   *to cover with foliage*
                    Paradise Lost I, 302-304

"Vallombrosa—I longed in thy shadiest wood
To slumber, reclined on the moss-covered floor!"
Fond wish that was granted at last, and the flood,
That lulled me asleep bids me listen once more.
5 Its murmur how soft! as it falls down the steep,
Near that cell—yon sequestered retreat high in air—
Where our Milton was wont lonely vigils to keep
For converse with God, sought through study and
                                                prayer.

The monks still repeat the tradition with pride,
10 And its truth who shall doubt? for his spirit is here;
In the cloud-piercing rocks doth her grandeur abide,
In the pines pointing heavenward her beauty austere;
In the flower-besprent* meadows his genius we trace   *besprinkled*
Turned to humbler delights, in which youth might
                                                confide,
15 That would yield him fit help while prefiguring that
                                                place
Where, if sin had not entered, love never had died.

When with life lengthened out came a desolate time,
And darkness and danger had compassed him round,
With a thought he would flee to these haunts of his
                      prime
20 And here once again a kind shelter be found.
And let me believe that when nightly the muse
Did waft him to Sion,* the glorified hill,   *holy site in*
Here also, on some favoured height, he would choose   *Jerusalem*
To wander, and drink inspiration at will.

25 Vallombrosa! of thee I first heard in the page
Of that holiest of bards, and the name for my mind
Had a musical charm, which the winter of age
And the changes it brings had no power to unbind.
And now, ye Miltonian shades! under you
30 I repose, nor am forced from sweet fancy to part,
While your leaves I behold and the brooks they will
                      strew,
And the realized vision is clasped to my heart.

Even so, and unblamed, we rejoice as we may
In forms that must perish, frail objects of sense;
35 Unblamed—if the soul be intent on the day
When the Being of Beings shall summon her hence.
For he and he only with wisdom is blest
Who, gathering true pleasures wherever they grow,
Looks up in all places, for joy or for rest,
40 To the fountain whence time and eternity flow.

NOTE Vallombrosa, literally "the vale of shades," is the site of a Benedictine abbey near
Florence, Italy. Both Wordsworth and Milton visited the abbey.

ANAPESTIC METER

    The basic *anapestic* foot of the poem appears to grow out of the pronunciation
of the opening word. The anapest is a metrical unit composed of three syllables,
the first two unaccented, the third accented as in line 1:

    "Vallombrósa—I longed in thy shadiest woód".

The meter is not perfectly regular, as in most poems, and Wordsworth's usual
variation is the introduction of an initial *iamb* instead of opening the line with an
anapest. This is to say that the poet omits one unstressed syllable at the beginning
of those lines. The use of the meter throughout emphasizes Wordsworth's fascination with the name.

QUESTIONS

1. How is the anapestic foot particularly appropriate to lines 4 and 5?
2. Describe the portrait of Milton in this poem.
3. What is the effect on the structure of the poem of the alternate end rhyme?
4. How does Wordsworth play on the literal meaning of Vallombrosa?
5. What is the antecedent of "her," line 36, and "he," line 37?
6. How does the poem reveal Milton as the ideal of which Wordsworth speaks in lines 37–40?

WHAT TO LOOK FOR IN THE ADDITIONAL READING

The discussions of Wordsworth's poetry have deliberately avoided the conventional labels "nature poetry" and "Romantic poet," for in some senses all poets are nature poets and Romanticism is of more interest to literary historians than to readers of Wordsworth's poetry. The discussions have encouraged direct confrontation of the poem without giving the reader a set of preconceived historical notions. Nonetheless, one ought to remember that Wordsworth's poetry is in strong reaction to the inherited tastes and conventions of the preceding century, which the reader ought to be able to deduce from poems like "A Poet!—He Hath Put His Heart to School." Wordsworth does write nature poetry, but the important thing to remember is that he uses nature and natural imagery in a way very different from that of Jonson and Pope. For Wordsworth the natural world is a live, organic, beneficent environment with powers of its own to chasten and encourage those men who love and praise it. It possesses a kind of moral power which can be discovered by sympathetic minds which have placed themselves into a state of serene repose.

Here you will find an additional *ballad*, an elegy, a *blank verse* epigram, and several sonnets, including one heroic sonnet in the Miltonic manner. In analyzing these poems, look for differences in diction, imagery, and even subject matter from the poetry of Jonson and Pope. In this inductive fashion you will soon discover for yourself how Wordsworth is different and what those characteristics are that make him a Romantic Poet. Although he reacts strongly against the overly stylized attitude towards poetry in the eighteenth century, he does not reject the past entirely, for his obvious model in the sonnet is the form as practiced by John Milton, and Milton is the subject of many of his poems. His rebellion, then, was not against all traditions. You may be interested, however, in comparing the vastly different elegies written by Milton and Wordsworth to see that Wordsworth was no slavish imitator of all things Miltonic.

—A simple child,
That lightly draws its breath,
And feels its life in every limb,
4 What should it know of death?

I met a little cottage girl:
She was eight years old, she said:
Her hair was thick with many a curl
8 That clustered round her head.

She had a rustic, woodland air,
And she was wildly clad:
Her eyes were fair, and very fair;
12 —Her beauty made me glad.

"Sisters and brothers, little maid,
How many may you be?"
"How many? Seven in all," she said
16 And wondering looked at me.

"And where are they? I pray you tell."
She answered, "Seven are we;
And two of us at Conway dwell,
20 And two are gone to sea.

"Two of us in the church-yard lie,
My sister and my brother;
And, in the church-yard cottage, I
24 Dwell near them with my mother."

"You say that two at Conway dwell,
And two are gone to sea,
Yet ye are seven!—I pray you tell,
28 Sweet maid, how this may be."

Then did the little maid reply,
"Seven boys and girls are we;
Two of us in the church-yard lie,
32 Beneath the church-yard tree."

"You run about, my little maid,
Your limbs they are alive;
If two are in the church-yard laid,
36 Then ye are only five."

"Their graves are green, they may be seen,"
The little maid replied,
"Twelve steps or more from my mother's door,
40 And they are side by side.

"My stockings there I often knit,
My kerchief there I hem;
And there upon the ground I sit,
44 And sing a song to them.

"And often after sunset, sir,
When it is light and fair,
I take my little porringer,
48 And eat my supper there.

"The first that died was sister Jane;
In bed she moaning lay,
Till God released her of her pain;
52 And then she went away.

"So in the church-yard she was laid;
And, when the grass was dry,
Together round her grave we played,
56 My brother John and I.

"And when the ground was white with snow,
And I could run and slide,
My brother John was forced to go,
60 And he lies by her side."

"How many are you, then," said I,
"If they two are in heaven?"
Quick was the little maid's reply,
64 "O master! we are seven."

"But they are dead; those two are dead!
Their spirits are in heaven!"
'T was throwing words away; for still
The little maid would have her will,
69 And said, "Nay, we are seven!"

Lines Left Upon a Seat in a Yew-Tree, Which Stands Near the Lake of Esthwaite, On a Desolate Part of the Shore, Commanding a Beautiful Prospect

Nay, traveller! rest. This lonely yew-tree stands
Far from all human dwelling: what if here
No sparkling rivulet spread the verdant herb?
What if the bee love not these barren boughs?
5 Yet, if the wind breathe soft, the curling waves,
That break against the shore, shall lull thy mind
By one soft impulse saved from vacancy.
                                        Who he was
That piled these stones and with the mossy sod
10 First covered, and here taught this aged tree
With its dark arms to form a circling bower,
I well remember—He was one who owned
No common soul. In youth by science nursed,
And led by nature into a wild scene
15 Of lofty hopes, he to the world went forth
A favoured Being, knowing no desire
Which genius did not hallow; 'gainst the taint
Of dissolute tongues, and jealousy, and hate,
And scorn,—against all enemies prepared,
20 All but neglect. The world, for so it thought,
Owed him no service; wherefore he at once
With indignation turned himself away,
And with the food of pride sustained his soul
In solitude.—Stranger! these gloomy boughs
25 Had charms for him; and here he loved to sit,
His only visitants a straggling sheep,
The stone-chat, or the glancing sand-piper:
And on these barren rocks, with fern and heath,
And juniper and thistle, sprinkled o'er,
30 Fixing his downcast eye, he many an hour
A morbid pleasure nourished, tracing here
An emblem of his own unfruitful life:
And, lifting up his head, he then would gaze
On the more distant scene,—how lovely 'tis
35 Thou see'st,—and he would gaze till it became
Far lovelier, and his heart could not sustain
The beauty, still more beauteous! Nor, that time,

When nature had subdued him to herself,
Would he forget those Beings to whose minds,
40 Warm from the labours of benevolence,
The world, and human life, appeared a scene
Of kindred loveliness; then he would sigh,
Inly* disturbed, to think that others felt   *deeply*
What he must never feel: and so, lost Man!
45 On visionary views would fancy feed,
Till his eye streamed with tears. In this deep vale
He died,—this seat his only monument.
    If Thou be one whose heart the holy forms
Of young imagination have kept pure,
50 Stranger! henceforth be warned; and know that pride
Howe'er disguised in its own majesty,
Is littleness; that he, who feels contempt
For any living thing, hath faculties
Which he has never used; that thought with him
55 Is in its infancy. The man whose eye
Is ever on himself doth look on one,
The least of Nature's works, one who might move
The wise man to that scorn which wisdom holds
60 Unlawful, ever. O be wiser, Thou!
Instructed that true knowledge leads to love;
True dignity abides with him alone
Who, in the silent hour of inward thought,
Can still suspect, and still revere himself,
65 In lowliness of heart.

In Memory of My Brother, John Wordsworth
Elegiac Verses

I

The sheep-boy whistled loud, and lo!
That instant, startled by the shock,
The buzzard mounted from the rock
Deliberate and slow:
5 Lord of the air, he took his flight;
Oh! could he on that woeful night
Have lent his wing, my brother dear,
For one poor moment's space to thee,
And all who struggled with the sea,
10 When safety was so near.

II

Thus in the weakness of my heart
I spoke (but let that pang be still)
When rising from the rock at will,
I saw the bird depart.
15 And let me calmly bless the power
That meets me in this unknown flower.
Affecting type of him I mourn!
With calmness suffer and believe,
And grieve, and know that I must grieve,
20 Not cheerless, though forlorn.

III

Here did we stop; and here looked round
While each into himself descends,
For that last thought of parting friends
That is not to be found.
25 Hidden was Grasmere Vale from sight,
Our home and his, his heart's delight,
His quiet heart's selected home.
But time before him melts away,
And he hath feeling of a day
30 Of blessedness to come.

IV

Full soon in sorrow did I weep,
Taught that the mutual hope was dust,
In sorrow, but for higher trust,
How miserably deep!
35 All vanished in a single word,
A breath, a sound, and scarcely heard:
Sea—ship—drowned—shipwreck—so it came,
The meek, the brave, the good, was gone;
He who had been our living John
40 Was nothing but a name.

That was indeed a parting! oh,
Glad am I, glad that it is past;
For there were some on whom it cast
Unutterable woe.
45 But they as well as I have gains;—
From many a humble source, to pains
Like these, there comes a mild release;
Even here I feel it, even this plant
Is in its beauty ministrant
50 To comfort and to peace.

VI

He would have loved thy modest grace,
Meek flower!* To him I would have said,
"It grows upon its native bed
Beside our parting-place;
55 There, cleaving to the ground, it lies
With multitude of purple eyes,
Spangling a cushion green like moss;
But we will see it, joyful tide!
Some day, to see it in its pride,
60 The mountain will we cross."

*moss campion:
a scarce and
beautiful flower*

VII

—Brother and friend, if verse of mine
Have power to make thy virtues known,
Here let a monumental stone
Stand—sacred as a shrine;
65 And to the few who pass this way,
Traveller or shepherd, let it say,
Long as these mighty rocks endure,—
Oh do not thou too fondly brood,
Although deserving of all good,
70 On any earthly hope, however pure!

To Toussaint L'Ouverture

Toussaint, the most unhappy man of men!
Whether the whistling rustic tend his plough
Within thy hearing, or thy head be now
4 Pillowed in some deep dungeon's earless den;—
O miserable chieftain! where and when
Wilt thou find patience? Yet die not; do thou
Wear rather in thy bonds a cheerful brow:
8 Though fallen thyself, never to rise again,
Live, and take comfort. Thou hast left behind
Powers that will work for thee; air, earth, and skies;
There's not a breathing of the common wind
12 That will forget thee; thou hast great allies;
Thy friends are exultations, agonies,
And love, and man's unconquerable mind.

NOTE   Toussaint L'Ouverture was a Haitian liberator and general (1743–1803).

It Is a Beauteous Evening, Calm and Free

It is a beauteous evening, calm and free,
The holy time is quiet as a nun
Breathless with adoration; the broad sun
4 Is sinking down in its tranquility;
The gentleness of heaven broods o'er the sea:
Listen! the mighty being is awake,
And doth with his eternal motion make
8 A sound like thunder—everlastingly.
Dear child! dear girl! that walkest with me here,
If thou appear untouched by solemn thought,
Thy nature is not therefore less divine:
12 Thou liest in Abraham's bosom all the year;
And worship'st at the Temple's inner shrine,
God being with thee when we know it not.

September 1, 1802

We had a female passenger who came
From Calais with us, spotless in array,—
A white-robed Negro, like a lady gay,
4 Yet downcast as a woman fearing blame;
Meek, destitute, as seemed, of hope or aim
She sate, from notice turning not away,
But on all proffered intercourse did lay
8 A weight of languid speech, or to the same
No sign of answer made by word or face:
Yet still her eyes retained their tropic fire,
That, burning independent of the mind,
12 Joined with the lustre of her rich attire
To mock the outcast.—O ye heavens, be kind!
And feel, thou earth, for his afflicted race!

With Ships the Sea Was Sprinkled Far and Nigh

With ships the sea was sprinkled far and nigh,
Like stars in heaven, and joyously it showed;
Some lying fast at anchor in the road,
4 Some veering up and down, one knew not why.
A goodly vessel did I then espy
Come like a giant from a haven broad;
And lustily along the bay she strode,
8 Her tackling rich, and of apparel high.
This ship was nought to me, nor I to her,
Yet I pursued her with a lover's look;
This ship to all the rest did I prefer:
12 When will she turn, and whither? She will brook
No tarrying; where she comes the winds must stir:
On went she, and due north her journey took.

Upon the Sight of a Beautiful Picture

Praised be the art whose subtle power could stay
Yon cloud, and fix it in that glorious shape;
Nor would permit the thin smoke to escape,
4 Nor those bright sunbeams to forsake the day;
Which stopped that band of travellers on their way,
Ere they were lost within the shady wood;
And showed the bark* upon the glassy flood   *boat
8 For ever anchored in her sheltering bay.
Soul-soothing art! whom morning, noontide, even,
Do serve with all their changeful pageantry;
Thou, with ambition modest yet sublime,
12 Here, for the sight of mortal man, hast given
To one brief moment caught from fleeting time
The appropriate calm of blest eternity.

NOTE   Wordsworth is viewing a landscape by Sir George Beaumont.

Surprised by Joy—Impatient as the Wind

Surprised by joy—impatient as the wind
I turned to share the transport—Oh! with whom
But thee,* deep buried in the silent tomb,   *the poet's daughter,
4 That spot which no vicissitude can find?   Catherine
Love, faithful love, recalled thee to my mind—
But how could I forget thee? Through what power,
Even for the least division of an hour,
8 Have I been so beguiled as to be blind
To my most grievous loss?—That thought's return
Was the worst pang that sorrow ever bore,
Save one, one only, when I stood forlorn,
12 Knowing my heart's best treasure was no more;
That neither present time, nor years unborn
Could to my sight that heavenly face restore.

Composed On Westminster Bridge, September 3, 1802

Earth has not anything to show more fair:
Dull would he be of soul who could pass by
A sight so touching in its majesty:
4 This City now doth, like a garment, wear
The beauty of the morning; silent, bare,
Ships, towers, domes, theatres, and temples lie
Open unto the fields, and to the sky;
8 All bright and glittering in the smokeless air,
Never did sun more beautifully steep
In his first splendour, valley, rock, or hill;
Ne'er saw I, never felt, a calm so deep!
12 The river glideth at his own sweet will:
Dear God! The very houses seem asleep;
And all that mighty heart is lying still!

TOPICS FOR WRITING AND DISCUSSION

FOR USE IN CLASS

1. Explain how the question in the opening stanza of "We Are Seven" is answered in the rest of the ballad.
2. Comment upon the humanitarian interests that Wordsworth displays in the additional reading.
3. Describe how Wordsworth's confrontation with the "meek flower" resolves the elegiac progression in his "Elegiac Verses."
4. Write a paraphrase of the sonnet "On the Sight of a Beautiful Picture" in which you describe in detail the painting Wordsworth observes and its significance for him.

FOR PREPARATION OUTSIDE OF CLASS

1. Write an essay entitled "Wordsworth's View of Nature."
2. Compare Wordsworth's moral values and his human ideals with those you see reflected in the poetry of Ben Jonson.
3. Describe the Miltonic characteristics in Wordsworth's sonnets.
4. Compare "Elegiac Verses" with Milton's "Lycidas."

Ode on a Grecian Urn

I

Thou still unravished bride of quietness,
   Thou foster-child of silence and slow time,
Sylvan historian, who canst thus express
   A flowery tale more sweetly than our rhyme:
5 What leaf-fringed legend haunts about thy shape
   Of deities or mortals, or of both,
     In Tempe* or the dale of Arcady*?   *mythological settings*
   What men or gods are these? What maidens loth?
What mad pursuit? What struggle to escape?
10   What pipes and timbrels*? What wild ecstasy?   *tambourines*

II

Heard melodies are sweet, but those unheard
   Are sweeter; therefore, ye soft pipes, play on;
Not to the sensual ear, but, more endeared,
   Pipe to the spirit ditties of no tone:
15 Fair youth, beneath the trees, thou canst not leave
   Thy song, nor ever can those trees be bare;
     Bold lover, never, never canst thou kiss,
Though winning near the goal—yet, do not grieve;
   She cannot fade, though thou hast not thy bliss,
20   Forever wilt thou love, and she be fair!

III

Ah, happy, happy boughs! that cannot shed
   Your leaves, nor ever bid the spring adieu;
And, happy melodist, unwearied,
   For ever piping songs for ever new;
25 More happy love! more happy, happy love!
   For ever warm and still to be enjoyed,
     Forever panting, and forever young;
All breathing human passion far above,
   That leaves a heart high-sorrowful and cloyed,
30   A burning forehead, and a parching tongue.

IV

Who are these coming to the sacrifice?
  To what green altar, O mysterious priest,
Lead'st thou that heifer lowing at the skies,
  And all her silken flanks with garlands drest?
35 What little town by river or sea shore,
    Or mountain-built with peaceful citadel,
      Is emptied of this folk, this pious morn?
And, little town, thy streets for evermore
    Will silent be; and not a soul to tell
40   Why thou art desolate, can e'er return.

V

O Attic* shape! Fair attitude! with brede°
  Of marble men and maidens overwrought,
With forest branches and the trodden weed;
  Thou, silent form, dost tease us out of thought
45 As doth eternity: Cold pastoral!
    When old age shall this generation waste,
      Thou shalt remain, in midst of other woe
Than ours, a friend to man, to whom thou say'st,
    "Beauty is truth, truth beauty,—that is all
50   Ye know on earth, and all ye need to know."

*of classic simplicity;
°border ornament

KEATS'S ENIGMATIC URN

Few perceptive readers deny the greatness of Keats's "Ode on a Grecian Urn," but many disagree on what the poem tells us, and especially on what the urn tells us, or does not tell us, in the poem. The urn is referred to as such only in the title, and as the fanciful image of the object unfolds in the poem, one is challenged beyond the limits of visualizing a literal object, so that the urn should be considered, perhaps, a creation of Keats's poetic fancy. If no one sculptured urn could embody all that the speaker attributes to it, then, the reader ought to regard the object of the *apostrophe* as an ideal Grecian urn. The concept of beauty with which the poem ends can be more easily associated with such an ideal than with a particular marble urn. Consider the attributes of the urn. It is a bride, a child, and a historian that tells us a tale. The puzzling tale (legend), leaf-fringed, may depict the actions of men or gods, perhaps one classical setting, perhaps another. The nature of pursuit, the escape, and the ecstasy it suggests can only be guessed at. In the second stanza, the speaker begins by recognizing the paradoxical nature of his experience: he can not literally hear the music being played by the figures on the urn, but he hears music nonetheless. The songs his imagination suggests to him, he thinks, are sweeter than any songs he could actually hear, for his imagined songs are all songs that have been and can be. The lover he sees on the urn is to be envied, he thinks, but even here he suggests a paradox; the lover's youth will never fade, and in that he is fortunate. However, in that static condition, he cannot move from where he stands, and his love for the marble maiden of perpetual beauty can never be consummated. In the third stanza, the speaker conveys something of his own ecstasy as he envies the immortal condition of the sculptor's art on the urn. The passion those figures seem to enjoy, he suggests, far exceeds human passion in quality, for human passion always involves sorrow and frustration. He seems to desire for himself something of the nature of that world figured on the urn. His imaginative discourse continues in stanza four, as he fancies that the figures form a kind of sacrificial procession, and he extends his vision beyond the urn to describe the deserted town from which the people have come. Actually the speaker knows nothing of the purpose, destination, or the origin of the marble figures, and the substance of the poem lies in the multiple suggestions his mind offers about them in his fanciful excursion. He stops then in stanza five to consider cooly and rationally what has been happening to him in the first four stanzas. He knows he has been indulging his imagination, for the evocative power of the urn has been so great it has "teased" him out of thought into fancy.

From here on the problems associated with the poem multiply, and more has been written about the final lines of this ode than about many epic poems. The first problem is how one explains the sense of "Cold pastoral." The urn, one might suggest, has always been cold to the touch, and warm only in the speaker's imagination. Only now does he seem to look at the pastoral figures on the urn as if they were exclusively cold, lifeless, marble—what they are in reality. Once he had praised and envied their lifelessness, for without life they could not die. But without life they could not kiss nor love; they were a "brede" (the pun is on *breed*) of marble men and maidens. The speaker is now beginning to realize that in spite of the fret and fever and worry of life, it is precious and of greater value than an imagined ideal condition. Another problem concerns the speaker in the final two lines. Although many readers have regarded the statement in the last two lines as Keats's aesthetic doctrine, the cliche is almost impossible to support in context. One must agree that the urn is speaking to the speaker or the reader at the beginning of line 49. The question is whether we attribute, through punctuation, both lines 49 and 50 to the urn, or only the statement "Beauty is truth, truth beauty." Even if we accept the latter reading, the problems are not completely solved. If the speaker utters the last phrases beginning "that is all . . ." we have the problem of the antecedent of the pronoun "ye." Is the speaker accepting and advocating the message of the urn as the ultimate aesthetic viewpoint, or does his statement imply that the generalities of "beauty" and "truth" are fine for the urn in its condition, but men in their condition need a great deal more? The poet's context can hardly support the former supposition. The message of the urn is one of only limited value for man, living as he does in a world of time and change.

The reading decided upon places quotation marks at the beginning of line 49 and at the end of line 50. Printed in this fashion, both lines must be read as a statement made by the urn to the speaker or the reader ("thou say'st" precedes the quotation). In all contemporary *transcripts* of the poem, including Keats's copies, there are no punctuation marks at all, and since the publication of the poem in 1820, editors and printers in their fascination with the famous pronouncement, have set it apart from the rest of the poem, whereas in context it satisfactorily resolves the major conflict in the poem.

QUESTIONS

1. Explain the appropriateness of the epithet "unravished."
2. Explain the phrase "foster-child" in line 2.
3. What is the effect of the series of rhetorical questions in lines 5–10?
4. What is the effect in stanza 3 of the repetition of the word "happy"?
5. Describe how the first three stanzas progressively intensify the speaker's emotional state.

*   *   *

To Autumn

I

Season of mists and mellow fruitfulness,
    Close bosom-friend of the maturing sun;
Conspiring with him how to load and bless
    With fruit the vines that round the thatch-eves run;
5 To bend with apples the mossed cottage-trees,
      And fill all fruit with ripeness to the core;
        To swell the gourd, and plump the hazel shells
    With a sweet kernel; to set budding more,
And still more, later flowers for the bees,
10 Until they think warm days will never cease,
      For Summer has o'er-brimmed their clammy cells.

II

Who hath not seen thee oft amid thy store?
   Sometimes whoever seeks abroad may find
Thee sitting careless on a granary floor,
15   Thy hair soft-lifted by the winnowing wind;
Or on a half-reaped furrow sound asleep,
    Drowsed with the fume of poppies, while thy hook
     Spares the next swath and all its twined flowers:
And sometimes like a gleaner thou dost keep
20   Steady thy laden head across a brook;
Or by a cider-press, with patient look,
    Thou watchest the last oozings hours by hours.

III

Where are the songs of Spring? Ay, where are they?
   Think not of them, thou hast thy music too,—
25 While barred clouds bloom the soft-dying day,
   And touch the stubble-plains with rosy hue;
Then in a wailful choir the small gnats mourn
    Among the river sallows, borne aloft
     Or sinking as the light wind lives or dies;
30 And full-grown lambs loud bleat from hilly bourn*;   *region*
    Hedge-crickets sing; and now with treble soft
    The red-breast whistles from a garden-croft*;   *plot*
     And gathering swallows twitter in the skies.

ANOTHER KEATS ODE

"To Autumn" is another of Keats's major odes, although the problems associated with it are nowhere near as complex as those encountered with the ode on the urn. "To Autumn" is much less personal than the other ode, and it is usually regarded as Keats's tribute to time and to the pleasures of this life. This is, as it were, a poetic statement of the resolution reached at the conclusion of the preceding ode. Here is no tormented speaker, envious of any other mode of existence, but one content with the richness and sensuality of his own lot. In a letter written to a friend, Keats praised the autumn season, and his prose account provides an interesting contrast to the poem. In fact, you may wish to compare the two, hoping to come to some conclusions about the very nature of poetry itself. Here is what Keats wrote:

"How beautiful the season is now—How fine the air. A temperate sharpness about it. Really, without joking, chaste weather—Dian skies— I never lik'd stubble so much as now—Aye better than the chilly green of spring. Somehow a stubble plain looks warm—in the same way that some pictures look warm—this struck me so much in my Sunday's walk that I composed upon it."

QUESTIONS

1. Describe how Keats develops the image of autumn fruitfulness in stanza one. What senses does the imagery especially appeal to?
2. List the verbs in the first stanza. What do they have in common, and what is their effect?
3. What is the rhyme scheme of the first stanza? How is it related to the rhyme scheme of a sonnet?
4. In stanza two autumn is personified and described in four different ways. Describe these four ways, and indicate how each is appropriate to the season.
5. What are the songs of autumn? Describe the sound patterns in stanza three.
6. The imagery of each stanza appeals to different senses. Compare the various ways that Keats appeals to the senses in the three stanzas.
7. Describe the tone of stanza three.

La Belle Dame Sans Merci

A Ballad

I

O, what can ail thee, knight-at-arms,
    Alone and palely loitering?
The sedge* has withered from the lake,   *water grass*
4   And no birds sing.

II

O, what can ail thee, knight-at-arms,
    So haggard and so woe-begone?
The squirrel's granary is full,
8   And the harvest's done.

III

I see a lily on thy brow,
    With anguish moist and fever dew;
And on thy cheeks a fading rose
12   Fast withereth too.

IV

I met a lady in the meads,
    Full beautiful—a faery's child,
Her hair was long, her foot was light,
16   And her eyes were wild.

V

I made a garland for her head,
    And bracelets too, and fragrant zone*;   *belt*
She looked at me as she did love,
20   And made sweet moan.

VI

I set her on my pacing steed,
    And nothing else saw all day long;
For sidelong would she bend, and sing
24   A faery's song.

VII

She found me roots of relish sweet,
    And honey wild, and manna* dew,   *heavenly*
And sure in language strange she said—
28   "I love thee true."

VIII

She took me to her elfin grot,*   *grotto*
    And there she wept and sighed full sore,
And there I shut her wild wild eyes
32   With kisses four.

X

And there she lulled me asleep
    And there I dreamed—Ah! woe betide!
The latest dream I ever dreamed
36   On the cold hill side.

X

I saw pale kings and princes too,
    Pale warriors, death-pale were they all;
They cried—"La Belle Dame sans Merci
40   Hath thee in thrall!"

XI

I saw their starved lips in the gloam,
   With horrid warning gaped wide,
And I awoke and found me here,
44   On the cold hill's side.

XII

And this is why I sojourn here
   Alone and palely loitering,
Though the sedge has withered from the lake,
48   And no birds sing.

A LITERARY BALLAD

Keats's ballad belongs to a well-established tradition of stories about men who fall in love with beautiful but cruel enchantresses. Homer's Calypso and Circe are early instances of a fay whose attraction was irresistible, but fatal. The English folk ballad tells us of similar women, women blameless for what happened to their lovers, for it was simply their nature to be "*sans merci*" (without mercy). Why they acted as they did, consequently, is never discussed, and besides it was characteristic of the ballad never to explain motivation. Many ballads deal with a fatal or tragic love, and the story of the man charmed by the beautiful sorceress was a natural one for the ballad.

The ballad tells a very simple story, and consequently every detail and every connotation must be carefully considered. Economy was a ballad characteristic, and the balladeer depended upon understatement to convey the subtleties of the narrative.

QUESTIONS

1. How does the ballad describe the knight's physical condition at the opening of the poem?

2. How is the season appropriate to the narrative?

3. What is the effect of employing a variation of stanza one as the concluding stanza of the poem?

4. Paraphrase stanzas four through eight.

5. What details in stanzas four through eight foreshadow the tragic nature of the encounter? Is the encounter only tragic for the knight? What details evoke sympathy for the lady?

6. Compare the *atmosphere* of stanzas 9–11 with that of stanzas 4–8.

7. What details establish the knight's attitude towards his experience?

8. What is the function of the first three stanzas spoken by a stranger who encounters the knight?

To Homer

Standing aloof in giant ignorance,
   Of thee I hear and of the Cyclades,*   *Greek islands*
As one who sits ashore and longs perchance
4   To visit dolphin-coral in deep seas.
So thou wast blind;—but then the veil was rent,
   For Jove uncurtained Heaven to let thee live,
And Neptune made for thee a spumy tent,
8   And Pan made sing for thee his forest-hive;
Aye on the shores of darkness there is light,
   And precipices show untrodden green,
There is a budding morrow in midnight,
12   There is a triple sight in blindness keen;
Such seeing hadst thou, as it once befell
To Dian, Queen of Earth, and Heaven, and Hell.

KEATS'S SONNETS

Keats wrote many sonnets, using both the Shakespearean and Italian forms, and perhaps achieving his greatest successes in the English mode. "To Homer," addressed to the spirit of that great natural genius, represents in miniature many of Keats's attitudes towards literature and the sonnet. Homer was for him a natural genius, untutored in literary modes and methods, who produced a masterpiece while "in giant ignorance." Keats begins his sonnet apostrophizing Homer and characterizing himself as one envious of Homer's abilities. His compressed image "dolphin-coral" has a Shakespearean compactness about it which leads one to envision both the color of coral and the grace of the dolphins who swim around it. The second quatrain introduces the traditional view that Homer was blind, but even in his blindness, as in his "ignorance," there is a kind of paradox. Ignorant, Homer knew more than most men. If normal light were denied him, supernatural light was his compensation. He saw into the secrets of the heavens, he investigated beneath the seas, and he heard the magical voices and the songs sung by all supernatural figures in the forests. The kingdom of sight was denied him. However, his inner sight spanned a triple kingdom. He could not see out far, but his blindness he could see in deep. The couplet introduces a mythological counterpart for the real Homer, and to conclude, Keats accepts the view that sees Diana a triple goddess with domains on earth, in heaven, and in hell.

This sonnet has a kind of intellectual and emotional progression. First it reveals the speaker's attraction to Homer, then his realization of Homer's blindness. That blindness then, suggests a paradox, and the speaker begins to realize that physical sight and physical perceptions are not important. What is important for the artist is "second sight"—that is, imaginative insight. The poet could live and see in his imagination, "standing aloof in giant ignorance," while he sang of the cosmic mysteries. The speaker's involvement in and his awareness of Homer's position increase as the poem develops.

On Seeing the Elgin Marbles

My spirit is too weak—mortality
    Weighs heavily on me like unwilling sleep,
    And each imagined pinnacle and steep
4 Of godlike hardship tells me I must die,
Like a sick eagle looking at the sky.
    Yet 'tis a gentle luxury to weep
    That I have not the cloudy winds to keep,
8 Fresh for the opening of the morning's eye.
Such dim-conceived glories of the brain
    Bring round the heart an undescribable feud;
    So do these wonders a most dizzy pain,
12   That mingles Grecian grandeur with the rude
Wasting of old Time—with a billowy main—
A sun—a shadow of a magnitude.

NOTE The Elgin Marbles are figures and friezes from the Parthenon acquired by Lord Elgin; they are displayed in the British Museum where Keats saw them in March, 1817.

QUESTIONS

1. What is the form of the sonnet? Describe how Keats handles the conventional divisions.

2. Paraphrase lines 3–5. What is the effect of the simile in line 5?

3. What is the "feud" which the speaker says is "undescribable"?

4. How are aspects of the eagle simile further developed in lines 6–9?

5. Describe as carefully as you can the nature of the speaker's experience as he views the antique sculpture.

6. Does the form Keats uses here seem more or less appropriate to the experience he describes than the Shakespearean mode might have been? (What is there about the experience which seems to dictate the Italian mode?)

Sonnet IX

Keen, fitful gusts are whispering here and there
    Among the bushes half leafless, and dry;
    The stars look very cold about the sky,
4 And I have many miles on foot to fare,
Yet feel I little of the cool bleak air,
    Or of the dead leaves rustling drearily,
    Or of those silver lamps that burn on high,
8 Or of the distance from home's pleasant lair:
For I am brimfull of the friendliness
    That in a little cottage I have found:
    Of fair-haired Milton's eloquent distress,
12   And all his love for gentle Lycid drowned;
Of lovely Laura* in her light green dress,
    And faithful Petrarch gloriously crowned.

*celebrated in
Petrarch's lyrics*

QUESTIONS

1. What is the form of this sonnet? Why is the form appropriate?
2. Describe the relationship between lines 1–4 and lines 5–8.
3. Paraphrase lines 9–14. How does the diction of these lines reveal the speaker's attitude towards literature?
4. Contrast the speaker's emotional attitude with the atmosphere of the season.

WHAT TO LOOK FOR IN THE ADDITIONAL READING

Both Wordsworth and Keats, along with other poets of their time, are conventionally labeled Romantic poets, but you have seen that they write very different kinds of poetry. Reading their poetry convinces one of their uniqueness rather than of their membership in the same group. But Keats was, after all, a second generation "Romantic," and Wordsworth was almost fifty when Keats began to publish his poems. The younger poet's interests and poetic techniques were very different from those of the older Wordsworth.

Keats's desire was to enter the world created by his imagination, and then to live there for as long as possible. He was, however, always aware that those poets who turned their backs on the real world of fever, fret, worry, and death were somehow betraying themselves and being dishonest to their vocation. Keats was constantly fascinated with what he knew was the permanence and *stasis* of art, and with the relationship of art to life. As much as he wished to ignore the real world and its systems of knowledge and its analytic modes of comprehension, he could not stay forever in "dolphin-coral." Out of the conflict between art and life, Keats created his best poetry.

To help make this world more bearable, man had, Keats believed, a potential and the capacity to love; love was the great emotion, and through it and its intensity, man could somehow rise above his limiting environment. Madeline and Prophyro, the heroine and hero of "The Eve of St. Agnes," are brought together on a magical night in which they are both ennobled far above other humankind. Psyche, in the ode to her, is finally reunited with her beloved, and she too is granted a status far above her original one. She appears to be Keats's ideal; she is the soul or imagination ennobled and purified by love and passion and tried in the world of suffering and hardship. She has not tried to escape (nor has Porphyro who, to capture his lady, moves into a hostile castle—his world) and has won her reward—immortality—in the world of men. It appears that somehow what Keats really wanted was a philosophy of sensation which would glorify human feelings and make intense passions holy: "The poetry of earth," he wrote, "is never dead." What Keats would do was to make a *romance* out of mortality.

Ode to Psyche

O Goddess! hear these tuneless numbers, wrung
    By sweet enforcement and remembrance dear,
And pardon that thy secrets should be sung
    Even into thine own soft-conched ear:
5 Surely I dreamt today, or did I see
    The winged Psyche with awakened eyes?
I wandered in a forest thoughtlessly,
    And, on the sudden, fainting with surprise,
Saw two fair creatures, couched side by side
10   In deepest grass, beneath the whispering roof
      Of leaves and trembled blossoms, where there ran
        A brooklet, scarce espied:

'Mid hushed, cool-rooted flowers, fragrant-eyed,
    Blue, silver-white, and budded Tyrian,*   *purple*
15 They lay calm-breathing on the bedded grass;
    Their arms embraced, and their pinions* too;   *wings*
    Their lips touched not, but had not bade adieu,
As if disjoined by soft-handed slumber,
And ready still past kisses to outnumber
20   At tender eye-dawn of aurorean* love: *beginning*
      The winged boy I knew;
    But who wast thou, O happy, happy dove?
      His Psyche true!

O latest born and loveliest vision far
25   Of all Olympus' faded hierarchy!
Fairer than Phoebe's* sapphire-regioned star,   *Diana, the moon*
    Or Vesper,* amorous glow-worm of the sky;   *the planet, Venus*
Fairer than these, though temple thou hast none,
    Nor altar heaped with flowers;
30 Nor virgin choir to make delicious moan
      Upon the midnight hours;
No voice, no lute, no pipe, no incense sweet
    From chain-swung censer teeming;
No shrine, no grove, no oracle, no heat
35   Of pale-mouthed prophet dreaming.

O brightest! though too late for antique vows,
    Too, too late for the fond believing lyre,
When holy were the haunted forest boughs,
    Holy the air, the water, and the fire;
40 Yet even in these days so far retired
    From happy pieties, thy lucent fans,*   *wings*
    Fluttering among the faint Olympians,
I see, and sing, by my own eyes inspired.
So let me be thy choir, and make a moan
45   Upon the midnight hours;
    Thy voice, thy lute, thy pipe, thy incense sweet
    From swinged censer teeming;
    Thy shrine, thy grove, thy oracle, thy heat
    Of pale-mouthed prophet dreaming.

50 Yes, I will be thy priest, and build a fane*   *temple*
    In some untrodden region of my mind,
Where branched thoughts, new grown with pleasant
      pain,
    Instead of pines shall murmur in the wind:
Far, far around shall those dark-clustered trees
55   Fledge the wild-ridged mountains steep by steep;
And there by zephyrs, streams, and birds, and bees,
    The moss-lain Dryads* shall be lulled to sleep;   *tree spirits*
And in the midst of this wide quietness
A rosy sanctuary will I dress
60 With the wreathed trellis of a working brain,
    With buds, and bells, and stars without a name,
With all the gardener Fancy e'er could feign,
    Who breeding flowers, will never breed the same:
And there shall be for thee all soft delight
65   That shadowy thought can win,
A bright torch, and a casement ope* at night,   *open*
    To let the warm Love in!

NOTE In Greek and Roman mythology, Psyche was a maiden who, after undergoing many hardships because of Venus' jealousy of her beauty, is reunited with Cupid and made immortal by Jupiter; she personifies the soul, and for Keats, the imagination.

The Eve of St. Agnes

I

St. Agnes' Eve—Ah, bitter chill it was!
The owl, for all his feathers, was a-cold;
The hare limped trembling through the frozen grass,
And silent was the flock in woolly fold:
5   Numb were the Beadsman's* fingers, while he told   *a holy man*
His rosary, and while his frosted breath,
Like pious incense from a censer old,
Seemed taking flight for heaven, without a death,
Past the sweet Virgin's picture, while his prayer he saith.

II

10   His prayer he saith, this patient, holy man;
Then takes his lamp, and riseth from his knees,
And back returneth, meagre, barefoot, wan,
Along the chapel aisle by slow degrees:
The sculptured dead, on each side, seem to freeze,
15   Emprisoned in black, purgatorial rails:
Knights, ladies, praying in dumb oratories,*   *an example of oxymoron*
He passeth by; and his weak spirit fails
To think how they may ache in icy hoods and mails.

III

Northward he turneth through a little door,
20   And scarce three steps, ere Music's golden tongue
Flattered to tears this aged man and poor;
But no—already had his deathbell rung:
The joys of all his life were said and sung:
His was harsh penance on St. Agnes' Eve:
25   Another way he went, and soon among
Rough ashes sat he for his soul's reprieve,
And all night kept awake, for sinners' sake to grieve.

IV

That ancient Beadsman heard the prelude soft?
And so it chanced, for many a door was wide,
30   From hurry to and fro. Soon, up aloft,
The silver, snarling trumpets 'gan to chide:
The level chambers, ready with their pride,
Were glowing to receive a thousand guests:
The carved angels, ever eager-eyed,
35   Stared, where upon their heads the cornice rests,
With hair blown back, and wings put cross-wise on
their breasts.

V

At length burst in the argent* revelry,   *sparkling*
With plume, tiara, and all rich array,
Numerous as shadows haunting faerily
40   The brain, new stuffed, in youth, with triumphs gay
Of old romance. These let us wish away,
And turn, sole-thoughted, to one Lady there,
Whose heart had brooded, all that wintry day,
On love, and winged St. Agnes' saintly care,
45   As she had heard old dames full many times declare.

VI

They told her how, upon St. Agnes' Eve,
Young virgins might have visions of delight,
And soft adorings from their loves receive
Upon the honied middle of the night,
50   If ceremonies due they did aright;
As, supperless to bed they must retire,
And couch supine their beauties, lily white;
Nor look behind, nor sideways, but require
Of Heaven with upward eyes for all that they desire.

VII

55   Full of this whim was thoughtful Madeline:
The music, yearning like a God in pain,
She scarcely heard: her maiden eyes divine,
Fixed on the floor, saw many a sweeping train

Pass by—she heeded not at all: in vain
60　Came many a tiptoe, amorous cavalier,
And back retired; not cooled by high disdain,
But she saw not: her heart was otherwhere:
She sighed for Agnes' dreams, the sweetest of the year.

VIII

She danced along with vague, regardless eyes,
65　Anxious her lips, her breathing quick and short:
The hallowed hour was near at hand: she sighs
Amid the timbrels, and the thronged resort
Of whisperers in anger, or in sport;
'Mid looks of love, defiance, hate, and scorn,
70　Hoodwinked with faery fancy; all amort,*　　　　　*oblivious*
Save to St. Agnes and her lambs unshorn,
And all the bliss to be before tomorrow morn.

IX

So, purposing each moment to retire,
She lingered still. Meantime, across the moors,
75　Had come young Porphyro, with heart on fire
For Madeline. Beside the portal doors,
Buttressed from moonlight, stands he, and implores
All saints to give him sight of Madeline,
But for one moment in the tedious hours,
80　That he might gaze and worship all unseen;
Perchance speak, kneel, touch, kiss—in sooth such
　　　things have been.

X

He ventures in: let no buzzed whisper tell:
All eyes be muffled, or a hundred swords
Will storm his heart, Love's feverous citadel:
85　For him, those chambers held barbarian hordes,
Hyena foemen, and hot-blooded lords,
Whose very dogs would execrations howl
Against his lineage: not one breast affords
Him any mercy, in that mansion foul,
90　Save one old beldame, weak in body and in soul.

XI

Ah, happy chance! the aged creature came,
Shuffling along with ivory-headed wand,
To where he stood, hid from the torch's flame,
Behind a broad hall-pillar, far beyond
95   The sound of merriment and chorus bland:
He startled her; but soon she knew his face,
And grasped his fingers in her palsied hand,
Saying, "Mercy, Prophyro! hie thee from this place:
"They are all here to-night, the whole blood-thirsty
race!

XII

100   "Get hence! get hence! there's dwarfish Hildebrand;
"He had a fever late, and in the fit
"He cursed thee and thine, both house and land:
"Then there's that old Lord Maurice, not a whit
"More tame for his gray hairs—Alas me! flit!
105   "Flit like a ghost away."—"Ah, Gossip* dear,   *companion*
"We're safe enough; here in this arm-chair sit,
"And tell me how"—"Good Saints! not here, not here;
"Follow me, child, or else these stones will be thy bier."

XIII

He followed through a lowly arched way,
110   Brushing the cobwebs with his lofty plume,
And as she muttered "Well-a—well-a-day!"
He found him in a little moonlight room,
Pale, latticed, chill, and silent as a tomb.
"Now tell me where is Madeline," said he,
115   "O tell me, Angela, by the holy loom
"Which none but secret sisterhood may see,
"When they St. Agnes' wool are weaving piously."

XIV

"St. Agnes! Ah; it is St. Agnes' Eve—
"Yet men will murder upon holy days:
120   "Thou must hold water in a witch's sieve,*   *i.e., perform magic*
"And be liege lord of all the Elves and Fays,

"To venture so: it fills me with amaze
"To see thee, Porphyro!—St. Agnes' Eve!
"God's help! my lady fair the conjuror plays
125 "This very night: good angels her deceive!
"But let me laugh awhile, I've mickle* time to grieve."   *much*

XV

Feebly she laugheth in the languid moon,
While Porphyro upon her face doth look,
Like puzzled urchin on an aged crone
130 Who keepeth closed a wond'rous riddle-book,
As spectacled she sits in chimney nook.
But soon his eyes grew brilliant, when she told
His lady's purpose; and he scarce could brook
Tears, at the thought of those enchantments cold,
135 And Madeline asleep in lap of legends old.

XVI

Sudden a thought came like a full-blown rose,
Flushing his brow, and in his pained heart
Made purple riot: then doth he propose
A stratagem, that makes the beldame start:
140 "A cruel man and impious thou art:
"Sweet lady, let her pray, and sleep, and dream
"Alone with her good angels, far apart
"From wicked men like thee. Go, go!—I deem
"Thou canst not surely be the same that thou didst
seem."

XVII

145 "I will not harm her, by all saints I swear."
Quoth Porphyro: "O may I ne'er find grace
"When my weak voice shall whisper its last prayer,
"If one of her soft ringlets I displace,
"Or look with ruffian passion in her face:
150 "Good Angela, believe me by these tears;
"Or I will, even in a moment's space,
"Awake, with horrid shout, my foemen's ears,
"And beard* them, though they be more fanged than
wolves and bears."   *challenge*

XVIII

"Ah, why wilt thou affright a feeble soul?
155   "A poor, weak, palsy-stricken, churchyard thing,
"Whose passing-bell may ere the midnight toll;
"Whose prayers for thee, each morn and evening,
"Were never missed."—Thus plaining,* doth she bring   *arguing*
A gentler speech from burning Porphyro;
160   So woeful, and of such deep sorrowing,
   That Angela gives promise she will do
Whatever he shall wish, betide her weal or woe.

XIX

Which was, to lead him, in close secrecy,
Even to Madeline's chamber, and there hide
165   Him in a closet, of such privacy
That he might see her beauty unespied,
And win perhaps that night a peerless bride,
While legioned faeries paced the coverlet,
And pale enchantment held her sleepy-eyed.
170   Never on such a night have lovers met,
Since Merlin paid his Demon all the monstrous debt.

XX

"It shall be as thou wishest," said the Dame:
"All cates* and dainties shall be stored there   *delicacies*
"Quickly on this feast-night: by the tambour* frame   *embroidery*
175   "Her own lute thou wilt see: no time to spare,
"For I am slow and feeble, and scarce dare
"On such a catering trust my dizzy head.
"Wait here, my child, with patience; kneel in prayer
"The while: Ah! thou must needs the lady wed,
180   "Or may I never leave my grave among the dead."

XXI

So saying, she hobbled off with busy fear.
The lover's endless minutes slowly passed;
The dame returned, and whispered in his ear
To follow her; with aged eyes aghast
185   From fright of dim espial. Safe at last,

Through many a dusky gallery, they gain
The maiden's chamber, silken, hushed, and chaste;
Where Porphyro took covert, pleased amain.
His poor guide hurried back with agues in her brain.

XXII

190 Her falt'ring hand upon the balustrade,
Old Angela was feeling for the stair,
When Madeline, St. Agnes' charmed maid,
Rose, like a missioned spirit, unaware:
With silver taper's light, and pious care,
195 She turned, and down the aged gossip led
To a safe level matting. Now prepare,
Young Porphyro, for gazing on that bed;
She comes, she comes again, like ring-dove frayed*   *frightened*
    and fled.

XXIII

Out went the taper as she hurried in;
200 Its little smoke, in pallid moonshine, died:
She closed the door, she panted, all akin
To spirits of the air, and visions wide:
No uttered syllable, or, woe betide!
But to her heart, her heart was voluble,
205 Paining with eloquence her balmy side;
As though a tongueless nightingale should swell
Her throat in vain, and die, heart-stifled, in her dell.

XXIV

A casement high and triple-arched there was,
All garlanded with carven imageries
210 Of fruits, and flowers, and bunches of knot-grass,
And diamonded with panes of quaint device,
Innumerable of stains and splendid dyes,
As are the tiger-moth's deep-damasked wings;
And in the midst, 'mong thousand heraldries,
215 And twilight saints, and dim emblazonings,
A shielded scutcheon blushed with blood of queens
    and kings.

XXV

Full on this casement shone the wintry moon,
And threw warm gules* on Madeline's fair breast,   *red patterns*
As down she knelt for heaven's grace and boon;
220 Rose-bloom fell on her hands, together prest,
And on her silver cross soft amethyst,
And on her hair a glory, like a saint:
She seemed a splendid angel, newly drest,
Save wings, for heaven:—Porphyro grew faint:
225 She knelt, so pure a thing, so free from mortal taint.

XXVI

Anon his heart revives: her vespers done,
Of all its wreathed pearls her hair she frees;
Unclasps her warmed jewels one by one;
Loosens her fragrant bodice; by degrees
230 Her rich attire creeps rustling to her knees:
Half-hidden, like a mermaid in seaweed,
Pensive awhile she dreams awake, and sees,
In fancy, fair St. Agnes in her bed,
But dares not look behind, or all the charm is fled.

XXVII

235 Soon, trembling in her soft and chilly nest,
In sort of wakeful swoon, perplexed she lay,
Until the poppied warmth of sleep oppressed
Her soothed limbs, and soul fatigued away;
Flown, like a thought, until the morrow-day;
240 Blissfully havened both from joy and pain;
Clasped like a missal where swart Paynims* pray;   *pagans*
Blinded alike from sunshine and from rain,
As though a rose should shut, and be a bud again.

XXVIII

Stolen to this paradise, and so entranced,
245 Porphyro gazed upon her empty dress,
And listened to her breathing, if it chanced
To wake into a slumberous tenderness;
Which when he heard, that minute did he bless,

And breathed himself: then from the closet crept,
250 Noiseless as fear in a wide wilderness,
And over the hushed carpet, silent, stept,
And 'tween the curtains peeped, where, lo!—how
    fast she slept.

XXIX

Then by the bedside, where the faded moon
Made a dim, silver twilight, soft he set
255 A table, and, half anguished, threw thereon
A cloth of woven crimson, gold, and jet:—
O for some drowsy Morphean* amulet!   *i.e., of Morpheus,
The boisterous, midnight, festive clarion,   God of Sleep
The kettle-drum, and far heard clarinet,
260 Affray his ears, though but in dying tone:—
The hall door shuts again, and all the noise is gone.

XXX

And still she slept an azure-lidded sleep,
In blanched linen, smooth, and lavendered,
While he from forth the closet brought a heap
265 Of candied apple, quince, and plum, and gourd;
With jellies soother than the creamy curd,
And lucent syrops, tinct* with cinnamon;   *flavored
Manna and dates, in argosy* transferred   *large ship
From Fez; and spiced dainties, every one,
270 From silken Samarcand to cedared Lebanon.

XXXI

These delicates he heaped with glowing hand
On golden dishes and in baskets bright
Of wreathed silver: sumptuous they stand
In the retired quiet of the night,
275 Filling the chilly room with perfume light.—
"And now, my love, my seraph fair, awake!
"Thou art my heaven, and I thine eremite:*   *worshipper
"Open thine eyes, for meek St. Agnes' sake,
"Or I shall drowse beside thee, so my soul doth ache."

XXXII

280 Thus whispering, his warm, unnerved arm
Sank in her pillow. Shaded was her dream
By the dusk curtains:—'twas a midnight charm
Impossible to melt as icéd stream:
The lustrous salvers* in the moonlight gleam;   *platters*
285 Broad golden fringe upon the carpet lies:
It seemed he never, never could redeem
From such a stedfast spell his lady's eyes;
So mused awhile, entoil'd in woofed* phantasies.   *woven*

XXXIII

Awakening up, he took her hollow lute,—
290 Tumultuous,—and, in chords that tenderest be,
He played an ancient ditty, long since mute,
In Provence called, "La belle dame sans merci:"
Close to her ear touching the melody;—
Wherewith disturbed, she uttered a soft moan:
295 He ceased—she panted quick—and suddenly
Her blue affrayed eyes wide open shone:
Upon his knees he sank, pale as smooth sculptured
    stone.

XXXIV

Her eyes were open, but she still beheld,
Now wide awake, the vision of her sleep:
300 There was a painful change, that high expelled
The blisses of her dream so pure and deep
At which fair Madeline began to weep,
And moan forth witless words with many a sigh;
While still her gaze on Porphyro would keep;
305 Who knelt, with joined hands and piteous eye,
Fearing to move or speak, she looked so dreamingly.

XXXV

"Ah, Porphyro!" said she, "but even now
"Thy voice was at sweet tremble in mine ear,
"Made tuneable with every sweetest vow;
310 "And those sad eyes were spiritual and clear;

"How changed thou art! how pallid, chill, and drear!
"Give me that voice again, my Porphyro,
"Those looks immortal, those complainings dear!
"Oh leave me not in this eternal woe,
315 "For if thou diest, my Love, I know not where to go."

XXXVI

Beyond a mortal man impassioned far
At these voluptuous accents, he arose,
Ethereal, flushed, and like a throbbing star
Seen mid the sapphire heaven's deep repose;
320 Into her dream he melted, as the rose
Blendeth its odour with the violet,—
Solution sweet: meantime the frost-wind blows
Like Love's alarum pattering the sharp sleet
Against the window panes; St. Agnes' moon hath set.

XXXVII

325 "'Tis dark: quick pattereth the flaw*-blown sleet: *squall*
"This is no dream, my bride, my Madeline!"
"'Tis dark: the icéd gusts still rave and beat:
"No dream, alas! alas! and woe is mine!
"Porphyro will leave me here to fade and pine.—
330 "Cruel! what traitor could thee hither bring?
"I curse not, for my heart is lost in thine,
"Though thou forsakest a deceived thing;—
"A dove forlorn and lost with sick unpruned wing."

XXXVIII

"My Madeline! sweet dreamer! lovely bride!
335 "Say, may I be for aye thy vassal blest?
"Thy beauty's shield, heart-shaped and vermeil*   *gilded*
    dyed?
"Ah, silver shrine, here will I take my rest
"After so many hours of toil and quest,
"A famished pilgrim,—saved by miracle.
340 "Though I have found, I will not rob thy nest
"Saving of thy sweet self; if thou think'st well
"To trust, fair Madeline, to no rude infidel.

XXXIX

"Hark! 'tis an elfin-storm from faery land,
"Of haggard seeming, but a boon indeed:
345   "Arise—arise! the morning is at hand;—
"The bloated wassaillers will never heed:—
"Let us away, my love, with happy speed;
"There are no ears to hear, or eyes to see,—
"Drowned all in Rhenish* and the sleepy mead;   *Rhine wine*
350   "Awake! arise! my love, and fearless be,
"For o'er the southern moors I have a home for thee."

XL

She hurried at his words, beset with fears,
For there were sleeping dragons all around,
At glaring watch, perhaps, with ready spears—
355   Down the wide stairs a darkling way they found.—
In all the house was heard no human sound.
A chain-drooped lamp was flickering by each door;
The arras*, rich with horseman, hawk, and hound,   *wall tapestry*
Fluttered in the besieging wind's uproar;
360 And the long carpets rose along the gusty floor.

XLI

They glide, like phantoms, into the wide hall;
Like phantoms, to the iron porch, they glide;
Where lay the Porter, in uneasy sprawl,
With a huge empty flagon by his side:
365   The wakeful bloodhound rose, and shook his hide,
But his sagacious eye an inmate owns:
By one, and one, the bolts full easy slide:—
The chains lie silent on the footworn stones;—
The key turns, and the door upon its hinges groans.

XLII

370   And they are gone: aye, ages long ago
These lovers fled away into the storm.
That night the Baron dreamt of many a woe,
And all his warrior-guests, with shade and form
Of witch, and demon, and large coffin worms,
375   Were long be-nightmared. Angela the old
Died palsy-twitched, with meagre face deform;
The Beadsman, after thousand aves told,
For aye unsought for slept among his ashes cold.

If By Dull Rhymes Our English Must Be Chained

If by dull rhymes our English must be chained,
And, like Andromeda, the sonnet sweet
Fettered, in spite of pained loveliness,
4 Let us find out, if we must be constrained,
Sandals more interwoven and complete
To fit the naked foot of poesy:
Let us inspect the lyre, and weigh the stress
8 Of every chord, and see what may be gained
By ear industrious, and attention meet;
Misers of sound and syllable, no less
Than Midas of his coinage, let us be
12 Jealous of dead leaves in the bay wreath crown;
So, if we may not let the Muse be free,
She will be bound with garlands of her own.

NOTE   In Greek mythology, Andromeda was a lady imprisoned by a sea monster.

To Sleep

O soft embalmer of the still midnight,
    Shutting, with careful fingers and benign,
Our gloom-pleased eyes, embowered from the light,
4   Enshaded in forgetfulness divine:
O smoothest Sleep! if so it please thee, close
    In midst of this thine hymn my willing eyes,
Or wait the amen, are thy poppy* throws   *sedative*
8   Around my bed its lulling charities.
Then save me, or the passed day will shine
Upon my pillow, breeding many woes,—
    Save me from curious conscience, that still lords
12 Its strength for darkness, burrowing like a mole;
    Turn the key deftly in the oiled wards,*   *a lock part*
And seal the hushed casket* of my soul.   *in one sense,*
                                                   jewel-box

On the Grasshopper and Cricket

The poetry of earth is never dead:
  When all the birds are faint with the hot sun,
  And hide in cooling trees, a voice will run
4 From hedge to hedge about the new-mown mead;
  That is the Grasshopper's—he takes the lead
  In summer luxury,—he has never done
  With his delights; for when tired out with fun
8 He rests at ease beneath some pleasant weed.
  The poetry of earth is ceasing never:
    On a lone winter evening, when the frost
      Has wrought a silence, from the stove there
        shrills
12 The Cricket's song, in warmth increasing ever,
    And seems to one in drowsiness half lost,
      The Grasshopper's among some grassy hills.

The Poet

At morn, at noon, at eve, and middle night
  He passes forth into the charmed air,
  With talisman to call up spirits rare
4 From plant, cave, rock, and fountain.—To his sight
  The husk of natural objects opens quite
    To the core; and every secret essence there
    Reveals the elements of good and fair;
8 Making him see, where Learning hath no light.
  Sometimes above the gross and palpable things
    Of this diurnal* sphere, his spirit flies   *daily*
    On awful* wing; and with its destined skies   *awesome*
12 Holds premature and mystic communings;
    Till such unearthly intercourses shed
      A visible halo round his mortal head.

On Sitting Down To Read King Lear Once Again

O golden tongued Romance, with serene lute!
  Fair plumed Syren*, Queen of far-away!   *i.e., siren*
  Leave melodizing on this wintry day,
4 Shut up thine olden pages, and be mute:
Adieu! for, once again, the fierce dispute
  Betwixt damnation and impassioned clay
  Must I burn through; once more humbly assay
8 The bitter-sweet of this Shakespearian fruit:
Chief Poet! and ye clouds of Albion*,   *England*
  Begetters of our deep eternal theme!
When through the old oak forest* I am gone,   *i.e., the Romance,*
                                          line 1
12   Let me not wander in a barren dream,
But, when I am consumed in the fire*,   *i.e., King Lear*
Give me new Phoenix wings to fly at my desire.

TOPICS FOR WRITING AND DISCUSSION

FOR USE IN CLASS

1. In an essay classify the varieties of imagery in "The Eve of St. Agnes."
2. Discuss the function of the minor characters, Angela and the Beadsman, in "The Eve of St. Agnes."
3. How is the stanzaic form, the *Spenserian stanza*, appropriate to "The Eve of St. Agnes"?
4. Describe Keats's attitude towards the sonnet in"If by dull rhymes our English must be chained."

FOR PREPARATION OUTSIDE OF CLASS

1. Write an essay comparing what Keats attempted in "Ode on a Grecian Urn" and what Wordsworth attempted in "Upon the Sight of a Beautiful Picture."
2. Discuss Keats's use of *oxymoron* and its effect.
3. Select one Shakespearian sonnet and one Italian sonnet in the additional reading and show how each form is appropriate to the development of the subject.
4. Compare Keats's nature imagery in "Ode to Psyche" with the treatment of nature in a Wordsworth poem of your choice.
5. Discuss Keats's attitude towards art and literature in the poems for additional reading.

The Poet

The poet in a golden clime was born,
  With golden stars above;
Dowered with the hate of hate, the scorn of scorn,
4   The love of love.

He saw through life and death, through good and ill,
  He saw through his own soul.
The marvel of the everlasting will,
8   An open scroll.

Before him lay: with echoing feet he threaded
  The secretest walks of fame:
The viewless arrows of his thoughts were headed
12   And winged with flame.

Like Indian reeds* blown from his silver tongue,   *darts*
  And of so fierce a flight,   *Gibraltar
From Calpe* unto Caucasus° they sung,   °*i.e., from west to*
16   Filling with light.   *east*

And vagrant melodies the winds which bore
  Them earthward till they lit;
Then, like the arrow-seeds of the field flower,
20   The fruitful wit.

Cleaving, took root, and springing forth anew
  Where'er they fell, behold,
Like to the mother plant in semblance, grew
24   A flower all gold.

And bravely* furnished all abroad to fling   *finely*
  The winged shafts of truth,
To throng with stately blooms the breathing spring
28   Of Hope and Youth.

So many minds did gird their orbs and beams,
  Though one did fling the fire.
Heaven flowed upon the soul in many dreams
32   Of high desire.

Thus truth was multiplied on truth, the world
    Like one great garden showed
And through the wreaths of floating dark upcurled,
36   Rare sunrise flowed.

And Freedom reared in that august sunrise
    Her beautiful bold brow,
When rites and forms before his burning eyes
40   Melted like snow.

There was no blood upon her maiden robes
    Sunned by those orient skies;
But round about the circles of the globes
44   Of her keen eyes.

And in her raiment's hem was traced in flame
    WISDOM, a name to shake
All evil dreams of power—a sacred name.
48   And when she spake.

Her words did gather thunder as they ran,
    And as the lightning to the thunder
Which follows it, riving the spirit of man,
52   Making earth wonder.

So was their meaning to her words. No sword
    Of wrath her right arm whirled,
But one poor poet's scroll, and with *his* word
56   She shook the world.

TENNYSON'S VIEW OF THE POET'S MISSION

"The Poet" emphasizes Tennyson's concept of the public and moral role of the artist; words and poems reflect a power of truth great enough to shake the world. Tennyson's portrait is an interesting one because of its idealized and highly stylized view of the poetic figure and of his origins. The first poet was a golden figure, composed of the quintessence of all things; as attributes he had the essence of hate, of scorn, and of love. Included among his abilities were the power to understand the secrets of existence and the wisdom to establish moral systems; gifted as he was, the poet's greatest ability was his own self-knowledge. He was a man who saw through all things, understanding himself and his mission. All his acts were naturally in tune with the divine will. He was the man who understood that will naturally and intuitively. His poems then, in a striking metaphor, are seen as shafts of light, making a singing sound as they dart through the air. Fortunately a few of these sounds, like vagrants, made their way to the earth where, like the seeds of flowers, they implanted themselves and grew to resemble the mother song of which they were a part. Of course, the flower is a golden one, and Tennyson continues to develop the image of the song as flower. The seeds from that flower spread on earth, the insights of the *archetypal* poet spread and grew. The image Tennyson uses is appropriate, but the important thing is not so much the literal image itself as what the use of a concrete image suggests. The truths poetry has to teach us, its insights, its moral intuitions—all these must be imaged in concrete terms or, in other words, the human poet (unlike his divine archetype) must speak in metaphor. Paradoxically, that is his only way of being direct, for metaphorical statement is indirect. Consequently this little poem by Tennyson tells us much more about the nature of the poet and poetry by the way it says what it says than a literal paraphrase would suggest. Students of literary history will be more interested in Tennyson's attitudes in the poem—that poetry serves the cause of freedom and morality. Readers of poetry, however, may find themselves more fascinated with how the poet works in the poem than with the poem's "statement." Throughout this book, the ideal reader is encouraged to combine both views.

The Poet's Mind

I

Vex not thou the poet's mind
   With thy shallow wit:
Vex not thou the poet's mind;
   For thou canst not fathom it.
5 Clear and bright it should be ever,
Flowing like a crystal river;
Bright as light, and clear as wind.

II

   Dark-browed sophist, come not anear;
     All the place is holy ground;
10   Hollow smile and frozen sneer
      Come not here.
   Holy water will I pour
   Into every spicy flower
Of the laurel-shrubs that hedge it around.
15 The flowers would faint at your cruel cheer.
   In your eye there is death,
   There is frost in your breath
   Which would blight the plants.

Where you stand you cannot hear
20   From the groves within
        The wild-bird's din.
In the heart of the garden the merry bird chants,
It would fall to the ground if you came in.
        In the middle leaps a fountain
25   Like sheet lightning.
        Ever brightening
With a low melodious thunder;
All day and all night it is ever drawn
From the brain of the purple mountain
30   Which stands in the distance yonder:
It springs on a level of bowery lawn,
And the mountain draws it from Heaven above,
And it sings a song of undying love;
And yet, though its voice be so clear and full,
35 You never would hear it; your ears are so dull;
So keep where you are: you are foul with sin;
It would shrink to the earth if you came in.

MORE ON THE POET'S MISSION

Here Tennyson argues against those shallow, logical, non-imaginative men (Keats called them "consecutive" thinkers) whose limited visions and coldly analytical powers would destroy the imaginative worlds created by the poets' imaginations. There are some men, the poem implies, who refuse to accept fictions and poetic visions. This poem argues a very Keatsian position. Keats had hoped to build in his mind a little shrine to his imagination, and to people it and landscape it and keep it cropped and clean, and every now and then to add a few extra flowers to honor it (see the last stanza of his "Ode to Psyche"). Those gardens of the imagination where poets and readers can taste and touch visionary flowers, or those imaginary seas where we may swim in "dolphin-coral," sound ridiculous out of context, but poets would insist that the worlds they create in the poem have more validity, and thus more reality, than the one in which we exist every day. The sophist, then, is warned not to meddle with or belittle the poetic mind. As beautiful as poetic worlds may be, they can be withered and destroyed by any man who refuses to accept the poetic vision as something apart from his own world. The poetic imagination, Tennyson suggests, requires a receptive and understanding listener, one who would willingly suspend his rational mind's plea that he disbelieve all fictions. Nevertheless, the implication at the poem's conclusion is that the poet will sing regardless of who listens.

With blackest moss the flower-plots
 Were thickly crusted, one and all;
The rusted nails fell from the knots
4 That held the pear to the garden-wall.
The broken sheds looked sad and strange:
 Unlifted was the clinking latch;
 Weeded and worn the ancient thatch
8 Upon the lonely moated grange.
  She only said, "My life is dreary,
   He cometh not," she said;
  She said, "I am aweary, aweary,
12   I would that I were dead!"

Her tears fell with the dews at even;
 Her tears fell ere the dews were dried;
She could not look on the sweet heaven,
16 Either at morn or eventide.
After the flitting of the bats,
 When thickest dark did trance the sky,
 She drew her casement-curtain by,
20 And glanced athwart the glooming flats.
  She only said, "The night is dreary,
   He cometh not," she said;
  She said, "I am aweary, aweary,
24   I would that I were dead!"

Upon the middle of the night,
 Waking she heard the night-fowl crow;
The cock sung out an hour ere light;
28 From the dark fen the oxen's low
Came to her; without hope of change,
 In sleep she seemed to walk forlorn,
 Till cold winds woke the grey-eyed morn
32 About the lonely moated grange.
  She only said, "The day is dreary,
   He cometh not," she said;
  She said, "I am aweary, aweary,
36   I would that I were dead!"

About a stone-cast from the wall
 A sluice with blackened waters slept,
And o'er it many, round and small,
40 The clustered marish-mosses crept.
Hard by a poplar shook alway,
 All silver-green with gnarled bark:
For leagues no other tree did mark
44 The level waste, the rounding gray.
  She only said, "My life is dreary,
   He cometh not," she said;
  She said, "I am aweary, aweary,
48   I would that I were dead!"

And ever when the moon was low,
 And the shrill winds were up and away,
In the white curtain, to and fro,
52 She saw the gusty shadow sway.
But when the moon was very low,
 And wild birds bound within their cell,
The shadow of the poplar fell
56 Upon her bed, across her brow.
  She only said, "The night is dreary,
   He cometh not," she said;
  She said, "I am aweary, aweary,
60   I would that I were dead!"

All day within the dreamy house,
 The doors upon their hinges creaked;
The blue fly sung in the pane; the mouse
64 Behind the mouldering wainscot shrieked,
Or from the crevice peered about.
 Old faces glimmered through the doors,
 Old footsteps trod the upper floors,
68 Old voices called her from without.
  She only said, "My life is dreary,
   He cometh not," she said;
  She said, "I am aweary, aweary,
72   I would that I were dead!"

The sparrow's chirrup on the roof,
　The slow clock ticking, and the sound
Which to the wooing wind aloof
76　The poplar made, did all confound
Her sense; but most she loathed the hour
　When the thick-moted sunbeam lay
Athwart the chambers, and the day
80　Was sloping toward his western bower.
Then, she said, "I am very dreary,
　He will not come," she said;
She wept, "I am aweary, aweary,
84　O God, that I were dead!"

KEATSIAN IMAGERY IN TENNYSON

This is another poem from about the same time in Tennyson's career as "The Poet" and "The Poet's Mind," but "Mariana" is more a descriptive lyric in a Keatsian vein than it is a statement about poetry. Many of Tennyson's early poems deal with the plight of deserted ladies, and here Tennyson has tried to suggest something of the condition of Mariana—her despair, her bleakness, her solitude. Tennyson concentrates on evoking the atmosphere surrounding Mariana through the use of extremely concrete, particularized images. The reader will notice that we know nothing at all about Mariana except her lover "cometh not." The refrain with variations conveys much of the bleakness of Mariana's condition.

QUESTIONS

1. What is the function of the time scheme employed in the lyric?
2. What elements or characteristics of Keats's imagery do you see in this poem by Tennyson?
3. Designate the rhyme scheme of the poem. What is the effect of coupling an *open* with a *closed quatrain*?
4. Discuss the effectiveness of the imagery of stanza 4.

The Lotos-Eaters

"COURAGE!" he said, and pointed toward the land,
"This mounting wave will roll us shoreward soon."
In the afternoon they came unto a land
In which it seemed always afternoon.
5 All round the coast the languid air did swoon,
Breathing like one that hath a weary dream.
Full-faced above the valley stood the moon;
And like a downward smoke, the slender stream
Along the cliff to fall and pause and fall did seem.

10 A land of streams! some, like a downward smoke,
Slow-dropping veils of thinnest lawn, did go;
And some through wavering lights and shadows broke,
Rolling a slumbrous sheet of foam below,
They saw the gleaming river seaward flow
15 From the inner land: far off, three mountain-tops,
Three silent pinnacles of aged snow,
Stood sunset-flushed; and, dewed with showery drops,
Up-clomb the shadowy pine above the woven copse.

The charmed sunset lingered low adown
20 In the red West; through mountain clefts the dale
Was seen far inland, and the yellow down
Bordered with palm, and many a winding vale
And meadow, set with slender galingale;*   *an herb*
A land where all things always seemed the same!
25 And round about the keel with faces pale,
Dark faces pale against that rosy flame,
The mild-eyed melancholy Lotos-eaters came.

Branches they bore of that enchanted stem,
Laden with flower and fruit, whereof they gave
30 To each, but whoso did receive of them,
And taste, to him the gushing of the wave
Far far away did seem to mourn and rave
On alien shores; and if his fellow spake,
His voice was thin, as voices from the grave;
35 And deep-asleep he seemed, yet all awake,
And music in his ears his beating heart did make.

They sat them down upon the yellow sand,
Between the sun and moon upon the shore;
And sweet it was to dream of Fatherland,
40 Of child, and wife, and slave; but evermore
Most weary seemed the sea, weary the oar,
Weary the wandering fields of barren foam.
Then some one said, "We will return no more;"
And all at once they sang, "Our island home*   *Ithaca*
45 Is far beyond the wave; we will no longer roam."

CHORIC SONG

I

There is sweet music here that softer falls
Than petals from blown roses on the grass,
Or night-dews on still waters between walls
Of shadowy granite, in a gleaming pass;
50 Music that gentlier on the spirit lies,
Than tired eyelids upon tired eyes;
Music that brings sweet sleep down from the blissful
    skies.
Here are cool mosses deep,
And through the moss the ivies creep,
55 And in the stream the long-leaved flowers weep,
And from the craggy ledge the poppy hangs in sleep.

II

Why are we weighed upon with heaviness,
And utterly consumed with sharp distress,
While all things else have rest from weariness?
60 All things have rest: why should we toil alone,
We only toil, who are the first of things,
And make perpetual moan,
Still from one sorrow to another thrown:
Nor ever fold our wings,
65 And cease from wanderings,
Nor steep our brows in slumber's holy balm;
Nor hearken what the inner spirit sings,
"There is no joy but calm!"
Why should we only toil, the roof and crown of
    things?

III

70 Lo! in the middle of the wood,
The folded leaf is wooed from out the bud
With winds upon the branch, and there
Grows green and broad, and takes no care,
Sun-steeped at noon, and in the moon
75 Nightly dew-fed; and turning yellow
Falls, and floats adown the air.
Lo! sweetened with the summer light,
The full-juiced apple, waxing over-mellow,
Drops in a silent autumn night.
80 All its allotted length of days,
The flower ripens in its place,
Ripens and fades, and falls, and hath no toil,
Fast-rooted in the fruitful soil.

IV

Hateful is the dark-blue sky,
85 Vaulted o'er the dark-blue sea.
Death is the end of life; ah, why
Should life all labour be?
Let us alone. Time driveth onward fast,
And in a little while our lips are dumb.
90 Let us alone. What is it that will last?
All things are taken from us, and become
Portions and parcels of the dreadful past.
Let us alone. What pleasure can we have
To war with evil? Is there any peace
95 In ever climbing up the climbing wave?
All things have rest, and ripen toward the grave
In silence; ripen, fall and cease:
Give us long rest or death, dark death, or dreamful
    ease.

V

How sweet it were, hearing the downward stream,
100 With half-shut eyes ever to seem
Falling asleep in a half-dream!
To dream and dream, like yonder amber light,
Which will not leave the myrrh-bush* on the height;   *aromatic bush*
To hear each other's whispered speech;
105 Eating the Lotos day by day,
To watch the crisping ripples on the beach,

And tender curving lines of creamy spray;
To end our hearts and spirits wholly
To the influence of mild-minded melancholy;
110 To muse and brook and live again in memory,
With those old faces of our infancy
Heaped over with a mound of grass,
Two handfuls of white dust, shut in an urn of brass!

VI

Dear is the memory of our wedded lives,
115 And dear the last embraces of our wives
And their warm tears: but all hath suffered change;
For surely now our household hearths are cold,
Our sons inherit us, our looks are strange,
And we should come like ghosts to trouble joy.
120 Or else the island princes over-bold
Have eat our substance, and the minstrel sings
Before them of the ten-years' war in Troy,
And our great deeds, as half-forgotten things.
Is there confusion in the little isle?
125 Let what is broken so remain.
The Gods are hard to reconcile;
'Tis hard to settle order once again.
There *is* confusion worse than death,
Trouble on trouble, pain on pain,
130 Long labour unto aged breath,
Sore task to hearts worn out with many wars
And eyes grown dim with gazing on the pilot-stars.

VII

But, propt on beds of amaranth* and moly,°   *purple flower
How sweet (while warm airs lull us, blowing lowly)   °aromatic plant
135 With half-dropt eyelids still,
Beneath a heaven dark and holy,
To watch the long bright river drawing slowly
His waters from the purple hill—
To hear the dewy echoes calling
140 From cave to cave through the thick-twined vine—
To watch the emerald-coloured water falling
Through many a wov'n acanthus-wreath* divine!   *i.e., wave-like
Only to hear and see the far-off sparkling brine,
Only to hear were sweet, stretched out beneath the
    pine.

VIII

145 The Lotos blooms below the barren peak,
The Lotos blows by every winding creek;
All day the wind breathes low with mellower tone;
Through every hollow cave and alley lone
Round and round the spicy downs the yellow
Lotos-dust is blown.
150 We have had enough of action, and of motion we,
Rolled to starboard, rolled to larboard, when the
surge was seething free,
Where the wallowing monster spouted his foam-
fountains in the sea.
Let us swear an oath, and keep it with an equal mind,
In the hollow Lotos-land to live and lie reclined
155 On the hills like gods together, careless of mankind.
For they lie beside their nectar, and the bolts are hurled
Far below them in the valleys, and the clouds are
lightly curled
Round their golden houses, girdled with the gleaming
world:
Where they smile in secret, looking over wasted lands,
160 Blight and famine, plague and earthquake, roaring
deeps and fiery sands,
Clanging fights, and flaming towns, and sinking ships,
and praying hands.
But they smile, they find a music centred in a doleful
song
Steaming up, a lamentation and an ancient tale of wrong,
Like a tale of little meaning though the words are strong;
165 Chanted from an ill-used race of men that cleave the soil,
Sow the seed, and reap the harvest with enduring toil,
Storing yearly little dues of wheat, and wine and oil;
Till they perish and they suffer—some, 'tis whispered
—down in hell
Suffer endless anguish, others in Elysian valleys dwell,
170 Resting weary limbs at last on beds of asphodel.*   *lily-like flowers*
Surely, surely, slumber is more sweet than toil, the shore
Than labour in the deep mid-ocean, wind and wave
and oar;
Oh rest ye, brother mariners, we will not wander more.

NOTE Tennyson was inspired to write several poems on Homeric subjects. Ulysses' adven-
tures in the Lotos-land, where many of his men ate of the lotos and consequently forgot
their homeland and wished only to exist in the pleasant, soporific condition brought on by
the fruit, suggested Tennyson's poem.

THE KEATSIAN TENNYSON AND THE VICTORIAN TENNYSON

For a poet who felt strongly about the moral and social responsibility of poetry, the statement of "The Lotos-Eaters" seems a kind of anomaly. In the midst of a historical period whose mottoes were "progress" and "expansion," and which prized work as a positive value, comes Tennyson's poem which seems to reject Victorian "progress" and cry instead for rest and escape. The Lotos-land, as extolled in the "Choric Song," was, after all, a place of perpetual peace where no one worried about social or moral responsibilities. Of course, Tennyson himself never seriously advocated the moral irresponsibility of Ulysses' mariners, for his was always a confidence in the movement of society and in the morality of progress. At heart his was a firm belief in the eventual perfectability of responsible man. Tennyson's everyday view was that those who evaded their social responsibility, like Ulysses, were the irresponsible men; the men who stayed at home, like Ulysses' son Telemachus, were Tennyson's heroes.

QUESTIONS

1. What evidence can you find that Tennyson is under Keats's influence here?
2. What stanzaic form does Tennyson use for the five stanzas which precede the "Choric Song" of the poem? Why is the form appropriate?
3. Analyze the appropriateness of the imagery which describes the lotos-land in the introductory five stanzas.
4. Do you find any pattern or patterns among the stanzas of the "Choric Song"? What is the effect of the patterns or lack of patterns?
5. Discuss how the "Choric Song" is organized.
6. What relevance to Tennyson and his time does the experience of Ulysses and his men have?

Tithonus

The woods decay, the woods decay and fall,
The vapours weep their burthen to the ground,
Man comes and tills the field and lies beneath,
And after many a summer dies the swan.
5 Me only cruel immortality
Consumes: I wither slowly in thine arms,
Here at the quiet limit of the world,
A white-haired shadow roaming like a dream
The ever silent spaces of the East,
10 Far-folded mists, and gleaming halls of morn.

Alas! for this grey shadow, once a man—
So glorious in his beauty and thy choice,
Who madest him thy chosen, that he seemed
To his great heart none other than a god!
15 I asked thee, "Give me immortality."
Then didst thou grant mine asking with a smile,
Like wealthy men who care not how they give.
But thy strong Hours indignant worked their wills,
And beat me down and marred and wasted me,
20 And though they could not end me, left me maimed
To dwell in presence of immortal youth,
Immortal age beside immortal youth,
And all I was, in ashes. Can thy love,
Thy beauty, make amends, though even now,
25 Close over us, the silver star, thy guide,
Shines in those tremulous eyes that fill with tears
To hear me? Let me go; take back thy gift.
Why should a man desire in any way
To vary from the kindly race of men,
30 Or pass beyond the goal of ordinance
Where all should pause, as is most meet for all?

A soft air fans the cloud apart; there comes
A glimpse of that dark world where I was born.
Once more the old mysterious glimmer steals
35 From thy pure brows, and from thy shoulders pure,
And bosom beating with a heart renewed.
Thy cheek begins to redden through the gloom,
Thy sweet eyes brighten slowly close to mine,
Ere yet they blind the stars, and the wild team
40 Which love thee, yearning for thy yoke, arise,
And shake the darkness from their loosened manes,
And beat the twilight into flakes of fire.

Lo! ever thus thou growest beautiful
In silence, then before thine answer given
45 Departest, and thy tears are on my cheek.

Why wilt thou ever scare me with thy tears,
And make me tremble lest a saying learnt,
In days far-off, on that dark earth, be true?
"The Gods themselves cannot recall their gifts."

50 Ay me! ay me! with what another heart
    In days far-off, and with what other eyes
    I used to watch—if I be he that watched—
    The lucid outline forming round thee; saw
    The dim curls kindle into sunny rings;
55 Changed with thy mystic change, and felt my blood
    Glow with the glow that slowly crimsoned all
    Thy presence and thy portals, while I lay,
    Mouth, forehead, eyelids, growing dewy-warm
    With kisses balmier than half-opening buds
60 Of April, and could hear the lips that kissed
    Whispering I knew not what of wild and sweet,
    Like that strange song I heard Apollo sing,
    While Ilion like a mist rose into towers.

    Yet hold me not for ever in thine East:
65 How can my nature longer mix with thine?
    Coldly thy rosy shadows bathe me, cold
    Are all thy lights, and cold my wrinkled feet
    Upon thy glimmering thresholds, when the steam
    Floats up from those dim fields about the homes
70 Of happy men that have the power to die,
    And grassy barrows of the happier dead.
    Release me, and restore me to the ground.
    Thou see'st all things, thou wilt my grave,
    Thou wilt renew thy beauty morn by morn;
75 I earth in earth forget these empty courts,
    And thee returning on thy silver wheels.

NOTE According to the myth, the Trojan Tithonus, who was loved by Eos, the goddess of
the dawn, asked for and was granted immortality, but was not granted eternal youth. After
centuries he was turned into a grasshopper.

MYTHOLOGY IN TENNYSON

This is another of Tennyson's "Greek poems," written about the same time as
"The Lotos-Eaters" and revealing Tennyson's fondness for Homeric subjects with
Keatsian images. The dramatic monologue, spoken by Tithonus to his beloved Eos,
poignantly reveals the condition of immortality without perpetual youth. The
burden of life was, after so many centuries, oppressive and terrible, and Tennyson's
extremely sympathetic treatment reveals Tithonus as a sharply characterized figure.
Probably Tennyson the man would have had little sympathy for the Trojan who
wished to be more than human, for Tennyson's ideal was man who had fulfilled all
his *human* potentialities and who would then be rewarded with eternal life at the end
of this world.

1. Characterize Tithonus. What are his feelings about his predicament, and how are those feelings described by Tennyson?

2. How is the myth of Tithonus related to the theme of Keats's "La Belle Dame Sans Merci"?

3. How is Tithonus' dialogue organized? Outline the monologue, pointing out the logic of its progression.

4. Describe the elements which establish the conversational tone of the monologue.

5. Whose modern novel uses line 4 as its title?

Tears, Idle Tears, I Know Not What They Mean

Tears, idle tears, I know not what they mean,
Tears from the depth of some divine despair
Rise in the heart, and gather to the eyes,
In looking on the happy autumn fields,
5 And thinking of the days that are no more.

Fresh as the first beam glittering on a sail,
That brings our friends up from the underworld,
Sad as the last which reddens over one
That sinks with all we love below the verge;
10 So sad, so fresh, the days that are no more.

Ah, sad and strange as in dark summer dawns
The earliest pipe of half-awakened birds
To dying ears, when unto dying eyes
The casement slowly grows a glimmering square;
15 So sad, so strange, the days that are no more.

Dear as remembered kisses after death,
And sweet as those by hopeless fancy feigned
On lips that are for others; deep as love,
Deep as first love, and wild with all regret;
20 O Death in Life, the days that are no more!

This song from *The Princess*, a long *romance*, is one of the outstanding examples of Tennyson's lyric ability. It may be the most discussed single lyric of the Victorian Period.

The poem is about a speaker who is surprised and bewildered to find that when he looks on autumn fields and thinks of the past, he sheds inexplicable tears. These tears arise from the depths of his being, from his very emotional center; he appears to be unaware of the *paradox* "divine despair" suggests, for it may be that the hopelessness of his present position has some value in it, some holy sanction indicated by the adjective "divine." In the second stanza the speaker employs two similes. In the first, he emphasizes the freshness of the past by comparing it to the freshness of the dawn, a dawn which we anticipate, for it brings hope (our first notice of the ship's sail). The emphasis in the simile is upon the nearness of the past to the speaker, upon its attractiveness and its clarity in his memory. The second simile continues the ship figure to suggest an opposite response; this time the speaker is sad rather than joyous. The fact that he uses the same terms— the light on ship's sail—for a contrasting response suggests that the twin emotions of joy and sadness are closely related. The speaker's feelings about the past, then, are ambiguous and conflicting. In the very next stanza he tells us that those feelings are strange. The entire stanza, which tells us about the strangeness of the dawn to a dying man is meant to indicate how, under certain circumstances, the familiar takes on a new quality. We are aware that the speaker's response to the past is one which is at once both sweet and sad.

The emotional effect of the final stanza is more intense than that in any of those previous. The intensity is achieved by the vividness of the way the imagery suggests the nearness of the past and by the sense of desperation and despair which runs through the lines. The past becomes as romantic and fabulous, as dear and sweet, as the future, but those deeply buried days are as alive as they are dead. The past ought to be tame, not "wild," but it is always capable of coming to the surface, of rising from the underworld to make us sad and "wild with regret." The poem's progression, however, is as much intellectual as emotional. The speaker comes to a gradual realization of the source and cause of his tears. From simply thinking of the "days that are no more" the speaker considers his ambiguous feelings and finally realizes what it is that constitutes the past. The days that are no more suggest themselves as a kind of paradox: one's memories of the past are a kind of death always with one in life.

Ask Me No More

Ask me no more: the moon may draw the sea;
  The cloud may stoop from heaven and take the shape,
  With fold to fold, of mountain or of cape;
But O too fond, when have I answered thee?
5   Ask me no more.

Ask me no more: what answer should I give?
  I love not hollow cheek or faded eye:
  Yet, O my friend, I will not have thee die!
Ask me no more, lest I should bid thee life;
10   Ask me no more.

Ask me no more: thy fate and mine are sealed;
  I strove against the stream and all in vain;
  Let the great river take me to the main.
No more, dear love, for at a touch I yield;
15   Ask me no more.

QUESTION

This song is a study in sound *modulation* and repetition. Describe the effect of *consonance* and *assonance* in this song.

WHAT TO LOOK FOR IN THE ADDITIONAL READING

To enable you to make some personal comparisons, "Mariana in the South" may be read along with "Mariana," and "St. Agnes' Eve" may be considered along with Keats's much longer poem of the same name. The conventionalized religious attitudes found in both poems by Tennyson are not apparent in Keats's poetry. The additional reading includes as well a tribute to Milton which you might consider a metrical experiment, and, as such, an excellent opportunity to practice *scansion*. In such limited space, it is difficult to include many examples of Tennyson's longer poems, especially any of the *Idylls of the King*, but here is one of his longer, more diffuse public poems, celebrating the English hero responsible for the defeat of Napoleon on the continent. This is the kind of public performance England expected of her laureates, and from Tennyson we have a valuable poetic image of the attitudes and conventions of an age. Tennyson was not a great sonneteer, but some of his sonnets are here to give you examples for comparison and to show that almost every poet tried his hand, at one time or another, at the form. The four sonnets here include one of each type: a personal dedication, a lyric with themes closely related to those of "Tears, Idle Tears," a comic *jeu d'esprit*, and, of course, a sonnet about poetry.

With one black shadow at its feet,
  The house thro' all the level shines,
Close-latticed to the brooding heat,
4   And silent in its dusty vines:
A faint-blue ridge upon the right,
  An empty river-bed before,
  And shallows on a distant shore,
8 In glaring sand and inlets bright.
  But "Ave Mary," made she moan,
    And "Ave Mary," night and morn,
    And "Ah," she sang, "to be all alone,
12   To live forgotten, and love forlorn."

She, as her carol sadder grew,
  From brow and bosom slowly down
Thro' rosy taper fingers drew
16 Her streaming curls of deepest brown
To left and right, and made appear,
  Still-lighted in a secret shrine,
  Her melancholy eyes divine,
20 The home of woe without a tear.
  And "Ave Mary," was her moan,
    "Madonna, sad is night and morn;"
    And "Ah," she sang, "to be all alone,
24   To live forgotten, and love forlorn."

Till all the crimson changed, and past
  Into deep orange o'er the sea,
Low on her knees herself she cast,
28 Before Our Lady murmured she:
Complaining, "Mother, give me grace
  To help me of my weary load."
  And on the liquid mirror glowed
32 The clear perfection of her face.
  "Is this the form," she made her moan,
    "That won his praises night and morn?"
    And "Ah," she said, "but I wake alone,
36   I sleep forgotten, I wake forlorn."

Nor bird would sing, nor lamb would bleat,
　　Nor any cloud would cross the vault,
But day increased from heat to heat,
40　　On stony drought and steaming salt;
Till now at noon she slept again,
　　And seemed knee-deep in mountain grass,
　　And heard her native breezes pass,
44　And runlets babbling down the glen.
　　She breathed in sleep a lower moan,
　　　And murmuring, as at night and morn,
　　She thought, "My spirit is here alone,
48　　Walks forgotten, and is forlorn."

Dreaming, she knew it was a dream:
　　She felt he was and was not there.
She woke; the babble of the stream
52　　Fell, and, without, the steady glare
Shrank one sick willow sere and small.
　　The river-bed was dusty-white;
　　And all the furnace of the light
56　Struck up against the blinding wall.
　　She whispered, with a stifled moan
　　　More inward than at night or morn,
　　"Sweet Mother, let me not here alone
60　　Live forgotten and die forlorn."

And, rising, from her bosom drew
　　Old letters, breathing of her worth,
For "Love", they said, "must needs be true,
64　　To what is loveliest upon earth."
An image seemed to pass the door,
　　To look at her with slight, and say,
　　"But now thy beauty flows away,
68　So be alone for evermore."
　　"O cruel heart," she changed her tone,
　　　"And cruel love, whose end is scorn,
　　Is this the end to be left alone,
72　　To live forgotten, and die forlorn?"

But sometimes in the falling day
 An image seemed to pass the door,
To look into her eyes and say,
76 "But thou shalt be alone no more."
And flaming downward over all
 From heat to heat the day decreased,
 And slowly rounded to the east
80 The one black shadow from the wall.
  "The day to night," she made her moan,
   "The day to night, the night to morn,
  And day and night I am left alone
84   To live forgotten, and love forlorn."

At eve a dry cicala* sung,   *i.e., cicada*
 There came a sound as of the sea;
Backward the lattice-blind she flung,
88 And leaned upon the balcony.
There all in spaces rosy-bright
 Large Hesper* glittered on her tears,   *Venus*
 And deepening thro' the silent spheres,
92 Heaven over Heaven rose the night.
  And weeping then she made her moan,
   "The night comes on that knows not morn,
  When I shall cease to be all alone,
96   To live forgotten, and love forlorn."

St. Agnes' Eve

Deep on the convent-roof the snows
 Are sparkling to the moon;
My breath to heaven like vapor goes;
4 May my soul follow soon!
The shadows of the convent-towers
 Slant down the snowy sward,*   *field*
Still creeping with the creeping hours
8 That lead me to my Lord.
Make Thou my spirit pure and clear
 As are the frosty skies,
Or this first snowdrop of the year
12 That in my bosom lies.

As these white robes are soiled and dark,
  To yonder shining ground;
As this pale taper's earthly spark,
16 To yonder argent round;* *surrounding
So shows my soul before the Lamb, moonlight*
  My spirit before Thee;
So in mine earthly house I am,
20 To that I hope to be.
Break up the heavens, O Lord! and far,
  Thro' all yon starlight keen,
Draw me, thy bride, a glittering star,
24 In raiment white and clean.

He lifts me to the golden doors;
  The flashes come and go;
All heaven bursts her starry floors,
28 And strows her lights below,
  And deepens on and up! the gates
  Roll back, and far within
For me the Heavenly Bridegroom waits,
32 To make me pure of sin.
The Sabbaths of Eternity,
  One Sabbath deep and wide—
A light upon the shining sea—
36 The Bridegroom with his bride!

Milton

O mighty-mouthed inventor of harmonies,
O skilled to sing of Time or Eternity,
  God-gifted organ-voice of England,
    Milton, a name to resound for ages;
5 Whose Titan angels, Gabriel, Abdiel,
Starred from Jehovah's gorgeous armories,
  Tower, as the deep-domed empyrean
    Rings to the roar of an angel onset!
Me rather all that bowery loneliness,
10 The brooks of Eden mazily murmuring,
  And bloom profuse and cedar arches
    Charm, as a wanderer out in ocean,
Where some refulgent sunset of India
Streams o'er a rich ambrosial ocean isle,
15   And crimson-hued the stately palm-woods
    Whisper in odorous heights of even.

The Kraken

Below the thunders of the upper deep;
Far far beneath in the abysmal sea,
His ancient, dreamless, uninvaded sleep
The Kraken sleepeth: faintest sunlights flee
5 About his shadowy sides: above him swell
Huge sponges of millennial growth and heights;
And far away into the sickly light,
From many a wondrous grot and secret cell
Unnumbered and enormous polypi
10 Winnow with giant fins the slumbering green.
There hath he lain for ages and will lie
Battening upon huge seaworms in his sleep,
Until the latter fire shall heat the deep;
Then once by men and angels to be seen,
15 In roaring he shall rise and on the surface die.

NOTE The kraken was a mythical sea monster, something like a giant squid, of which
Tennyson had read.

Ode on the Death of the Duke of Wellington

I

Bury the Great Duke
  With an empire's lamentation,
Let us bury the Great Duke
  To the noise of the mourning of a mighty nation,
5 Mourning when their leaders fall,
Warriors carry the warrior's pall,
And sorrow darkens hamlet and hall.

II

Where shall we lay the man whom we deplore?*   *mourn*
Here, in streaming London's central roar.
10 Let the sound of those he wrought for,
And the feet of those he fought for,
Echo round his bones for evermore.

III

Lead out the pageant: sad and slow,
As fits an universal woe,
15 Let the long long procession go,
And let the sorrowing crowd about it grow,
And let the mournful martial music blow;
The last great Englishman is low.

IV

Mourn, for to us he seems the last,
20 Remembering all his greatness in the past.
No more in soldier fashion will he greet
With lifted hand the gazer in the street.
O friends, our chief state-oracle is mute:
Mourn for the man of long-enduring blood,
25 The statesman-warrior, moderate, resolute,
Whole in himself, a common good.
Mourn for the man of amplest influence,
Yet clearest of ambitious crime,
Our greatest yet with least pretence,
30 Great in council and great in war,
Foremost captain of his time,
Rich in saving common-sense,
And, as the greatest only are,
In his simplicity sublime.
35 O good grey head which all men knew,
O voice from which their omens all men drew,
O iron nerve to true occasion true,
O fall'n at length that tower of strength
Which stood four-square to all the winds that blew!
40 Such was he whom we deplore.
The long self-sacrifice of life is o'er.
The great World-victor's victor will be seen no more.

V

All is over and done:
Render thanks to the Giver,
45 England, for thy son.
Let the bell be tolled.
Render thanks to the Giver,
And render him to the mould.

Under the cross of gold
50 That shines over city and river,
There he shall rest for ever
Among the wise and the bold.
Let the bell be tolled:
And a reverent people behold
55 The towering car, the sable steeds:
Bright let it be with its blazoned deeds,
Dark in its funeral fold.
Let the bell be tolled:
And a deeper knell in the heart be knolled;
60 And the sound of the sorrowing anthem rolled
Thro' the dome of the golden cross;
And the volleying cannon thunder his loss;
He knew their voices of old.
For many a time in many a clime
65 His captain's-ear has heard them boom
Bellowing victory, bellowing doom:
When he with those deep voices wrought,
Guarding realms and kings from shame;
With those deep voices our dead captain taught
70 The tyrant, and asserts his claim
In that dread sound to the great name,
Which he has worn so pure of blame,
In praise and in dispraise the same,
A man of well-attempered frame.
75 O civic muse, to such a name,
To such a name for ages long,
To such a name,
Preserve a broad approach of fame,
And ever-echoing avenues of song.

VI

80 Who is he that cometh, like an honoured guest,
With banner and with music, with soldier and with priest,
With a nation weeping, and breaking on my rest?
Mighty Seaman*, this is he   *Nelson
Was great by land as thou by sea.
85 Thine island loves thee well, thou famous man,
The greatest sailor since our world began.
Now, to the roll of muffled drums,
To thee the greatest soldier comes;

For this is he
90 Was great by land as thou by sea;
His foes were thine; he kept us free;
O give him welcome, this is he
Worthy of our gorgeous rites,
And worthy to be laid by thee;
95 For this is England's greatest son,
He that gained a hundred fights,
Nor ever lost an English gun;
This is he that far away
Against the myriads of Assaye
100 Clashed with his fiery few and won;
And underneath another sun,
Warring on a later day,
Round affrighted Lisbon drew
The treble works, the vast designs
105 Of his laboured rampart-lines,
Where he greatly stood at bay,
Whence he issued forth anew,
And ever great and greater grew,
Beating from the wasted vines
110 Back to France her banded swarms,
Back to France with countless blows,
Till o'er the hills her eagles flew
Beyond the Pyrenean pines,
Followed up in valley and glen
115 With blare of bugle, clamour of men,
Roll of cannon and clash of arms,
And England pouring on her foes.
Such a war had such a close.
Again their ravening eagle rose
120 In anger, wheeled on Europe-shadowing wings,
And barking for the thrones of kings;
Till one that sought but Duty's iron crown
On that loud sabbath shook the spoiler down;
A day of onsets of despair!
125 Dashed on every rocky square
Their surging charges foamed themselves away;
Last, the Prussian trumpet blew;
Thro' the long-tormented air
Heaven flashed a sudden jubilant ray,
130 And down we swept and charged and overthrew.
So great a soldier taught us there,
What long-enduring hearts could do

In that world's-earthquake, Waterloo!
Mighty Seaman, tender and true,
135 And pure as he from taint of craven guile,
O saviour of the silver-coasted isle,
O shaker of the Baltic and the Nile,
If aught of things that here befall
Touch a spirit among things divine,
140 If love of country move thee there at all,
Be glad, because his bones are laid by thine!
And thro' the centuries let a people's voice
In full acclaim,
A people's voice,
145 The proof and echo of all human fame,
A people's voice, when they rejoice
At civic revel and pomp and game,
Attest their great commander's claim
With honour, honour, honour, honour to him,
150 Eternal honour to his name.

VII

A people's voice! we are a people yet.
Tho' all men else their nobler dreams forget,
Confused by brainless mobs and lawless Powers;
Thank Him who isled us here, and roughly set
155 His Briton in blown seas and storming showers,
We have a voice with which to pay the debt
Of boundless love and reverence and regret
To those great men who fought, and kept it ours.
And keep it ours, O God, from brute control;
160 O Statesmen, guard us, guard the eye, the soul
Of Europe, keep our noble England whole,
And save the one true seed of freedom sown
Betwixt a people and their ancient throne,
That sober freedom out of which there springs
165 Our loyal passion for our temperate kings;
For, saving that, ye help to save mankind
Till public wrong be crumbled into dust,
And drill the raw world for the march of mind,
Till crowds at length be sane and crowns be just.
170 But wink no more in slothful overtrust.
Remember him who led your hosts;
He bad you guard the sacred coasts.
Your cannons moulder on the seaward wall;

His voice is silent in your council-hall
175 For ever; and whatever tempests lour*   *scowl*
For ever silent, even if they broke
In thunder, silent; yet remember all
He spoke among you, and the Man who spoke;
Who never sold the truth to serve the hour,
180 Nor paltered with Eternal God for power;
Who let the turbid streams of rumour flow
Thro' either babbling world of high and low;
Whose life was work, whose language rife
With rugged maxims hewn from life;
185 Who never spoke against a foe;
Whose eighty winters freeze with one rebuke
All great self-seekers trampling on the right:
Truth-teller was our England's Alfred* named;   *Alfred the Great*
Truth-lover was our English Duke;   *(849–899)*
190 Whatever record leap to light
He never shall be shamed.

VIII

Lo, the leader in these glorious wars
Now to glorious burial slowly borne,
Followed by the brave of other lands,
195 He, on whom from both her open hands
Lavish Honour showered all her stars,
And affluent Fortune emptied all her horn.
Yea, let all good things await
Him who cares not to be great,
200 But as he saves or serves the state.
Not once or twice in our rough island-story,
The path of duty was the way to glory:
He that walks it, only thirsting
For the right, and learns to deaden
205 Love of self, before his journey closes,
He shall find the stubborn thistle bursting
Into glossy purples, which outredden
All voluptuous garden-roses.
Not once or twice in our fair island-story,
210 The path of duty was the way to glory:
He, that ever following her commands,
On with toil of heart and knees and hands,
Thro' the long gorge to the far light has won
His path upward, and prevailed,

215 Shall find the toppling crags of Duty scaled
   Are close upon the shining table-lands
   To which our God Himself is moon and sun.
   Such was he: his work is done,
   But while the races of mankind endure,
220 Let his great example stand
   Colossal, seen of every land,
   And keep the soldier firm, the statesman pure:
   Till in all lands and thro' all human story
   The path of duty be the way to glory:
225 And let the land whose hearths he saved from shame
   For many and many an age proclaim
   At civic revel and pomp and game,
   And when the long-illumined cities flame,
   Their every-loyal iron leader's fame,
230 With honour, honour, honour, honour to him,
   Eternal honour to his name.

IX

   Peace, his triumph will be sung
   By some yet unmoulded tongue
   Far on in summers that we shall not see:
235 Peace, it is a day of pain
   For one about whose patriarchal knee
   Late the little children clung:
   O peace, it is a day of pain
   For one, upon whose hand and heart and brain
240 Once the weight and fate of Europe hung.
   Ours the pain, be his the gain!
   More than is of man's degree
   Must be with us, watching here
   At this, our great solemnity.
245 Whom we see not we revere,
   We revere, and we refrain
   From talk of battles loud and vain,
   And brawling memories all too free
   For such a wise humility
250 As befits a solemn fane:
   We revere, and while we hear
   The tides of Music's golden sea
   Setting toward eternity,
   Uplifted high in heart and hope are we,
255 Until we doubt not that for one so true
   There must be other nobler work to do

Than when he fought at Waterloo,
And Victor he must ever be.
For tho' the Giant Ages heave the hill
260 And break the shore, and evermore
Make and break, and work their will;
Tho' world on world in myriad myriads roll
Round us, each with different powers,
And other forms of life than ours,
265 What know we greater than the soul?
On God and Godlike men we build our trust.
Hush, the Dead March wails in the people's ears:
The dark crowd moves, and there are sobs and tears:
The black earth yawns: the mortal disappears;
270 Ashes to ashes, dust to dust;
He is gone who seemed so great.—
Gone; but nothing can bereave him
Of the force he made his own
Being here, and we believe him
275 Something far advanced in State,
And that he wears a truer crown
Than any wreath that man can weave him.
Speak no more of his renown,
Lay your earthly fancies down,
280 And in the vast cathedral leave him.
God accept him, Christ receive him.

To ———

As when with downcast eyes we muse and brood,
And ebb into a former life, or seem
To lapse far back in some confused dream
4 To states of mystical similitude,
If one but speaks or hems or stirs his chair,
Ever the wonder waxeth more and more,
So that we say, "All this hath been before,
8 All this hath been, I know not when or where";
So, friend, when first I looked upon your face,
Our thought gave answer each to each, so true—
Opposed mirrors each reflecting each—
12 That, tho' I knew not in what time or place,
Methought that I had often met with you,
And either lived in either's heart and speech.

NOTE   This sonnet is probably addressed to Arthur Henry Hallam, Tennyson's young friend;
Hallam's death was the occasion for Tennyson's greatest poem, *In Memoriam*.

Could I Outwear My Present State of Woe

Could I outwear my present state of woe
With one brief winter, and indue i' the spring
Hues of fresh youth, and mightily outgrow
4 The wan dark coil of faded suffering—
Forth in the pride of beauty issuing
A sheeny snake, the light of vernal bowers,
Moving his crest to all sweet plots of flowers
8 And watered valleys where the young birds sing;
Could I thus hope* my lost delight's renewing,   *hope for*
I straightly would command the tears to creep
From my charged lids; but inwardly I weep:
12 Some vital heat as yet my heart is wooing:
This to itself hath drawn the frozen rain
From my cold eyes and melted it again.

Sonnet

There are three things which fill my heart with sighs,
And steep my soul in laughter (when I view
Fair maiden-forms moving like melodies)
4 Dimples, roselips, and eyes of any hue.
There are three things beneath the blessed skies
For which I live, black eyes and brown and blue:
I hold them all most dear, but oh! black eyes,
8 I live and die, and only die for you.
Of late such eyes looked at me—while I mused,
At sunset, underneath a shadowy plane,
In old Bayona* nigh the southern sea—   *a city in SW France*
12 From an half-open lattice looked at *me.*
I saw no more—only those eyes—confused
And dazzled to the heart with glorious pain.

Poets and Their Bibliographies

Old poets fostered under friendlier skies,
  Old Virgil* who would write ten lines, they say,
  At dawn, and lavish all the golden day
4 To make them wealthier in his readers' eyes;
  And you, old popular Horace*, you the wise   *Latin Poets*
  Adviser of the nine-years-pondered lay,
  And you, that wear a wreath of sweeter bay,
8 Catullus*, whose dead songster never dies;
  If glancing downward on the kindly sphere
  That once had rolled you round and round the sun,
  You see your Art still shrined in human shelves,
12 You should be jubilant that you flourish'd here
  Before the Love of Letters, overdone,
Had swampt the sacred poets with themselves.

TOPICS FOR WRITING AND DISCUSSION

FOR USE IN CLASS

1. Discuss how the diction and the imagery in "The Kraken" are used to present the poet's apocalyptic vision.

2. How do the diction and imagery establish the tone of the sonnet "There Are Three Things Which Fill My Heart With Sighs"?

3. Compare the attitude towards poetry in "Poets and their Bibliographies" with that in Wordsworth's sonnet, "There is a Pleasure in Poetic Pains."

4. Discuss the effect of the white imagery in "St. Agnes' Eve."

FOR PREPARATION OUTSIDE OF CLASS

1. Compare the color imagery in "Mariana in the South" with the color imagery in "Mariana."

2. Compare the musings in the sonnet "To ———" with the musings in "Tears, Idle Tears."

3. Discuss the public attitudes of Tennyson which are evident in his "Ode on the Death of the Duke of Wellington."

4. Discuss the evidence of Keats's influence on Tennyson.

10 READING THE POETRY OF Robert Browning [1812–1889]

Meeting at Night

I

The gray sea and the long black land;
And the yellow half-moon large and low;
And the startled little waves that leap
In fiery ringlets from their sleep,
5 As I gain the cove with pushing prow,
And quench its speed i' the slushy sand.

II

Then a mile of warm sea-scented beach;
Three fields to cross till a farm appears;
A tap at the pane, the quick sharp scratch
10 And blue spurt of a lighted match,
And a voice less loud, through its joys and fears,
Than the two hearts beating each to each!

Parting at Morning

Round the cape of a sudden came the sea,
And the sun looked over the mountain's rim:
And straight was a path of gold for him,
And the need of a world of men for me.

TWO LOVE POEMS

These two poems by Browning are intended as companion pieces. "Meeting at Night" is the lover's narrative as he approaches the place of his rendezvous. The short lyric gains most of its strength from the sharp, compact, and highly suggestive images; in fact, without the particularizing detail (like "gray," "black," "yellow," "startled," etc.) the poem would be little less than a matter of fact report. The details in each stanza suggest a gradual narrowing of the speaker's scope until they focus upon a perfectly realized detail: the "fiery ringlets" of the first stanza and the "blue spurt" of the second. The wealth of detail and the gradual narrowing of the poem from the expanse of sea and land to "two hearts beating each to each" suggest something of the lover's attitude towards his experience; everything centers upon and focuses upon his love. It is as if everything he sees is directed towards and takes its characteristics from his romantic passion. The "fiery ringlets" of little waves suggest light dancing upon his lady's hair and the "warm sea-scented beach" suggests something of the sensuousness of their passion. The intensity of the lover's emotions has illuminated the landscape. The poem depends, then, for its success upon the skillful and evocative use of detail to create a sharp, precise, self-sufficient image.

For every meeting at night, Browning suggests, there is a "Parting at Morning," for not all lovers fade away into eternity, never having to face the dawn as did Keats's Madeline and Porphyro. In Browning's poem the world (the sea and the sun) now confronts the lover. He no longer controls and designates planets by the strength of his passion. They serve to remind him that a world exists outside the one he had created the night before, and he remembers that love is not sufficient unto itself and that he must join the world imposed on him from without.

QUESTIONS "MEETING AT NIGHT"

1. Point out several examples of effective sound patterns.
2. What do the "tap at the pane" and the quiet, fearful voice from within tell the reader about the nature of the meeting?
3. What is the effect of the hyperbole in the final two lines?

"PARTING AT MORNING"

How do lines 3 and 4 establish a realistic attitude towards the place of love in the world?

In Three Days

I

So, I shall see her in three days
And just one night, but nights are short,
Then two long hours, and that is morn.
See how I come, unchanged, unworn!
5 Feel, where my life broke off from thine,
How fresh the splinters keep and fine,—
Only a touch and we combine!

II

Too long, this time of year, the days!
But nights, at least the nights are short.
10 As night shows where her one moon is,
A hand's-breath of pure light and bliss,
So life's night gives my lady birth
And my eyes hold her! What is worth
The rest of heaven, the rest of earth?

III

15 O loaded curls, release your store
Of warmth and scent, as once before
The tingling hair did, lights and darks
Outbreaking into fairy sparks,
When under curl and curl I pried
20 After the warmth and scent inside,
Through lights and darks how manifold—
The dark inspired, the light controlled!
As early Art embrowns the gold.

IV

What great fear, should one say, "Three days
25 That change the world might change as well
Your fortune; and if joy delays,
Be happy that no worse befell!"
What small fear, if another says,
"Three days and one short night beside
30 May throw no shadow on your ways;
But years must teem with change untried,
With chance not easily defied,
With an end somewhere undescried."
No fear!—or if a fear be born
35 This minute, it dies out in scorn.
Fear? I shall see her in three days
And one night, now the nights are short,
Then just two hours, and that is morn.

ANOTHER LOOK AT LOVE

Browning was always interested in attempting to convey something of the reality of love, without at the same time denying all romantic tradition. "In Three Days" is his poetic presentation of a lover's monologue as the man anticipates seeing his beloved. The lover's song in which he hopes that time will pass quickly is a traditional one, and lovers are ever troubled, as Browning's is, with fears of what might happen in the time that elapses until the next assignation. This lover anticipates his listener's comments by conceding that days and years will undoubtedly bring changes, but his rapturous visions of anticipation drown out all misgivings. Browning's attitude is implicit towards the speaker, and the title conveys something of the poem's ambiguity. The reader is asked to judge the lover and to realize that time will eventually change the nature of the relationship regardless of what the lover believes at this moment. What makes this poem different from more traditional ones is that in the tradition we never question the fiction that young, romantic love will last forever, but here Browning insists that we not suspend our disbelief. Here the lover admits, by not arguing the point, that time will bring change, but that three days is, after all, a very short time, and little change can occur in that period. There is a certain charm and irony implicit in the lover's attitude and in the title.

Respectability

I

Dear, had the world in its caprice
    Deigned to proclaim "I know you both,
    Have recognized your plighted troth,
4 Am sponsor for you: live in peace!"—
    How many precious months and years
        Of youth had passed, that speed so fast,
        Before we found it out at last,
8 The world, and what it fears?

II

How much of priceless life were spent
    With men that every virtue decks,
    And women models of their sex,
12 Society's true ornament,—
    Ere we dared wander, nights like this,
        Through wind and rain, and watch the Seine,
        And feel the Boulevard break again
16 To warmth and light and bliss?

III

I know! the world proscribes not love;
    Allows my fingers to caress
    Your lips' contour and downiness,
20 Provided it supply a glove.
    The world's good word!—the Institute!
        Guizot receives Montalembert!
        Eh? Down the court three lampions flare:
24 Put forward your best foot!

NOTE In lines 21-23, the "Institute" is the Institute of France on the Left Bank, which the lovers pass in their stroll. Guizot's welcoming of Montalembert is the lover's example of hypocrisy in the name of propriety, for although Guizot and Montalembert were political enemies, Guizot approved Montalembert's membership in the French Academy. The Academy met in the Institute, and as he passed that building, the speaker remembered the incident. "Lampions" are elaborate lamps in the Institute's courtyard.

UNCONVENTIONAL LOVE

In this dramatic monologue an outspoken lover taunts the world of convention with his unconventional *affair d'amour*. The setting is the Left Bank of Paris, as we listen to a lover's emotional and finally sarcastic flaunts.

QUESTIONS

1. Paraphrase stanza I.
2. Describe the lover's attitude towards polite society in stanza II.
3. Paraphrase lines 18–20. Explain the glove metonymy.
4. Explain the last line of the poem. Has the lover's tone changed from the beginning of his statement?
5. How is the ironic tone of stanza III established?
6. Explain the *irony* in the relationship of the title to the poem.

Porphyria's Lover

The rain set early in to-night,
   The sullen wind was soon awake,
It tore the elm-tops down for spite,
   And did its worst to vex the lake:
5   I listened with heart fit to break.
When glided in Porphyria; straight
   She shut the cold out and the storm,
And kneeled and made the cheerless grate
   Blaze up, and all the cottage warm;
10   Which done, she rose, and from her form
Withdrew the dripping cloak and shawl,
   And laid her soiled gloves by, untied
Her hat and let the damp hair fall,
   And, last, she sat down by my side
15   And called me. When no voice replied,
She put my arm about her waist,
   And made her smooth white shoulder bare,
And all her yellow hair displaced,
   And, stooping, made my cheek lie there,
20   And spread, o'er all, her yellow hair,
Murmuring how she loved me—she
   Too weak, for all her heart's endeavor,
To set its struggling passion free
   From pride, and vainer ties dissever,
25   And give herself to me forever.

But passion sometimes would prevail,
    Nor could to-night's gay feast restrain
A sudden thought of one so pale
    For love of her, and all in vain:
30   So, she was come through wind and rain.
Be sure I looked up at her eyes
    Happy and proud; at last I knew
Porphyria worshipped me: surprise
    Made my heart swell, and still it grew
35   While I debated what to do.
That moment she was mine, mine, fair,
    Perfectly pure and good: I found
A thing to do, and all her hair
    In one long yellow string I wound
40   Three times her little throat around,
And strangled her. No pain felt she;
    I am quite sure she felt no pain.
As a shut bud that holds a bee,
    I warily oped her lids: again
45   Laughed the blue eyes without a stain.
And I untightened next the tress
    About her neck; her cheek once more
Blushed bright beneath my burning kiss:
    I propped her head up as before,
50   Only, this time my shoulder bore
Her head, which droops upon it still:
    The smiling rosy little head,
So glad it has its utmost will,
    That all it scorned at once is fled,
55   And I, its love, am gained instead!
Porphyria's love: she guessed not how
    Her darling one wish would be heard.
And thus we sit together now,
    And all night long we have not stirred,
60   And yet God has not said a word!

THE MAD LOVER

By now it ought to be apparent that Browning dealt in his poems with many varieties of love. Love, as such, never interested him as much as the psychology of the lover, and we remember Browning as the poet who could portray dramatically and vividly a speaker revealing himself to us; he was a poet fascinated with the drama of psychological revelation. All sorts of psyches interested him, even the bizarre and macabre aspects of the necrophiliac's experience. Once entitled "Mad House Cell," "Porphyria's Lover" is the statement of a homicidal psychopath whose revelations are all the more chilling and frightening because of the way Browning understates them. The poem shocks us because of the contrast between what we know has happened and the matter of fact way in which the event is reported. This method of understatement reveals the nature of the psychopath's mind. One thing simply happens after another, and, as he comments, "God has not said a word."

QUESTIONS

1. How does the speaker characterize Porphyria?
2. Point out some particularly effective understatement.
3. What is the effect of the final line?

Soliloquy of the Spanish Cloister

I

Gr-r-r—there go, my heart's abhorrence!
    Water your damned flower-pots, do!
If hate killed men, Brother Lawrence,
4   God's blood, would not mine kill you!
What? your myrtle-bush wants trimming?
    Oh, that rose has prior claims—
Needs its leaden vase filled brimming?
8   Hell dry you up with its flames!

II

At the meal we sit together:
    *Salve tibi!** I must hear   *Hail to thee*
Wise talk of the kind of weather,
12   Sort of season, time of year:
Not a plenteous cork-crop: scarcely   *a growth on oak*
    *Dare we hope oak-galls,** I doubt:*   *leaves valuable for*
What's the Latin name for "parsley"?   *tannic acid*
16   What's the Greek name for Swine's Snout?

III

Whew! We'll have our platter burnished,
   Laid with care on our own shelf!
With a fire-new spoon we're furnished,
20   And a goblet for ourself,
Rinsed like something sacrificial
   Ere 'tis fit to touch our chaps—
Marked with L for our initial!
24   (He-he! There his lily snaps!)

IV

Saint, forsooth! While brown Dolores
   Squats outside the Convent bank
With Sanchicha, telling stories,
28   Steeping tresses in the tank,
Blue-black, lustrous, thick like horsehairs,
   —Can't I see his dead eye glow,
Bright as 'twere a Barbary corsair's*?   *pirate*
32   (That is, if he'd let it show!)

V

When he finishes refection,
   Knife and fork he never lays
Cross-wise, to my recollection,
36   As do I, in Jesu's praise.
I the Trinity illustrate,
   Drinking watered orange-pulp—
In three sips the Arian* frustrate;   *heretic*
40   While he drains his at one gulp.

VI

Oh, those melons? If he's able
   We're to have a feast! so nice!
One goes to the Abbot's table,
44   All of us get each a slice.
How go on your flowers? None double?
   Not one fruit-sort* can you spy?   *pollinated bud*
Strange!—And I, to, at such trouble,
48   Keep them close-nipped on the sly!

VII

There's a great text in Galatians,
   Once you trip on it, entails
Twenty-nine distinct damnations,
52   One sure, if another fails:
If I trip him just a-dying,
   Sure of heaven as sure can be,
Spin him round and send him flying
56   Off to hell, a Manichee*?   *heretic*

VIII

Or, my scrofulous French novel,
   On gray paper with blunt type!
Simple glance at it, you grovel
60   Hand and foot in Belial's* gripe: *a devil*
If I double down its pages
   At the woeful sixteenth print*   *page*
When he gathers his greengages,
64   Ope a sieve and slip it in't?

IX

Or, there's Satan—one might venture
   Pledge one's soul to him, yet leave
Such a flaw in the indenture
68   As he'd miss till, past retrieve,
Blasted lay that rose-acacia
   We're so proud of! *Hy, Zy, Hine.*＊   *sound of bells*
'St, there's Vespers! *Plena gratiâ,*
72   *Ave, Virgo!*＊ Gr-r-r—you swine!   *Hail Mary, full
of grace*

NOTE The italicized phrase in line 10 and the italicized lines 13-15 indicate words spoken by Brother Lawrence to the speaker.

A DRAMATIC MONOLOGUE

Browning was as fascinated with the life of the Middle Ages as he was with the Italian Renaissance. In this early dramatic monologue, the unidentified speaker is an ecclesiast with an overwhelmingly comic and tragic hatred for Brother Lawrence, a cloistered colleague. The cloistered life has produced in the speaker petty jealousies and hatreds, and his daily life is composed of silently degrading Brother Lawrence in devilishly ludicrous plots. The speaker's paranoia reaches the ridiculous in his progressively ingenious plans for capturing the soul of Brother Lawrence (stanzas 7–9).

1. Describe the tonal shifts in stanzas 1 and 2. How are these manipulations accomplished?

2. Characterize Brother Lawrence as the speaker sees him. What does he hate most about Brother Lawrence?

3. How much do we know about the speaker himself? (Be sure to differentiate between what we are sure of and what is implied.)

4. In stanzas 3 and 6, what are the petty acts the speaker commits?

5. Describe the three ways the speaker hopes to trap Brother Lawrence's soul in stanzas 7–9. How is the progression a significant one?

Andrea Del Sarto

(CALLED "THE FAULTLESS PAINTER")

But do not let us quarrel any more,
No, my Lucrezia; bear with me for once:
Sit down and all shall happen as you wish.
You turn your face, but does it bring your heart?
5   I'll work then for your friend's friend, never fear,
Treat his own subject after his own way,
Fix his own time, accept too his own price,
And shut the money into this small hand
When next it takes mine. Will it? tenderly?
10 Oh, I'll content him,—but to-morrow, Love!
I often am much wearier than you think,
This evening more than usual, and it seems
As if—forgive now—should you let me sit
Here by the window with your hand in mine
15 And look a half-hour forth on Fiesole,
Both of one mind, as married people use,
Quietly, quietly the evening through,
I might get up to-morrow to my work
Cheerful and fresh as ever. Let us try.
20 To-morrow, how you shall be glad for this!
Your soft hand is a woman of itself,
And mine the man's bared breast she curls inside.
Don't count the time lost, neither; you must serve
For each of the five pictures we require:
25 It saves a model. So! keep looking so—
My serpentining beauty, rounds on rounds!
—How could you ever prick those perfect ears,

Even to put the pearl there! oh, so sweet—
My face, my moon, my everybody's moon,
30 Which everybody looks on and calls his,
And, I suppose, is looked on by in turn,
While she looks—no one's: very dear, no less.
You smile? why, there's my picture ready made,
There's what we painters call our harmony!
35 A common grayness silvers everything,—
All in a twilight, you and I alike
—You, at the point of your first pride in me
(That's gone you know),—but I, at every point;
My youth, my hope, my art, being all toned down
40 To yonder sober pleasant Fiesole.
There's the bell clinking from the chapel-top;
That length of convent-wall across the way
Holds the trees safer, huddled more inside;
The last monk leaves the garden; days decrease,
45 And autumn grows, autumn in everything.
Eh? the whole seems to fall into a shape
As if I saw alike my work and self
And all that I was born to be and do,
A twilight-piece. Love, we are in God's hand.
50 How strange now, looks the life he makes us lead;
So free we seem, so fettered fast we are!
I feel he laid the fetter: let it lie!
This chamber for example—turn your head—
All that's behind us! You don't understand
55 Nor care to understand about my art,
But you can hear at least when people speak:
And that cartoon,* the second from the door   *preliminary sketch
—It is the thing, Love! so such things should be—
Behold Madonna!—I am bold to say.
60 I can do with my pencil what I know,
What I see, what at bottom of my heart
I wish for, if I ever wish so deep—
Do easily, too—when I say, perfectly,
I do not boast, perhaps: yourself are judge,
65 Who listened to the Legate's* talk last week,   *papal envoy
And just as much they used to say in France.
At any rate 'tis easy, all of it!
No sketches first, no studies, that's long past:
I do what many dream of, all their lives,
70 —Dream? strive to do, and agonize to do,
And fail in doing. I could count twenty such

On twice your fingers, and not leave this town,
Who strive—you don't know how the others strive
To paint a little thing like that you smeared
75 Carelessly passing with your robes afloat,—
Yet do much less, so much less, Someone* says,   *Michelangelo*
(I know his name, no matter)—so much less!
Well, less is more, Lucrezia: I am judged.
There burns a truer light of God in them,
80 In their vexed beating stuffed and stopped-up brain,
Heart, or whate'er else, than goes on to prompt
This low-pulsed forthright craftsman's hand of mine.
Their works drop groundward, but themselves, I know,
Reach many a time a heaven that's shut to me,
85 Enter and take their place there sure enough,
Though they come back and cannot tell the world.
My works are nearer heaven, but I sit here.
The sudden blood of these men! at a word—
Praise them, it boils, or blame them, it boils too.
90 I, painting from myself and to myself,
Know what I do, am unmoved by men's blame
Or their praise either. Somebody remarks
Morello's* outline there is wrongly traced,   *a mountain near*
His hue mistaken; what of that? or else,   *Florence*
95 Rightly traced and well ordered; what of that?
Speak as they please, what does the mountain care?
Ah, but a man's reach should exceed his grasp,
Or what's a heaven for? All is silver-gray
Placid and perfect with my art: the worse!
100 I know both what I want and what might gain,
And yet how profitless to know, to sigh
"Had I been two, another and myself,
Our head would have o'erlooked the world!" No doubt.
Yonder's a work now, of that famous youth
105 The Urbinate* who died five years ago.   *Raphael*
('Tis copied, George Vasari* sent it me.)   *a biographer of*
Well, I can fancy how he did it all,   *painters*
Pouring his soul, with kings and popes to see,
Reaching, that heaven might so replenish him,
110 Above and through his art—for it gives way;
That arm is wrongly put—and there again—
A fault to pardon in the drawing's lines,
Its body, so to speak: its soul is right,
He means right—that, a child may understand.
115 Still, what an arm! and I could alter it:

But all the play, the insight and the stretch—
Out of me, out of me! And wherefore out?
Had you enjoined them on me, given me soul,
We might have risen to Rafael, I and you!
120 Nay, Love, you did give all I asked, I think—
More than I merit, yes, by many times.
But had you—oh, with the same perfect brow,
And perfect eyes, and more than perfect mouth,
And the low voice my soul hears, as a bird
125 The fowler's pipe, and follows to the snare—
Had you, with these the same, but brought a mind!
Some women do so. Had the mouth there urged
"God and the glory! never care for gain.
The present by the future, what is that?
130 Live for fame, side by side with Agnolo*!   *Michelangelo*
Rafael is waiting: up to God, all three!"
I might have done it for you. So it seems:
Perhaps not. All is as God over-rules.
Beside, incentives come from the soul's self;
135 The rest avail not. Why do I need you?
What wife had Rafael, or has Agnolo?
In this world, who can do a thing, will not;
And who would do it, cannot, I perceive:
Yet the will's somewhat—somewhat, too, the power—
140 And thus we half-men struggle. At the end,
God, I conclude, compensates, punishes.
'Tis safer for me, if the award be strict,
That I am something underrated here.
Poor this long while, despised, to speak the truth.
145 I dared not, do you know, leave home all day,
For fear of chancing on the Paris lords.
The best is when they pass and look aside;
But they speak sometimes; I must bear it all.
Well may they speak! That Francis,* that first time,   *Francis I of France*
150 And that long festal year at Fontainebleau!
I surely then could sometimes leave the ground,
Put on the glory, Rafael's daily wear,
In that humane great monarch's golden look,—
One finger in his beard or twisted curl
155 Over his mouth's good mark that made the smile,
One arm about my shoulder, round my neck,
The jingle of his gold chain in my ear,
I painting proudly with his breath on me,
All his court round him, seeing with his eyes,

160 Such frank French eyes, and such a fire of souls
    Profuse, my hand kept plying by those hearts—
    And, best of all, this, this, this face beyond,
    This in the background, waiting on my work,
    To crown the issue with a last reward!
165 A good time, was it not, my kingly days?
    And had you not grown restless . . . but I know—
    'Tis done and past; 'twas right, my instinct said;
    Too live the life grew, golden and not gray,
    And I'm the weak-eyed bat no sun should tempt
170 Out of the grange whose four wall make his world.
    How could it end in any other way?
    You called me, and I came home to your heart.
    The triumph was—to reach and stay there; since
    I reached it ere the triumph, what is lost?
175 Let my hands frame your face in your hair's gold,
    You beautiful Lucrezia that are mine!
    "Rafael did this, Andrea painted that;
    The Roman's is the better when you pray,
    But still the other's Virgin was his wife—"
180 Men will excuse me. I am glad to judge
    Both pictures in your presence; clearer grows
    My better fortune, I resolve to think.
    For, do you know, Lucrezia, as God lives,
    Said one day Agnolo, his very self,
185 To Rafael . . . I have known it all these years . . .
    (When the young man was flaming out his thoughts
    Upon a palace-wall for Rome to see,
    Too lifted up in heart because of it)
    "Friend, there's a certain sorry little scrub
190 Goes up and down our Florence, none cares how,
    Who, were he set to plan and execute
    As you are, pricked on by your popes and kings,
    Would bring the sweat into that brow of yours!"
    To Rafael's—And indeed the arm is wrong.
195 I hardly dare . . . yet, only you to see,
    Give the chalk here—quick, thus the line should go!
    Ay, but the soul! he's Rafael! rub it out!
    Still, all I care for, if he spoke the truth,
    (What he? why, who but Michel Agnolo?
200 Do you forget already words like those?)
    If really there was such a chance, so lost—
    Is, whether you're—not grateful—but more pleased.
    Well, let me think so. And you smile indeed!

This hour has been an hour! Another smile?
205 If you would sit thus by me every night
I should work better, do you comprehend?
I mean that I should earn more, give you more.
See, it is settled dusk now; there's a star;
Morello's gone, the watch-lights show the wall,
210 The cue-owls speak the name we call them by.
Come from the window, love,—come in, at last,
Inside the melancholy little house
We built to be so gay with. God is just.
King Francis may forgive me: oft at nights
215 When I look up from painting, eyes tired out,
The walls become illumined, brick from brick
Distinct, instead of mortar, fierce bright gold,
That gold of his I did cement them with!
Let us but love each other. Must you go?
220 That Cousin here again? he waits outside?
Must see you—you, and not with me? Those loans?
More gaming debts to pay? you smiled for that?
Well, let smiles buy me! have you more to spend?
While hand and eye and something of a heart
225 Are left me, work's my ware, and what's it worth?
I'll pay my fancy. Only let me sit
The gray remainder of the evening out,
Idle, you call it, and muse perfectly
How I could paint, were I but back in France,
230 One picture, just one more—the Virgin's face,
Not yours this time! I want you at my side
To hear them—that is, Michel Agnolo—
Judge all I do and tell you of its worth.
Will you? To-morrow, satisfy your friend.
235 I take the subjects for his corridor,
Finish the portrait out of hand—there, there,
And throw him in another thing or two
If he demurs; the whole should prove enough
To pay for this same Cousin's freak. Beside,
240 What's better and what's all I care about,
Get you the thirteen scudi for the ruff!
Love, does that please you? Ah, but what does he,
The Cousin! What does he to please you more?

I am grown peaceful as old age to-night.
245 I regret little, I would change still less.
Since there my past life lies, why alter it?

The very wrong to Francis!—it is true
I took his coin, was tempted and complied,
And built this house and sinned, and all is said.
250 My father and my mother died of want.
Well, had I riches of my own? you see
How one gets rich! Let each one bear his lot.
They were born poor, lived poor, and poor they died:
And I have labored somewhat in my time
255 And not been paid profusely. Some good son
Paint my two hundred pictures—let him try!
No doubt, there's something strikes a balance. Yes,
You loved me quite enough, it seems to-night.
This must suffice me here. What would one have?
260 In heaven, perhaps, new chances, one more chance—
Four great walls in the New Jerusalem,
Meted* on each side by the angel's reed,   *allotted*
For Leonard, Rafael, Agnolo and me
To cover—the three first without a wife,
265 While I have mine! So-still they overcome
Because there's still Lucrezia,—as I choose.

Again the Cousin's whistle! Go, my Love.

THE TRAGEDY OF PERFECTION: A DRAMATIC MONOLOGUE

"Andrea del Sarto" reflects Browning's perpetual interest in painting and the
Italian Renaissance. The monologue dramatizes the life and attitudes that Browning
attributes to Andrea del Sarto, and by mentioning other painters of the Renaissance
he creates an intimate sense of the period. Browning has successfully captured an
artist's entire life here as del Sarto reminisces over his golden past and accepts
his silver gray future. His was the tragedy of choosing a goal he could accomplish;
his reach never exceeded his grasp, he never attempted more than he could
accomplish, and what he accomplished was always the perfect example of its kind.
But for Browning, the majesty of the vision was more valuable than the perfection
of execution. Andrea del Sarto lacked the vision, and if he once promised great
things, he has now chosen Lucrezia and the mediocrities for which she stands. It is,
however, by his choice, and he is fated forever to correct the draftsmanship of
artists whose visions far exceeded his. Perhaps, he hopes, in heaven there will be
one great wall set aside for him and his "perfect" art.

This simple summary of Browning's statement in the poem reveals nothing of
the artistry in sustaining a monologue of more than 250 lines. He has succeeded in
capturing the subtle tonal manipulations of his speaker's confession. The imagined
listener, Lucrezia, although she says nothing, plays a significant part here. We
assume that she reacts in various ways with eye movements and nodding of head

and that even at moments may be prepared to speak. Del Sarto's monologue, then, is dramatic because he anticipates future arguments from his listener and brings up matters which they have shared in the past. Browning has also organized the monologue in a series of crescendos with calmer, more introspective moments in between, and he has employed a consistent pattern of imagery (especially the gold-gray motif) to designate the past and the present of the painter.

QUESTIONS

1. Characterize Lucrezia as you see her in the poem.
2. Has Andrea del Sarto virtues other than his ability to draft a perfect picture?
3. Trace the gray-gold imagery in the poem.
4. What does del Sarto mean when he says that the days with King Francis were "my kingly days"?
5. What is the effect of the line (266), "Because there's still Lucrezia—as I choose"?
6. How does del Sarto allude to Michelangelo on three occasions?

WHAT TO LOOK FOR IN THE ADDITIONAL READINC

Here you will find three more dramatic monologues, two of which contain significant statements about Browning's aesthetics. The other, "The Bishop Orders His Tomb at St. Praxed's Church," is one of Browning's most brilliant evocations of the Renaissance. Of this poem John Ruskin wrote: "I know of no other piece of modern English, prose or poetry, in which there is so much told, as in these lines, of the Renaissance spirit,—its wordliness, inconsistency, pride, hypocrisy, ignorance of itself, love of art, of luxury, and of good Latin. It is nearly all that I have said of the central Renaissance in thirty pages of the *Stones of Venice*, put into as many lines, Browning's also being also the antecedent work." Pay particular attention as you read this poem to the subtle tonal shifts and the ways in which Browning manipulates the tone of the speaking voice; for here as in so many of the monologues the drama is conveyed by the tone of the poem rather than by the content. The other monologues will interest you, especially "Abt Vogler," which reintroduces the theme of the imperfect as you saw it in "Andrea del Sarto" as the organist extemporizes and builds from the notes he strikes a "great palace." He is forever attempting to build a palace greater than the one before, and as an extemporizer be begins each work anew, always trying to outdo the previous performance.

"The Lost Leader" may come as something of a shock, but many poets viewed Wordsworth's later years and career as evidence that the old poet was something of a turncoat. Byron accused him of it, Shelley made the same charges, but their claims were basically political. For Browning, however, Wordsworth's "defection" was a spiritual and moral matter, for the old poet had become a Judas for the establishment.

The Bishop Orders His Tomb at Saint Praxed's Church
Rome, 15—

<table>
<tr><td>Vanity, saith the preacher, vanity!*,</td><td>See Ecclesiastes 1, 2</td></tr>
<tr><td>Draw round my bed: is Anselm keeping back?</td><td></td></tr>
<tr><td>Nephews*—sons mine . . . ah God, I know not! Well—</td><td>a euphemism for
illegitimate sons</td></tr>
<tr><td>She, men would have to be your mother once,</td><td></td></tr>
<tr><td>5 Old Gandolf* envied me, so fair she was!</td><td>a rival cleric</td></tr>
</table>

What's done is done, and she is dead beside,
Dead long ago, and I am Bishop since,
And as she died so must we die ourselves,
And thence ye may perceive the world's a dream.
10 Life, how and what is it? As here I lie
In this state-chamber, dying by degrees,
Hours and long hours in the dead night, I ask
"Do I live, am I dead?" Peace, peace seems all.
Saint Praxed's ever was the church for peace;
15 And so, about this tomb of mine. I fought
With tooth and nail to save my niche, ye know:

—Old Gandolf cozened* me, despite my care;   cheated

Shrewd was that snatch from out the corner South
He graced his carrion with, God curse the same!
20 Yet still my niche is not so cramped but thence
One sees the pulpit o' the epistle-side,
And somewhat of the choir, those silent seats,
And up into the aery dome where live
The angels, and a sunbeam's sure to lurk:
25 And I shall fill my slab of basalt there,
And 'neath my tabernacle take my rest,
With those nine columns round me, two and two,
The odd one at my feet where Anselm stands:
Peach-blossom marble all, the rare, the ripe
30 As fresh-poured red wine of a mighty pulse.
—Old Gandolf with his paltry onion-stone,
Put me where I may look at him! True peach,
Rosy and flawless: how I earned the prize!
Draw close: that conflagration of my church
35 —What then? So much was saved if aught were missed!
My sons, ye would not be my death? Go dig
The white-grape vineyard where the oil-press stood,
Drop water gently till the surface sink,
And if ye find . . . Ah, God I know not, I! . . .
40 Bedded in store of rotten fig-leaves soft,

And corded up in a tight olive-frail*,   *basket*
Some lump, ah God, of *lapis lazuli,*
Big as a Jew's head cut off at the nape,
Blue as a vein o'er the Madonna's breast . . .
45 Sons, all have I bequeathed you, villas, all,
That brave Frascati villa with its bath,
So, let the blue lump poise between my knees,
Like God the Father's globe on both his hands
Ye worship in the Jesu Church so gay,
50 For Gandolf shall not choose but see and burst!
Swift as a weaver's shuttle fleet our years:
Man goeth to the grave, and where is he?
Did I say basalt for my slab, sons? Black—
'Twas ever antique-black I meant! How else
55 Shall ye contrast my frieze to come beneath?
The bas-relief in bronze ye promised me,
Those Pans and Nymphs ye wot of, and perchance
Some tripod, thyrsus* with a vase or so,   *pagan ornaments*
The Saviour at his sermon on the mount,
60 Saint Praxed in a glory, and one Pan
Ready to twitch the Nymph's last garment off,
And Moses with the tables . . . but I know
Ye mark me not! What do they whisper thee,
Child of my bowels, Anselm? Ah ye hope
65 To revel down my villas while I gasp
Bricked o'er with beggar's mouldy travertine*   *cheap stone*
Which Gandolf from his tomb-top chuckles at!
Nay, boys, ye love me—all of jasper, then!
'Tis jasper ye stand pledged to, lest I grieve.
70 My bath must needs be left behind, alas!
One block, pure green as a pistachio-nut,
There's plenty jasper somewhere in the world—
And have I not Saint Praxed's ear to pray
Horses for ye, and brown Greek manuscripts,
75 And mistresses with great smooth marbly limbs?
—That's if ye carve my epitaph aright,
Choice Latin, picked phrase, Tully's* every word,   *Cicero*
No gaudy ware like Gandolf's second line—
Tully, my masters? Ulpian* serves his need!   *inferior Latin writer*
80 And then how I shall lie through centuries,
And hear the blessed mutter of the mass,
And see God made and eaten all day long,
And feel the steady candle-flame, and taste

Good strong thick stupefying incense-smoke!
85 For as I lie here, hours of the dead night,
Dying in state and by such slow degrees,
I fold my arms as if they clasped a crook,
And stretch my feet forth straight as stone can point,
And let the bedclothes, for a mortcloth, drop
90 Into great laps and folds of sculptor's-work:
And as yon tapers dwindle, and strange thoughts
Grow, with a certain humming in my ears,
About the life before I lived this life,
And this life too, popes, cardinals and priests,
95 Saint Praxed at his sermon on the mount,
Your tall pale mother with her talking eyes,
And new-found agate urns as fresh as day,
And marble's language, Latin pure, discreet,
—Aha, ELUCESCEBAT* quoth our friend?   *Ulpian's error for
100 No Tully, said I, Ulpian at the best!   ELUCEBAT: "he
Evil and brief hath been my pilgrimage.   was honored."
All *lapis*, all, sons! Else I give the Pope
My villas! Will ye ever eat my heart?
Ever your eyes were as a lizard's quick,
105 They glitter like your mother's for my soul,
Or ye would heighten my impoverished frieze,
Piece out its starved design, and fill my vase
With grapes, and add a vizor and a term*,   *additional ornaments
And to the tripod ye would tie a lynx
110 That in his struggle throws the thyrsus down,
To comfort me on my entablature
Whereon I am to lie till I must ask
"Do I live, am I dead?" There, leave me, there!
For ye have stabbed me with ingratitude
115 To death—ye wish it—God, ye wish it!
    Stone—
Gritstone, a-crumble! Clammy squares which sweat
As if the corpse they keep were oozing through—
And no more *lapis* to delight the world!
120 Well, go! I bless ye. Fewer tapers there,
But in a row: and, going, turn your backs
—Ay, like departing altar-ministrants,
And leave me in my church, the church for peace,
That I may watch at leisure if he leers—
125 Old Gandolf—at me, from his onion-stone,
As still he envied me, so fair she was!

The Lost Leader

Just for a handful of silver he left us,
    Just for a riband to stick in his coat—
Found the one gift of which fortune bereft us,
4   Lost all the others she let us devote;
They, with the gold to give, doled him out silver,
    So much was theirs who so little allowed:
How all our copper had gone for his service!
8   Rags—were they purple, his heart had been proud!
We that had loved him so, followed him, honored him,
    Lived in his mild and magnificent eye,
Learned his great language, caught his clear accents,
12   Made him our pattern to live and to die!
Shakespeare was of us, Milton was for us,
    Burns, Shelley, were with us—they watch from
                            their graves!
He alone breaks from the van and the freemen,
16   —He alone sinks to the rear and the slaves!
We shall march prospering,—not thro' his presence;
    Songs may inspirit us,—not from his lyre;
Deeds will be done,—while he boasts his quiescence,
20   Still bidding crouch whom the rest bade aspire:
Blot out his name, then, record one lost soul more,
    One task more declined, one more footpath untrod,
One more devils' triumph and sorrow for angels,
24   One wrong more to man, one more insult to God!
Life's night begins: let him never come back to us!
    There would be doubt, hesitation and pain,
Forced praise on our part—the glimmer of twilight,
28   Never glad confident morning again!
Best fight on well, for we taught him—strike gallantly,
    Menace our heart ere we master his own;
Then let him receive the new knowledge and wait us,
32   Pardoned in heaven, the first by the throne!

NOTE Browning, who once admired Wordsworth, wrote this poem on the occasion of Wordsworth's appointment as Poet Laureate. With the office went its emblem (a riband) and a pension (a handful of silver).

How It Strikes a Contemporary

I only knew one poet in my life:
And this, or something like it, was his way.

You saw go up and down Valladolid*,   *a city in Spain*
A man of mark, to know next time you saw.
His very serviceable suit of black
Was courtly once and conscientious still,
And many might have worn it, though none did:
The cloak, that somewhat shone and showed the threads,
Had purpose, and the ruff, significance.
He walked and tapped the pavement with his cane,
Scenting the world, looking it full in face,
An old dog, bald and blindish, at his heels.
They turned up, now, the alley by the church,
That leads nowhither; now they breathed themselves
On the main promenade just at the wrong time:
You'd come upon his scrutinizing hat,
Making a peaked shade blacker than itself
Against the single window spared some house
Intact yet with its mouldered Moorish work,—
Or else surprise the ferrel of his stick
Trying the mortar's temper 'tween the chinks
Of some new shop a-building, French and fine.
He stood and watched the cobbler at his trade,
The man who slices lemons into drink,
The coffee-roaster's brazier, and the boys
That volunteer to help him turn its winch.
He glanced o'er books on stalls with half an eye,
And fly-leaf ballads on the vendor's string,
And broad-edge bold-print posters by the wall.
He took such cognizance of men and things,
If any beat a horse, you felt he saw;
If any cursed a woman, he took note;
Yet stared at nobody,—you stared at him,
And found, less to your pleasure than surprise,
He seemed to know you and expect as much.
So, next time that a neighbor's tongue was loosed,
It marked the shameful and notorious fact,
We had among us, not so much a spy,
As a recording chief-inquisitor,
The town's true master if the town but knew!

We merely kept a governor for form,
While this man walked about and took account
Of all thought, said and acted, then went home,
And wrote it fully to our Lord the King
45 Who has an itch to know things, he knows why,
And reads them in his bedroom of a night.
Oh, you might smile! there wanted not a touch,
A tang of . . . well, it was not wholly ease
As back into your mind the man's look came.
50 Stricken in years a little,—such a brow
His eyes had to live under!—clear as flint
On either side the formidable nose
Curved, cut and colored like an eagle's claw.
Had he to do with A.'s surprising fate?
55 When altogether old B. disappeared
And young C. got his mistress,—was't our friend,
His letter to the King, that did it all?
What paid the bloodless man for so much pains?
Our Lord the King has favorites manifold,
60 And shifts his ministry some once a month;
Our city gets new governors at whiles,—
But never word or sign, that I could hear,
Notified to this man about the streets
The King's approval of those letters conned
65 The last thing duly at the dead of night.
Did the man love his office? Frowned our Lord,
Exhorting when none heard—"Beseech me not!
Too far above my people,—beneath me!
I set the watch,—how should the people know?
70 Forget them, keep me all the more in mind!"
Was some such understanding 'twixt the two?

I found no truth in one report at least—
That if you tracked him to his home, down lanes
Beyond the Jewry, and as clean to pace,
75 You found he ate his supper in a room
Blazing with lights, four Titians on the wall,
And twenty naked girls to change his plate!
Poor man, he lived another kind of life
In that new stuccoed third house by the bridge,
80 Fresh-painted, rather smart than otherwise!
The whole street might o'erlook him as he sat,
Leg crossing leg, one foot on the dog's back,

Playing a decent cribbage with his maid
(Jacynth*, you're sure her name was) o'er the cheese   *exotic name*
85 And fruit, three red halves of starved winter-pears,
Or treat of radishes in April. Nine,
Ten, struck the church clock, straight to bed went he.

My father, like the man of sense he was,
Would point him out to me a dozen times;
90 "'St—'St," he'd whisper, "the Corregidor*!"   *chief magistrate*
I had been used to think that personage
Was one with lacquered breeches, lustrous belt,
And feathers like a forest in his hat,
Who blew a trumpet and proclaimed the news,
95 Announced the bull-fights, gave each church its turn,
And memorized the miracle in vogue!
He had a great observance from us boys;
We are in error; that was not the man.

I'd like now, yet had haply been afraid,
100 To have just looked, when this man came to die,
And seen who lined the clean gay garret-sides
And stood about the neat low truckle-bed,
With the heavenly manner of relieving guard.
Here had been, mark, the general-in-chief,
105 Thro' a whole campaign of the world's life and death,
Doing the King's work all the dimday long,
In his old coat and up to knees in mud,
Smoked like a herring, dining on a crust,—
And, now the day was won, relieved at once!
110 No further show or need for that old coat,
You are sure, for one thing! Bless us, all the while
How sprucely we are dressed out, you and I!
A second, and the angels alter that.
Well, I could never quite write a verse,—could you?
115 Let's to the Prado and make the most of time.

Abt Vogler

(AFTER HE HAS BEEN EXTEMPORIZING UPON THE MUSICAL INSTRUMENT OF HIS INVENTION.)

I

Would that the structure brave, the manifold music I build,
  Bidding my organ obey, calling its keys to their work,
Claiming each slave of the sound, at a touch, as when
    Solomon willed
4   Armies of angels that soar, legions of demons that lurk,
Man, brute, reptile, fly,—alien of end and of aim,
  Adverse, each from the other heaven-high, hell-deep
    removed,—
Should rush into sight at once as he named the
    ineffable Name,
8   And pile him a palace straight, to pleasure the
    princess he loved!

II

Would it might tarry like his, the beautiful building of mine,
  This which my keys in a crowd pressed and
    importuned to raise!
Ah, one and all, how they helped, would dispart now
    and now combine,
12   Zealous to hasten the work, heighten their master
    his praise!
And one would bury his brow with a blind plunge
    down to hell,
  Burrow awhile and build, broad on the roots of things,
Then up again swim into sight, having based me my
    palace well,
16   Founded it, fearless of flame, flat on the nether springs.

III

And another would mount and march, like the excellent
    minion he was,
  Ay, another and yet another, one crowd but with
    many a crest,
Raising my rampired* walls of gold as transparent as   *with ramparts*
    glass,

20   Eager to do and die, yield each his place to the rest:
For higher still and higher (as a runner tips with fire,
    When a great illumination surprises a festal night—
Outlining round and round Rome's dome from space
    to spire)
24   Up, the pinnacled glory reached, and the pride of
    my soul was in sight.

IV

In sight? Not half! for it seemed, it was certain, to match
    man's birth,
    Nature in turn conceived, obeying an impulse as I;
And the emulous heaven yearned down, made effort to
    reach the earth,
28   As the earth had done her best, in my passion, to
    scale the sky:
Novel splendors burst forth, grew familiar and dwelt
    with mine,
    Not a point nor peak but found and fixed its
    wandering star;
Meteor-moons, balls of blaze: and they did not pale
    nor pine,
32   For earth had attained to heaven, there was no more
    near nor far.

V

Nay more; for there wanted not who walked in the
    glare and glow,
    Presences plain in the place; or, fresh from the
    Protoplast*,   *first matter*
Furnished for ages to come, when a kindlier wind
    should blow.
36   Lured now to begin and live, in a house to their
    liking at last;
Or else the wonderful Dead who have passed through
    the body and gone,
    But were back once more to breathe in an old
    world worth their new:
What never had been, was now; what was, as it shall
    be anon;
40   And what is,—shall I say, matched both? for I was
    made perfect too.

VI

All through my keys that gave their sounds to a wish
 of my soul,
 All through my soul that praised as its wish flowed
  visibly forth,
 All through music and me! For think, had I painted
  the whole,
44 Why, there it had stood, to see, nor the process so
  wonder-worth:
Had I written the same, made verse—still, effect
  proceeds from cause,
 Ye know why the forms are fair, ye hear how the
  tale is told;
It is all triumphant art, but art in obedience to laws,
48 Painter and poet are proud in the artist-list enrolled:—

VII

But here is the finger of God, a flash of the will that can,
 Existent behind all laws, that made them and, lo,
  they are!
And I know not if, save in this, such gift be allowed
  to man,
52 That out of three sounds he frame, not a fourth
  sound, but a star.
Consider it well: each tone of our scale in itself is naught;
 It is everywhere in the world—loud, soft, and all is said:
Give it to me to use! I mix it with two in my thought:
56 And, there! Ye have heard and seen: consider and
  bow the head!

VIII

Well, it is gone at last, the palace of music I reared;
 Gone! and the good tears start, the praises that
  come too slow;
For one is assured at first, one scarce can say that he feared,
60 That he even gave it a thought, the gone thing was
  to go.

Never to be again! But many more of the kind
    As good, nay, better perchance: is this your comfort
        to me?
To me, who must be saved because I cling with my mind
64   To the same, same self, same love, same God: ay,
        what was, shall be.

IX

Therefore to whom turn I but to thee, the ineffable
    Name?
    Builder and maker, thou, of houses not made with
        hands!
What, have fear of change from thee who art ever
    the same?
68   Doubt that thy power can fill the heart that thy
        power expands?
There shall never be good, with, for evil, so much
    good more;
    The evil is null, is naught, is silence implying sound;
What was good shall be good, with, for evil, so much
    good more;
72   On the earth the broken arcs; in the heaven, a perfect
        round.

X

All we have willed or hoped or dreamed of good shall
    exist;
    Not its semblance, but itself, no beauty, nor good,
        nor power
Whose voice has gone forth, but each survives for the
    melodist
76   When eternity affirms the conception of an hour.
The high that proved too high, the heroic for earth
    too hard,
    The passion that left the ground to lose itself in the sky,
Are music sent up to God by the lover and the bard;
80   Enough that he heard it once; we shall hear it
        by-and-by.

XI

And what is our failure here but a triumph's evidence
  For the fulness of the day's? Have we withered or
    agonized?
Why else was the pause prolonged but that singing
    might issue thence?
84   Why rushed the discords in but that harmony should
    be prized?
Sorrow is hard to bear, and doubt is slow to clear,
  Each sufferer says his say, his scheme of the weal
    and woe:
But God has a few of us whom he whispers in the ear;
88   The rest may reason and welcome: 'tis we
    musicians know.

XII

Well, it is earth with me; silence resumes her reign:
  I will be patient and proud, and soberly acquiesce.
Give me the keys. I feel for the common chord again,
92   Sliding by semitones, till I sink to the minor,—yes,
And I blunt it into a ninth, and I stand on alien ground,
  Surveying awhile the heights I rolled from into the
    deep;
Which, hark, I have dared and done, for my resting-
    place is found,
96   The C Major of this life: so, now I will try to sleep.

NOTE Abt Vogler (1749-1814) was a German musician, famous for his extemporizing; he invented the portable organ.

TOPICS FOR WRITING AND DISCUSSION

FOR USE IN CLASS

    1. Discuss Browning's use of irony in "The Bishop Orders His Tomb."
    2. Write a character sketch of Browning's Bishop of St. Praxed's.
    3. Discuss the color imagery in "The Bishops Orders His Tomb" as it is related to stone.
    4. Describe city life in Valladolid as it is described in "How It Strikes a Contemporary."

FOR PREPARATION OUTSIDE OF CLASS

1. Discuss Browning's concept of the function of the poet or artist using evidence from three poems by Browning.

2. Trace as carefully as you can the music metaphor in "Abt Vogler."

3. Compare the views of monastic life as you find it described in Wordsworth's "Vallambrosa" and Browning's "Soliloquy of a Spanish Cloister."

4. Write a character analysis of Browning's Andrea del Sarto.

5. Compare the views of love in the five love poems by Browning in this collection with that in Wordsworth's Lucy Poems.

Spring

Nothing is so beautiful as spring—
  When weeds, in wheels, shoot long and lovely and lush;
  Thrush's eggs look little low heavens, and thrush
4 Through the echoing timber does so rinse and wring
The ear, it strikes like lightnings to hear him sing;
  The glassy peartree leaves and blooms, they brush
  The descending blue; that blue is all in a rush
8 With richness; the racing lambs too have fair their fling.

What is all this juice and all this joy?
  A strain of the earth's sweet being in the beginning
In Eden garden.—Have, get, before it cloy,
12   Before it cloud, Christ, lord, and sour with sinning,
Innocent mind and Mayday in girl and boy,
Most, O maid's child, thy choice and worthy the
                          winning.

HOPKINS' IDIOSYNCRACIES

As one begins to read Hopkins, he is immediately confronted with some of the poet's idiosyncracies—among them Hopkins' fondness for coining compounds, his wrenched syntax, his archaic, obscure, and sometimes strange diction, his religious allusions, and his unusually rich ambiguities. Many readers, however, find these distinctive characteristics less a barrier to reading Hopkins than the very reason for reading him. These traits are often compounded to provide an exciting atmosphere for the poem, and the suggestive possibilities which result convey a depth greater than a prose paraphrase can suggest.

In one of Hopkins' less complicated sonnets—another of the many English poems on spring—one can find instances of his distinctive traits. Usually Hopkins begins a sonnet with a direct statement, and his fondness for alliterative patterns is especially obvious here. The reader will notice two clear-cut compounds—"peartree" and "Mayday"—which succeed in compressing an image so that Hopkins suggests more compactly the essence of spring than if he had printed them as separate words. His compound "Mayday" acts as a metaphor for the innocence and joy of the child's consciousness. It suggests youth, freshness, vitality, and cleanness. The final four lines present both an ambiguity and an instance of Hopkins' wrenched syntax. Initially, the reader finds it difficult to find subject and verb, but close attention reveals that the imperatives appear directed to Christ; that is, the final lines are a plea to the "maid's child" to possess the mind of the child before it clouds with sinning. On second or third reading, however, one sees the possibility that Hopkins implores the child to reach out for the innocence of Christ. Of course, neither of the possibilities is exclusive, for Hopkins hopes we will hold both in balance. In line 8 Hopkins has forced the adjective "fair" into the position of an adverb, allowing the word to function in a wrenched manner as both parts of speech. The lambs have a *fair* fling because it is a fling they *deserve*; their fling is *fair* because it is theirs *naturally*. The lamb also serves as a significant religious allusion, preparing us for the introduction of religious subject matter in the sestet.

This sonnet also illustrates something of Hopkins' poetic technique. Most often Hopkins opens his poem with a stanza, or, in the case of the sonnet, with an octave which describes a natural scene. One should remember that, besides being a religious poet, Hopkins is a significant nature poet as well. In the sonnet, the reader should look for a religious allusion near line 8, for it is through a subtle suggestion that he usually introduces his religious theme. The sestet, then, contains the obviously religious material as the speaker implores God or Christ to preserve the beauty of nature. It is as if the speaker has found behind natural beauty a divine spirit. This pattern is repeated again and again in Hopkins' poetry.

QUESTIONS

1. How do the words "wheels" and "shoot" suggest the vitality of spring in addition to the visible patterns of growth during this season? How do the sound patterns reinforce the effect of line 2?

2. What is the effect of leaving out a word in line 3? What word?

3. How does the imagery of line 3 introduce the religious theme of the poem?

4. Explain the terms of the metaphor in line 4; the simile in line 5.

5. What progression is made from line 3 to line 8 in the religious allusion?

6. Describe how Hopkins succeeds in conveying spring in motion throughout the octave.

7. How has the reader been prepared for the word "juice" at the beginning of the sestet?

* * *

The Starlight Night

Look at the stars! look, look up at the skies!
  O look at all the fire-folk sitting in the air!
  The bright boroughs, the circle-citadels there!
4 Down in dim woods the diamond delves! the elves'-eyes!
  The grey lawns cold where gold, where quickgold lies!
    Wind-beat whitebeam! airy abeles* set on a flare!   *poplars*
    Flake-doves sent floating forth at a farmyard scare!—
8 Ah well! it is all a purchase, all is a prize.

  Buy then! bid then!—What?—Prayer, patience, alms, vows.
  Look, look: a May-mess, like on orchard boughs!
    Look! March-bloom, like on mealed-with-yellow sallows!
12 These are indeed the barn; withindoors house
  The shocks. This piece-bright paling shuts the spouse
    Christ home, Christ and his mother and all his hallows*.   *saints*

ANOTHER NATURE—RELIGIOUS POEM

"The Starlight Night" follows something of the same pattern as "Spring." Directing our vision up to the stars, the speaker describes the scene he sees there in terrestrial terms. We are asked to image the stars as the council fires of cities in the sky, and then as our eye sweeps across the skies, we are, as it were, looking down into diamond mines. The scene is brought even closer to earth as the octave progresses. The sky is imaged as an early morning lawn covered with golden dew. That scene, in turn, suggests another, and Hopkins gains his effect by multiplying suggestions. The effect of the octave is to impress us with the closeness of the heavens, and those groups of stars which are metaphorized as "flake-doves" (that is, they look as if they were swept across the sky like feathers from doves) introduce the religious theme the reader should look for at the end of the octave. The dove is the standard symbol for the Holy Ghost.

QUESTIONS

    1. In line 8, how are the words "purchase" and "prize" related?
    2. How is the transition between the end of the octave and the beginning of the sestet accomplished?
    3. Describe the appropriateness of the image which describes the willow trees (line 11).

4. Explain the appropriateness of the harvest image in the last three lines.

5. Find and explain a pun in line 13.

6. Explain the relationship of the harvest image to the religious theme with which the sonnet concludes.

The Candle Indoors

Some candle clear burns somewhere I come by.
I muse at how its being puts blissful back
With yellowy moisture mild night's blear-all black,
4 Or to fro tender trambeams truckle at the eye.
By that window what task what fingers ply,
I plod wondering, a wanting, just for lack
Of answer the eagerer a wanting Jessy or Jack
8 There God to aggrandise, God to glorify.—

Come you indoors, come home; your fading fire
Mend first and vital candle in close heart's vault:
You there are master, do your own desire;
12 What hinders? Are you beam-blind, yet to a fault
In a neighbour deft-handed? are you that liar
And, cast by conscience out, spendsavour salt?

BIBLICAL ALLUSION

The underlying allusion throughout this sonnet is to the Sermon on the Mount. A reading of Matthew, Chapter 5, will enlarge the meaning of the last three lines, and also the prevailing image of the candle. The octave opens with a literal observation of a candle in a window and concludes with the introduction of the religious subject matter which relates the lighted candle to Christ's sermon—"Let your light so shine before men, that they may see your good works, and glorify your Father which is in heaven." The language and imagery of lines 12–14 are related to that portion of the Sermon on the Mount which reads, "Ye are the salt of the earth, but if the salt shall have lost his savour, wherewith shall it be salted," and " ... why beholdest thou the mote that is in thy brother's eye, but considerest not the beam that is in thine own eye." As Christ considered his Disciples to be the "salt of the earth" and "the light of the world," so the speaker in the sestet cautions himself to lead an exemplary life to glorify God.

The Lantern Out of Doors

Sometimes a lantern moves along the night,
   That interests our eyes. And who goes there?
   I think; where from and bound, I wonder, where,
4 With, all down darkness wide, his wading light?

Men go by me whom either beauty bright
   In mould or mind or what not else makes rare:
   They rain against our much-thick and marsh air
8 Rich beams, till death or distance buys them quite.

Death or distance soon consumes them: wind
   What most I may eye after, be in at the end
   I cannot, and out of sight is out of mind.

12 Christ minds; Christ's interest, what to avow or amend
   There, eyes them, heart wants, care haunts, foot
                    follows kind,
   Their ransom, their rescue, and first, fast, last friend.

Carrion Comfort

Not, I'll not, carrion comfort, Despair, not feast on thee;
Not untwist—slack they may be—these last strands of man
In me or, most weary, cry I can no more. I can;
4   Can something, hope, wish day come, not choose not to be.
But ah, but O thou terrible, why wouldst thou rude on me
Thy wring world right foot rock? lay a lion limb against me? scan
With darksome devouring eyes my bruised bones? and fan,
8   O in turns of tempest, me heaped there; me frantic to avoid thee and flee?
Why? That my chaff might fly; my grain lie, sheer and clear.
Nay in all that toil, that coil, since (seems) I kissed the rod,
Hand rather, my heart lo! lapped strength, stole joy, would laugh, cheer.
12 Cheer whom though? the hero whose heaven handling flung me, foot trod
Me? or me that fought him? O which one? is it each one? That night, that year
Of now done darkness I wretch lay wrestling with (my God!) my God.

HOPKINS' SYNTAX

This sonnet poses more syntactical problems than the typical Hopkins' poem. The wrenched syntax suggests something of the tortured condition of the speaker as he experiences his own "dark night of the soul." His experience of religious despair is described in terms of nightmares and tempests as Hopkins wrestles with his beliefs and the torments that accompany them. The syntax of the first quatrain, for instance, especially the disjointed nature of line 1, conveys something of the fitful, almost spastic nature of the religious experience of near despair. The speaker insists that despite his condition he can endure it and will live until his "morning." The second quatrain intensifies the description with its heavy use of alliteration and its insistence upon the separateness of each word. The alliteration, the use of one part of speech for another (e.g., "rude" for rudely) and the many words which both end and begin with consonants help convey the intensity of the experience. Such devices characterize the voice of the speaker; he is methodical and careful, but obviously excited as he tries his best to control his emotions. The words which begin and end with consonants suggest a purposefulness about the speaker as he suffers despair.

In the sestet the winds the speaker has experienced in the tempests of despair are seen under another aspect. Not only do they torture, they also are the winnowing powers to separate the grain from the chaff. The realization that man is tested by despair and, having passed the test, can be stronger than before allows his soul to laugh and cheer. His has, indeed, been a divine struggle as he, like Jacob, lay wrestling with divinity.

QUESTIONS

1. Explain the adjective "carrion" (line 1).
2. Paraphrase lines 5 and 6.
3. What is the effect of the two compounds "wring world" and "lion limb" (line 6)?
4. What is the effect of the internal rhyme in lines 9 and 10?
5. What are the connotations of "coil" (line 10)?
6. Discuss the tone of the final line of the sonnet.

The Windhover
To Christ Our Lord

I caught this morning morning's minion, kingdom of daylight's dauphin, dapple-dawn-drawn Falcon,
  in his riding
Of the rolling level underneath him steady air, and
  striding
4 High there, how he rung upon the rein of a wimpling
  wing*
In his ecstasy! then off, off forth on swing,
  As a skate's heel sweeps smooth on a bow-bend: the
  hurl and gliding
Rebuffed the big wind. My heart in hiding
8 Stirred for a bird,—the achieve of, the mastery of the
  thing!

Brute beauty and valour and act, oh, air, pride, plume,
  here
  Buckle! and the fire that breaks from thee then, a
  billion
Times told lovelier, more dangerous, O my chevalier!

*circled at the end of
a tether*

12   No wonder of it: sheer plod makes plough down
      sillion*   *furrow*
Shine, and blue-bleak embers, ah my dear,
Fall, gall themselves, and gash gold-vermilion.

HOPKINS AT HIS MOST DIFFICULT

"The Windhover," one of Hopkins' most difficult and best known poems, rewards one's careful reading, but many of the poem's characteristic features ought to be familiar since no new devices will be found here. The poem's subject is the kestrel, or small hawk, often trained for hunting, but the poem is dedicated, or directed, to Christ. The speaker, then, sees something in the kestrel's nature and activity which reminds him of divinity. The bird suggests power and glory, excitement and strength, romance and chivalry, and the imagery of the opening quatrain helps convey the numerous feudal associations. The speaker watches the bird soar through the air, gliding against the headwinds of the sky. The speaker's heart, "in hiding" (that is, within his body or denied and in bondage to his order) suggests many things, but most of all the speaker implies that he would like to emulate the wildly romantic instinctual activity of the bird. As a priest, Hopkins had, after all, denounced the more romantic paths open to the poet, for he became Christ's poet, bound by the rules of his order. The role of the wild, romantic minstrel was not to be his no matter how much he coveted it.

The sestet presents many problems, most of them with the definition of "buckle" (line 10). The word does immediately appear to mean "to fasten" or "to inclose" but it may also mean "to crumple" or "to crush." The line, then, becomes ambiguous, for Hopkins may mean that his "cloistered" life is more beautiful and more romantic than the obviously wild life epitomized by the kestrel, for his is a life of duty and obedience to God. On the other hand, critics have argued, the priest-speaker, who has denied himself the more romantic existence of the troubador, is crushed by the sight of a bird which he takes as a symbol of the way of life no longer open to him. Probably something of both readings is true, for it is unnecessary to decide upon an exclusive reading. Hopkins wants to convey the contradictory nature of his own feelings. Dedication to what he sees as the common life of the priesthood need not rule out feelings of nostalgia for the life that might have been. What he succeeds in doing at the conclusion of the sonnet is to convince himself and us that even within his life of order and restraint exists the possibility of heroism and beautiful action; the crucifixion imagery which concludes the poem reminds us of the world's greatest act of heroism, an act accomplished meekly through order and discipline.

QUESTIONS

1. What diction throughout the sonnet contributes to the establishment of imagery associated with feudalism?

2. What is the effect of compound adjectives in this poem? What is the effect of the adjective series (line 3)?

3. Explain the ice-skating image in line 6.

4. Explain the fire imagery of the sestet.

WHAT TO LOOK FOR IN THE ADDITIONAL READING

Few new problems should be encountered in the additional reading. "Hurrahing in Harvest" celebrates Hopkins' joy in harvesting God in the world. This sonnet is organized around his typical pattern: an octave of natural descriptions followed by a sestet concerned with the religious significance of the scene he describes. The reader will wish to compare certain attitudes and techniques in "The Caged Skylark" with themes in "The Windhover," and the bleak sonnets "No Worst, There Is None" and "I Wake and Feel the Fell of Dark" may be compared with the more powerful description of despair in "Carrion Comfort." Hopkins surprises by the variety of diction and imagery, but his themes are very few. Once you have acquainted yourself with his numerous idiosyncrasies, these poems should delight you with the poet's ability to be forever fresh.

Spring and Fall
To a Young Child

Margaret, are you grieving
Over Goldengrove unleaving?
Leaves, like the things of man, you
With your fresh thoughts care for, can you?
5   Ah! as the heart grows older
It will come to such sights colder
By and by, nor spare a sigh
Though worlds of wanwood leafmeal lie;
And yet you will weep and know why.
10 Now no matter, child, the name:
Sorrow's are the same.
Nor mouth had, no nor mind, expressed
What heart heard of, ghost guessed.
It is the blight man was born for,
15 It is Margaret you mourn for.

Hurrahing in Harvest

Summer ends now; now, barbarous in beauty, the
    stooks arise
Around; up above, what wind-walks! what lovely
    behaviour
Of silk-sack clouds! has wilder, wilful-wavier
4 Meal-drift moulded ever and melted across skies?

I walk, I lift up, I lift up heart, eyes,
Down all that glory in the heavens to glean our
    Saviour;
And, eyes, heart, what looks, what lips yet gave you a
8 Rapturous love's greeting of realer, of rounder replies?

And the azurous hung hills are his world-wielding
    shoulder
Majestic—as a stallion stalwart, very-violet-sweet!—
These things, these things were here and but the
    beholder
12 Wanting which two when they once meet,
The heart rears wings bold and bolder
And hurls for him, O half hurls earth for him off
    under his feet.

The May Magnificat

May is Mary's month, and I
Muse at that and wonder why:
Her feasts follow reason,
4 Dated due to season –

Candlemas, Lady Day;
But the Lady Month, May,
Why fasten that upon her,
8 With a feasting in her honour?

Is it only its being brighter
Than the most are must delight her?
Is it opportunest
12 And flowers finds soonest?

Ask of her, the mighty mother:
Her reply puts this other
Question: What is Spring?—
16 Growth in every thing—

Flesh and fleece, fur and feather,
Grass and greenworld all together;
Star-eyed strawberry-breasted
20 Throstle above her nested

Cluster of bugle blue eggs thin
Forms and warms the life within;
And bird and blossom swell
24 In sod or sheath or shell

All things rising, all things sizing
Mary sees, sympathising
With that world of good,
28 Nature's motherhood.

Their magnifying of each its kind
With delight calls to mind
How she did in her stored
32 Magnify the Lord.

Well but there was more than this:
Spring's universal bliss
Much, had much to say
36 To offering Mary May.

When drop-of-blood-and-foam-dapple
Bloom lights the orchard-apple
And thicket and thorp are merry
40 With silver-surfèd cherry

And azuring-over greybell makes
Wood banks and brakes wash wet like lakes
And magic cuckoocall
44 Caps, clears, and clinches all—

This ecstacy all through mothering earth
Tells Mary her mirth till Christ's birth
To remember and exultation
48 In God who was her salvation.

The Caged Skylark

As a dare gale skylark scanted in a dull cage
Man's mounting spirit in his bone house, mean house,
 dwells—
That bird beyond the remembering his free fells;
4 This in drudgery, day labouring out life's age.

Though aloft on turf or perch or poor low stage,
Both sing sometimes the sweetest, sweetest spells,
Yet both droop deadly sometimes in their cells
8 Or wring their barriers in bursts of fear or rage.

Not that the sweet fowl, song fowl, needs no rest—
Why, hear him, hear him babble and drop down to
 his nest,
But his own nest, wild nest, no prison.

12 Man's spirit will be flesh-bound when found at best,
But uncumbered: meadow-down is not distressed
For a rainbow footing it nor he for his bones risen.

I Wake and Feel the Fell of Dark

I wake and feel the fell of dark, not day.
What hours, O what black hours we have spent
This night! what sighs you, heart, saw; ways you
 went!
4 And more must, in yet longer light's delay.
With witness I speak this. But where I say
Hours I mean years, mean life. And my lament
Is cries countless, cries like dead letters sent
8 To dearest him that lives alas! away.

I am gall, I am heartburn. God's most deep decree
Bitter would have me taste: my taste was me;
Bones built in me, flesh filled, blood brimmed
 the curse.
12 Selfyeast of spirit a dull dough sours. I see
The lost are like this, and their scourge to be
As I am mine, their sweating selves; but worse.

No Worst, There Is None

No worst, there is none. Pitched past pitch of grief,
More pangs will, schooled at forepangs, wilder wring.
Comforter, where, where is your comforting?
4 Mary, mother of us, where is your relief?

My cries heave, herds-long, huddle in a main, a chief
Woe, world-sorrow; on an age-old anvil wince and sing—
Then lull, then leave off. Fury had shrieked " No
     lingering!
8 Let me be fell: force I must be brief."

O the mind, mind has mountains; cliffs of fall
Frightful, sheer, no-man-fathomed. Hold them cheap
May who ne'er hung there. Nor does long our small
12 Durance deal with that steep or deep. Here! creep,
Wretch, under a comfort serves in a whirlwind: all
Life death does end and each day dies with sleep.

TOPICS FOR WRITING AND DISCUSSION

FOR USE IN CLASS

1. Discuss how Hopkins uses the harvest imagery in "Hurrahing in Harvest."
2. Discuss the attitude towards spring in "The May Magnificat."
3. Discuss the connotative qualities of some of the diction of "The Caged Skylark."
4. Discuss the tone of the sonnet of "No Worst, There is None"; concentrate especially on tonal changes.

FOR PREPARATION OUTSIDE OF CLASS

1. Compare Hopkins' treatment of original sin in "Spring and Fall" with Yeats's in "Adam's Curse."
2. Compare the treatment of the theme of mortality in Hopkins' "Spring and Fall" with Wordsworth's in "We are Seven."
3. Compare Hopkins and Wordsworth as nature poets.
4. Compare Hopkins and Donne as religious poets.

Adam's Curse

We sat together at one summer's end,
That beautiful mild woman, your close friend,
And you and I, and talked of poetry.
I said, "A line will take us hours maybe;
5 Yet if it does not seem a moment's thought,
Our stitching and unstitching has been naught.

Better go down upon your marrow-bones
And scrub a kitchen pavement, or break stones
Like an old pauper, in all kinds of weather;
10 For to articulate sweet sounds together
Is to work harder than all these, and yet
Be thought an idler by the noisy set
Of bankers, schoolmasters, and clergymen
The martyrs call the world."

15   And thereupon
That beautiful mild woman for whose sake
There's many a one shall find out all heartache
On finding that her voice is sweet and low
Replied, "To be born woman is to know—
20 Although they do not talk of it at school—
That we must labour to be beautiful."

I said, "It's certain there is no fine thing
Since Adam's fall but needs much labouring.
There have been lovers who thought love should be
25 So much compounded of high courtesy
That they would sigh and quote with learned looks
Precedents out of beautiful old books;
Yet now it seems an idle trade enough."

We sat grown quiet at the name of love;
30 We saw the last embers of daylight die,
And in the trembling blue-green of the sky
A moon, worn as if it had been a shell
Washed by time's waters as they rose and fell
About the stars and broke in days and years.

35 I had a thought for no one's but your ears:
    That you were beautiful, and that I strove
    To love you in the old high way of love;
    That it had all seemed happy, and yet we'd grown
    As weary-hearted as that hollow moon.

IMPERFECT MAN'S IDEALS

This poem is about love and the poet's mission. Both are conceived of as ideals, out of the grasp of ordinary mortals, but to be aspired to by exceptional lovers and poets. The speaker, in a quiet conversation with two women, comments on the poet's problems. The imagery in lines 6–8 is appropriate in the conversation with women: the reworking of a poem is "stitching and unstitching," and versifying is likened to the household chore of scrubbing a kitchen. According to the poet, though, the labor of poetry is more onerous than these household chores, but a labor considered idleness by the rest of the world. One of his companions responds that being beautiful is a labor. The beauty of which she speaks is probably a kind of ideal spiritual perfection. The speaker replies by introducing the concept of man's imperfection because of Adam's fall; to create any fine thing requires labor. He goes on to allude to the chivalric ideal of courtly love through which man had striven for perfection and fulfillment by laboring to idealize his beloved. At the mention of this far away ideal of love, the company grows silent, aware of their own inadequacy. Their emotional state is perfectly mirrored in the dramatic context: it is the season's end, the day's end, the moon is worn out, and all spirits have been eroded by the passage of time. At the conclusion of the poem the speaker attempts to materialize his ideals by loving "in the old high way," but, a man of his day, he is weary, a victim of Adam's curse. This is not to say that ideals of poetry, beauty, and love are not to be striven for, but they elude man in his imperfect condition; their constant elusiveness may make man weary of his attempts to "articulate sweet sounds."

QUESTIONS

1. Compare Yeats's handling of the heroic couplet with that of Pope's.
2. What elements of metrics and diction does Yeats employ to achieve an informal, conversational tone?
3. Describe the effect of enjambment in the poem.
4. What implicit observations does the poem make on the world of the poet's day?
5. What is the effect of calling one of the company "That beautiful mild woman"?
6. What progression do you detect in the poet's concluding thoughts in the final four lines?

When You Are Old

When you are old and grey and full of sleep,
And nodding by the fire, take down this book,
And slowly read, and dream of the soft look
4 Your eyes had once, and of their shadows deep;

How many loved your moments of glad grace,
And loved your beauty with love false or true,
But one man loved the pilgrim soul in you,
8 And loved the sorrows of your changing face;

And bending down beside the glowing bars,
Murmur, a little sadly, how Love fled
And paced upon the mountains overhead
12 And hid his face amid a crowd of stars.

A VIEW OF LOVE

In this poem Yeats's speaker compounds his passionless contemplation of
love to ask a former lover to remember, when she is old, how love once fled in
the past. The speaker reminds his former love, not that he had loved her only
in the flush of youth, but that he had "loved the sorrows of [her] changing face."
The correlative setting in this poem is a glowing fireplace to warm an old woman.

QUESTIONS

1. Describe the progression that the three stanzas make.
2. How is the speaker's love characterized by the phrase "loved the pilgrim
soul in you"?
3. What view of love is expressed in lines 10–12?
4. What is the effect of beginning so many of the lines with "and"?

Ephemera

"Your eyes that once were never weary of mine
Are bowed in sorrow under pendulous lids,
Because our love is waning."
                                    And then she:
5 "Although our love is waning, let us stand
By the lone border of the lake once more,
Together in that hour of gentleness
When the poor tired child, Passion, falls asleep:
How far away the stars seem, and how far
10 Is our first kiss, and ah, how old my heart!"
Pensive they paced along the faded leaves,
While slowly he whose hand held hers replied:
"Passion has often worn our wandering hearts."

The woods were round them, and the yellow leaves
15 Fell like faint meteors in the gloom, and once
A rabbit old and lame limped down the path;
Autumn was over him: and now they stood
On the lone border of the lake once more:
Turning, he saw that she had thrust dead leaves
20 Gathered in silence, dewy as her eyes,
In bosom and hair.
                         "Ah, do not mourn," he said,
That we are tired, for other loves await us;
Hate on and love through unrepining hours.
25 Before us lies eternity; our souls
Are love, and a continual farewell."

ANOTHER VIEW OF LOVE

Love is another kind of burden in this poem. Whereas in "Adam's Curse"
ideal love grows wearisome, in this poem passion is tiring. Both poems emphasize that love is a mutable experience, and something of the same world weariness
infects these lovers as well. Although many poets have dealt with the intensity
of first love, Yeats sometimes prefers to dramatize situations where love is over,
changed, or waning. Nostalgically, his lovers find themselves recounting the
pleasures of the past and indulgently bemoaning a passionless present. Again, as in
"Adam's Curse," the emotions of the lovers have natural correlatives—far away
stars, faded and falling leaves, and an old lame rabbit.

QUESTIONS

1. How does the title relate to the theme of the poem?
2. What is the cumulative effect of the adjectives used in the poem—"weary," "bowed," "pendulous," "waning," "lone," "tired," "old," "dead"?
3. How does the speaker's once beloved ornament herself appropriately in the dramatic situation?
4. What is the effect of the speaker's concluding comments?

When Helen Lived

We have cried in our despair
That men desert,
For some trivial affair
4 Or noisy, insolent, sport,
Beauty that we have won
From bitterest hours;
Yet we, had we walked within
8 Those topless towers
Where Helen walked with her boy,
Had given but as the rest
Of the men and women of Troy,
12 A word and a jest.

THE REAL AND THE IDEAL

Here Yeats compares an aspect of his own time with an attitude he ascribes to the Trojans of Homer's epic poem, the *Iliad*. The twelve-line poem is actually made up of three open quatrains, but Yeats has not treated them as three separate units. Lines 1 through 6 describe the present period, 7 through 12, Troy and Helen. The middle quatrain, then, is a transitional one; the first two lines serve to complete the opening quatrain syntactically, and the second two lines introduce the contrast between an age that cries out in despair and one that offered "a word and a jest" at a situation which led to the Trojans' ultimate destruction. Yeats characterizes his age as one in despair, for its small men have deserted its ideals for "trivial . . . insolent sport." The ideals, however, the beauty "won from bitterest hours," remain. It is not difficult to determine the speaker's attitude towards his country's despair.

QUESTIONS

1. What is the effect in line 9 of calling Paris Helen's "boy"?
2. How are the lines of varying length used in the poem?

No Second Troy

Why should I blame her that she filled my days
With misery, or that she would of late
Have taught to ignorant men most violent ways,
4   Or hurled the little streets upon the great,
Had they but courage equal to desire?
What could have made her peaceful with a mind
That nobleness made simple as a fire,
8   With beauty like a tightened bow, a kind
That is not natural in an age like this,
Being high and solitary and most stern?
Why, what could she have done, being what she is?
12 Was there another Troy for her to burn?

NOTE Yeats was a violently nationalistic poet, and when he was young he fell in love with Maud Gonne, a ravishing beauty involved in Irish revolutionary movements directed against England. Yeats proposed to her several times and each time she refused.

QUESTIONS

1. What is the function of the metonymy in line 4?
2. How does the speaker characterize his countrymen associated with the lady?
3. How are the similes in lines seven and eight appropriate?
4. Explain the meaning of the title and its relationship to the last line of the poem.
5. Describe how the speaker's monologue progresses from quatrain to quatrain.

To a Shade

If you have revisited the town, thin Shade,
Whether to look upon your monument
(I wonder if the builder has been paid)
4   Or happier-thoughted when the day is spent
To drink of that salt breath out of the sea
When grey gulls flit about instead of men,
And the gaunt houses put on majesty:
8   Let these content you and be gone again;
For they are at their old tricks yet.

                            A man
Of your own passionate serving kind who had brought
In his full hands what, had they only known,
12   Had given their children's children loftier thought,
Sweeter emotion, working in their veins
Like gentle blood, has been driven from the place,
And insult heaped upon him for his pains,
16   And for his open-handedness, disgrace;
Your enemy, an old foul mouth, had set
The pack upon him.
                            Go, unquiet wanderer,
20   And gather the Glasnevin* coverlet   *a Dublin cemetery*
About your head till the dust stops your ear,
The time for you to taste of that salt breath
And listen at the corners has not come;
24   You had enough of sorrow before death—
Away, away! You are safer in the tomb.

NOTES   The shade addressed in the poem is that of Charles Stewart Parnell, who died in 1891, and whose efforts were greatly responsible in gaining Irish independence. Because of a scandalous love affair, Parnell was repudiated by the Church, and ever since Irishmen have been torn between admiration of their hero and obedience to their Church.
     The other man mentioned in the poem (line 10) was Yeats's friend, Hugh Lane, an Irish art dealer who had hoped to introduce Ireland to French impressionist painting. Yeats undertook to champion Lane's many causes, political and artistic.
     "The old foul mouth" (line) 17 may have been William Martin Murphy, a newspaper publisher.

YEATS AND THE HERO

     This poem is one of Yeats's best expressions of his attitudes towards heroic men. The strain of disillusionment with his own people which runs through so much of his early poetry combines here with a sense of nostalgia and a quiet poignancy as he addresses the spirit of Ireland's lost leader. The people have quickly forgotten their hero and ignored both his monument and his ideals, but here the speaker's contempt for the people is overshadowed by his sympathy for Parnell. By putting his friend, Hugh Lane in company with Parnell, he honors his colleague with what may be Ireland's greatest compliment. Like Parnell, Lane lived only to serve, and for his sacrifices and patriotism he was betrayed. Ireland, the speaker implies, seems to deny those who love her best, preferring ignorance, stupidity, narrowness, and foul-mouthed leaders. Lane and Parnell offered her the way to majesty and nobility, but Ireland does not appear ready for greatness.
     The reverie concludes when the speaker dismisses Parnell's thin spirit, for he fears that what he must say is too much additional sorrow for the shade to endure. Poignantly Parnell is again denied by an Irishman, but this time he is denied to save him greater disillusionment.

1. How are Yeats's views organized in this poem? (How many lines are devoted to praising Parnell and Lane, and how many to condemning their enemies?)
2. Describe how each stanza reaches a climax and describe the progressive intensity of the climaxes, emphasizing especially the climax of stanza 3.
3. Point out an example of sarcastic irony. Why is the tone effective?
4. What is appropriate about the epithet "thin" (line 1)?
5. How would you describe the overall tone of this poem? What devices does Yeats employ to achieve this tone?
6. What is the effect of the realistic detail, especially the nature imagery?
7. To what extent are Yeats's views in this poem antidemocratic?

Sailing to Byzantium

I

That is no country for old men. The young
In one another's arms, birds in the trees,
—Those dying generations—at their song,
4 The salmon-falls, the mackerel-crowded seas,
Fish, flesh, or fowl, commend all summer long
Whatever is begotten, born, and dies.
Caught in that sensual music all neglect
8 Monuments of unageing intellect.

II

An aged man is but a paltry thing,
A tattered coat upon a stick, unless
Soul clap its hands and sing, and louder sing
12 For every tatter in its mortal dress,
Nor is there singing school but studying
Monuments of its own magnificence;
And therefore I have sailed the seas and come
16 To the holy city of Byzantium.

III

O sages standing in God's holy fire
As in the gold mosaic of a wall,
Come from the holy fire, perne in a gyre,
20 And be the singing-masters of my soul.
Consume my heart away; sick with desire
And fastened to a dying animal
It knows not what it is; and gather me
24 Into the artifice of eternity.

Once out of nature I shall never take
My bodily form from any natural thing,
But such a form as Grecian goldsmiths make
28 Of hammered gold and gold enamelling
To keep a drowsy Emperor awake;
Or set upon a golden bough to sing
To lords and ladies of Byzantium
32 Of what is past, or passing, or to come.

NOTES In lines 17 through 19 the speaker envisions the holy men of the Church portrayed in Byzantine mosaics; that is, they appear as deeply colored figures against a golden background. That golden background may include individual halos, and those halos Yeats metaphorizes as "God's holy fire." The figures in Byzantine art are highly stylized, not at all naturalistic.
　　To "perne in a gyre" is to move downwards in a spiral motion. The word "perne" may be from an old Irish word meaning spool.

YEATS IN AN IDEAL WORLD

For a poet whose poems had already rejected his countrymen and his country's narrow mindedness, "Sailing to Byzantium" is a natural culmination. In this poem Yeats commends himself to the world of art and artifice, which is symbolized for him in Byzantium. In "Sailing to Byzantium" an old man retreats completely from a world which neglects "monuments of unageing intellect." In opposition to the sensual music of the young, Yeats poses the soul music, or imaginative music, of his decaying body. An old man, he feels, cannot compete with sensual music, and in the mutable world he is a paltry thing. In the world of art, however, he can create monuments to the soul's magnificence, immortalizing the human imagination and singing of things immutable. For Yeats the whole aesthetic complex associated with Byzantium suggested that Byzantium was an ideal culture where immortal artifacts could be fashioned out of mortal circumstances and where man experienced at once the past, the present, and the future. In Byzantium the artist was formed in the image of things immortal, and that vision is sufficient consolation for an old man who feels he is worthless in a world dedicated to the young. In his ideal world, age is no longer significant, and men are measured and valued for their abilities to create things immortal, not things mutable.

In "Adam's Curse" Yeats retreated to the ideal of chivalric love, in "When Helen Lived" to the ideal of Trojan heroism, in "No Second Troy" to the ideal of supreme beauty, and in this poem he retreats to the glorious religious and artistic ideals of Byzantium (Constantinople) of the past. Whereas Keats in "Ode on a Grecian Urn" concluded that a life lived in an ideal world was too limiting and too restricting for an artist (especially for an artist in his twenties), for an old Yeats (in his sixties) such a life represented the ultimate experience.

1. Why does Yeats use the pronoun "that" instead of "this" in line 1?
2. How does the speaker characterize, in stanza one, the world he rejects?
3. In stanza one, what does the speaker contrast with the mutable world?
4. Why might the world of ancient Byzantium be particularly attractive for a speaker fleeing from the real to an ideal world?
5. Explain the effectiveness of the ellipses in stanza two.
6. Describe the appropriateness of the metaphor in line 10.
7. In what ways is Byzantium a "holy city"?
8. Trace the music imagery throughout the poem. How does it contribute to the structure of the poem?
9. Describe the opposition between nature and art in the poem.
10. What is the appropriateness of Yeats's audience in stanza four, in which he elects to sing to a "drowsy Emperor" or "lords and ladies" as a golden bird?

WHAT TO LOOK FOR IN THE ADDITIONAL READING

Here you will find some examples of how Yeats treats the conventional ballad form. Remember that a ballad is a short narrative form, usually in quatrains (ballad measure), and often about a tragic love affair. Balladeers seldom comment upon or interpret the action they describe. You will wish to compare Yeats's handling of this traditional form with that of Wordsworth and Keats. Yeats, as you have seen in your preceding reading, is a skillful love poet, and three of his carefully phrased love lyrics are included in the additional reading. Probably one of the most well known of Yeats's poems is the one entitled "The Second Coming." Yeats was as convinced in the twentieth century as Donne was in the seventeenth that "the centre cannot hold." Both poets strongly believed that the forces of chaos and anarchy were the dominant forces in the world. Where Ben Jonson looked out and saw evenness, and symmetry, and harmony, Donne and Yeats saw only asymmetry and cacophony. Donne found his refuge in Christianity and its promise of eventual contentment; Yeats found his hope in art and in the artist's song. At least there he could create an object removed from the dislocations and mutability of the temporal world and patterned after unageing monuments of the intellect. Although in many poems it may appear that Yeats and Donne saw their respective worlds in a similar way, Yeats's affinities with Ben Jonson are no less strong, especially in his intimate poem, "A Prayer for My Daughter." Although we remember that Ben Jonson has a famous stanza beginning "Tis not growing like a tree", here Yeats hopes his daughter will remember "a flourishing, hidden tree . . . rooted in one dear perpetual place." But it is Yeats's insistence in the final stanza on custom and ceremony that makes him sound like his fellow-poet of over three hundred years ago. Jonson would have agreed that innocence and beauty, that all proportion and all order—all which is ideal—depend upon custom and ceremony. The more poetry one reads, the more one is convinced that the works of poets make up a kind of continual and many-voiced dialogue.

The Ballad of Father Gilligan

The old priest Peter Gilligan
Was weary night and day;
For half his flock were in their beds,
4 Or under green sods lay.

Once, while he nodded on a chair,
At the moth-hour of eve,
Another poor man sent for him,
8 And he began to grieve.

"I have no rest, nor joy, nor peace,
For people die and die";
And after cried he, "God forgive!
12 My body spake, not I!"

He knelt, and leaning on the chair
He prayed and fell asleep;
And the moth-hour went from the fields,
16 And stars began to peep.

They slowly into millions grew,
And leaves shook in the wind;
And God covered the world with shade,
20 And whispered to mankind.

Upon the time of sparrow-chirp
When moths came once more,
The old priest Peter Gilligan
24 Stood upright on the floor.

"Mavrone, mavrone! the man has died
While I slept on the chair";
He roused his horse out of its sleep,
28 And rode with little care.

He rode now as he never rode,
By rocky lane and fen;
The sick man's wife opened the door:
32 "Father! you come again!"

"And is the poor man dead?" he cried.
"He died an hour ago."
The old priest Peter Gilligan
36 In grief swayed to and fro.

"When you were gone, he turned and died
As merry as a bird."
The old priest Peter Gilligan
40 He knelt him at that word.

"He Who hath made the night of stars
For souls who tire and bleed,
Sent one of His great angels down
44 To help me in my need.

"He Who is wrapped in purple robes,
With planets in His care,
Had pity on the least of things
48 Asleep upon a chair."

The Fiddler of Dooney

When I play on my fiddle in Dooney,
Folk dance like a wave of the sea;
My cousin is priest in Kilvarnet,
4 My brother in Mocharabuiee.

I passed my brother and cousin:
They read in their books of prayer;
I read in my books of songs
8 I bought at the Sligo fair.

When we come at the end of time
To Peter sitting in state,
He will smile on the three old spirits,
12 But call me first through the gate;

For the good are always the merry,
Save by an evil chance,
And the merry love the fiddle,
16 And the merry love to dance:

And when the folk there spy me,
They will all come up to me,
With "Here is the fiddler of Dooney!"
20 And dance like a wave of the sea.

He Gives His Beloved Certain Rhymes

Fasten your hair with a golden pin,
And bind up every wandering tress;
I bade my heart build these poor rhymes:
It worked at them, day out, day in,
5   Building a sorrowful loveliness
Out of the battles of old times.

You need but lift a pearl-pale hand,
And bind up your long hair and sigh;
And all men's hearts must burn and beat;
10   And candle-like foam on the dim sand,
And stars climbing the dew-dropping sky,
Live but to light your passing feet.

A Poet To His Beloved

I bring you with reverent hands
The books of my numberless dreams,
White woman that passion has worn
4   As the tide wears the dove-grey sands,
And with heart more old than the horn
That is brimmed from the pale fire of time:
White woman with numberless dreams,
8   I bring you my passionate rhyme.

He Wishes His Beloved Were Dead

Were you but lying cold and dead,
And lights were paling out of the West,
You would come hither, and bend your head,
4   And I would lay my head on your breast;
And you would murmur tender words,
Forgiving me, because you were dead:
Nor would you rise and hasten away,
8   Though you have the will of the wild birds,
But know your hair was bound and wound
About the stars and moon and sun:
O would, beloved, that you lay
12   Under the dock-leaves in the ground,
While lights were paling one by one.

The Second Coming

Turning and turning in the widening gyre
The falcon cannot hear the falconer;
Things fall apart; the centre cannot hold;
Mere anarchy is loosed upon the world,
5 The blood-dimmed tide is loosed, and everywhere
The ceremony of innocence is drowned;
The best lack all conviction, while the worst
Are full of passionate intensity.

Surely some revelation is at hand;
10 Surely the Second Coming is at hand.
The Second Coming! Hardly are those words out
When a vast image out of Spiritus Mundi
Troubles my sight: somewhere in sands of the desert
A shape with lion body and the head of a man,
15 A gaze blank and pitiless as the sun,
Is moving its slow thighs, while all about it
Reel shadows of the indignant desert birds.
The darkness drops again; but now I know
That twenty centuries of stony sleep
20 Were vexed to nightmare by a rocking cradle,
And what rough beast, its hour come round at last,
Slouches towards Bethlehem to be born?

A Prayer for My Daughter

Once more the storm is howling, and half hid
Under this cradle-hood and coverlid
My child sleeps on. There is no obstacle
4 But Gregory's wood and one bare hill
Whereby the haystack—and roof-levelling wind,
Bred on the Atlantic, can be stayed;
And for an hour I have walked and prayed
8 Because of the great gloom that is in my mind.

I have walked and prayed for this young child an hour
And heard the sea-wind scream upon the tower,
And under the arches of the bridge, and scream
12 In the elms above the flooded stream;
Imagining in excited reverie
That the future years had come,
Dancing to a frenzied drum,
16 Out of the murderous innocence of the sea.

May she be granted beauty and yet not
Beauty to make a stranger's eye distraught,
Or hers before a looking-glass, for such,
20 Being made beautiful overmuch,
Consider beauty a sufficient end,
Lose natural kindness and maybe
The heart-revealing intimacy
24 That chooses right, and never find a friend.

Helen being chosen found life flat and dull
And later had much trouble from a fool,
While that great Queen, that rose out of the spray,
28 Being fatherless could have her way
Yet chose a bandy-legged smith for man.
It's certain that fine women eat
A crazy salad with their meat
32 Whereby the Horn of Plenty is undone.

In courtesy I'd have her chiefly learned;
Hearts are not had as a gift but hearts are earned
By those that are not entirely beautiful;
36 Yet many, that have played the fool
For beauty's very self, has charm made wise,
And many a poor man that has roved,
Loved and thought himself beloved,
40 From a glad kindness cannot take his eyes.

May she become a flourishing hidden tree
That all her thoughts may like the linnet be,
And have no business but dispensing round
44 Their magnanimities of sound,
Nor but in merriment begin a chase,
Nor but in merriment a quarrel.
O may she live like some green laurel
48 Rooted in one dear perpetual place.

My mind, because the minds that I have loved,
The sort of beauty that I have approved,
Prosper but little, has dried up of late,
52 Yet knows that to be choked with hate
May well be of all evil chances chief.
If there's no hatred in a mind
Assault and battery of the wind
56 Can never tear the linnet from the leaf.

An intellectual hatred is the worst,
So let her think opinions are accursed.
Have I not seen the loveliest woman born
60 Out of the mouth of Plenty's horn,
Because of her opinionated mind
Barter that horn and every good
By quiet natures understood
64 For an old bellows full of angry wind?

Considering that, all hatred driven hence,
The soul recovers radical innocence
And learns at last that it is self-delighting,
68 Self-appeasing, self-affrighting,
And that its own sweet will is Heaven's will;
She can, though every face should scowl
And every windy quarter howl
72 Or every bellows burst, be happy still.

And may her bridegroom bring her to a house
Where all's accustomed, ceremonious;
For arrogance and hatred are the wares
76 Peddled in the thoroughfares.
How but in custom and in ceremony
Are innocence and beauty born?
Ceremony's a name for the rich horn,
80 And custom for the spreading laurel tree.

TOPICS FOR WRITING AND DISCUSSION

FOR USE IN CLASS

1. "He Wishes His Beloved Were Dead" is a strange love poem. Write an essay in which you discuss the nature of the poem.

2. Discuss Yeats's attitude towards his poetry in "He Gives His Beloved Certain Rhymes" or "A Poet to His Beloved."

3. What qualities does Yeats pray for in "A Prayer for My Daughter"? How are those qualities defined in the poem?

FOR PREPARATION OUTSIDE OF CLASS

1. Write an essay describing Yeats's attitude towards his own time, concentrating especially upon "The Second Coming."
2. Write an essay on Yeats's use of the ballad form.
3. Compare Yeats and Browning as love poets.
4. Discuss Yeats's views on the relationship of the hero to the masses, based on the views in this collection of his poetry.

Terms Used in the Discussions of Poetry

Note: The definitions of the literary terms here have been specially edited after their selection for this volume from the more comprehensive *A Student's Guide to Literary Terms*, by James G. Taaffe (T1186 of the World Publishing Company's *New World Language and Linguistics Series*).

Alliteration: The repetition of a sound, usually the initial sound and most often a consonant, in words of one line or of successive lines of verse.

Allusion: Indirect reference to an event, person, thing, place or quality. An allusion may serve, by suggestion, to extend the significance of a poetic image.

Ambiguity: The use of a word, phrase, sentence, or passage with two or more separate, often contradictory, meanings in such a way that the sense of the statement remains in doubt.

Analogy: A similarity in some respects between things otherwise unlike; a partial resemblance.

Anapest: A metrical unit, or foot, of three syllables, two unaccented followed by one accented.

Apostrophe: Words addressed to one or more persons or things generally in an exclamatory tone.

Apotheosis: The act of making a god of a person; a glorification.

Archetypal: Literally, the original pattern, the model from which all similar things were made. The term designates a concept held by a group of modern critics who contend that certain poems evoke strong reactions from us because of the relationships we feel to the archetypes inherent in their imagery. For instance, a strong reaction to a rising and falling pattern is said to reflect our feelings about the archetypes of the pattern, birth and death.

Argument: A short statement of subject matter, or a summary of material that is to follow.

Assonance: A kind of partial rhyme characterized by correspondence of vowel sounds but not of consonants (e.g., lady – Baby).

Atmosphere: A pervasive color or tone of a literary work; the term is used especially to characterize the air of a narrative poem (e.g., a fateful atmosphere).

Ballad: A narrative poem, characteristically in simple diction and short stanzas with a refrain. Often the refrain line will be significantly modified as the ballad proceeds.

Blank verse: Unrhymed iambic pentameter.

Cadence: Measured movement; a poet's cadences can fall into any of several patterns (pentameter, hexameter, etc.)

Caesura: A pause in the verse rhythm.

Circle metaphor: A figure of speech in which the imagery suggests a circular or spiral pattern.

Cliché: A trite expression; a platitude.

Closed quatrain: A four-line stanza with a rhyme scheme *abba*.

Connotation: Specific associations carried by words apart from their literal meaning.

Consonance: The harmony, congruity, or rhyme which occurs when vowel sounds differ and final consonantal sounds agree (e.g., call – pull).

Correlative: Reciprocally dependent; a scene, image, pattern, sound, etc., closely related to something else.

Couplet: Two successive verses of the same length and meter, usually with end rhyme.

Denotation: The direct, explicit meaning or reference of a word or term, as distinguished from its connotations.

Diction: A writer's vocabulary; his choice of particular words and phrases over others.

Dramatic situation: The situation, background, environment, or occasion of a poem.

Elegy: A poem of lament and praise of the dead.

Elision: The omission or slurring over of a vowel or other sound to make the meter smoother; often found with *the* as in *th'house* with the result that two sounds become one.

Ellipsis: The omission of a word or words necessary for complete grammatical construction but understood in context.

Encomium: A poem of tribute and commendation; a work in praise of a person or event.

Enjambment: The omission of a pause at the end of a line; the running of a sentence from one verse into the next.

Epic poem: A long, dignified, formal narrative poem celebrating the exploits of a folk or national hero, frequently including warfare, supernatural events, and a setting involving heaven, hell, and earth.

Epigram: A succinct, terse, often witty saying or a brief satirical poem.

Epitaph: A short composition in verse or prose in honor of someone who has died; from the Greek, "upon the stone."

Euphemism: The use of a word or expression considered less offensive, less blunt and harsh, than another (e.g., "passed away" for "died").

Feminine ending: An alternate term for *feminine rhyme.*

Feminine rhyme: Rhyme of two or three syllables, of which only the first is accented (e.g., fashion – passion).

Foot: In prosody, the unit of meter, consisting of two or more syllables (occasionally, a single syllable) with a given accentual pattern. Commonly a foot has one accented syllable and one or two unaccented syllables in a specified order.

Genre: Literally, from the French, a class or kind,—hence, a literary type with its conventions and traditions (e.g., the *essay* is a prose genre).

Gloss: A note or comment upon textual material, or a collection of such notes.

Heroic couplet: Two verses of end-rhymed iambic pentameter.

Homophone: One of two or more words pronounced alike but different in meaning (e.g. to, too, two).

Hyperbole: Exaggeration for effect (e.g., "I could eat a horse").

Iamb: In prosody, a metrical unit composed of two syllables, one unaccented followed by one accented.

Image: An image may be a figure of speech, a simile or metaphor, or a simple visual and physical matter, as in a poem whose printed lines actually are arranged in a definite shape (e.g., a pillar or a bird). A poem may present all its attitudes in terms of specific flowers or birds, or it may abound in figurative reference to human organs like the heart or eye. Such references are part of the imagery.

Irony: Verbal irony is a method of expression, sometimes humorous or sarcastic, in which the intended meaning of the words used is the direct opposite of their usual sense. Dramatic irony or irony of situation is a combination of circumstances or a result that is the opposite of what might be expected or considered appropriate.

Italian sonnet: A fourteen-line iambic pentameter poem, divided into two sections: the *octave*, lines 1–8, rhyming *abba, abba;* and the *sestet*, lines 9–14, rhyming *cde, cde;* often, however, the rhyme scheme of the sestet varies (e.g., *cd, cd, cd*).

Jeu d'esprit: The term is often used to characterize a poem or a section of a poem which appears playful and spirited, "tossed off" as if it were in the mood of a game.

Literary ballad: An attempt to imitate the folk ballad. See *Ballad.*

Lyric: Originally something "from the lyre"; now an inclusive term for a poem expressing a personal emotion revealing something of the speaker's sentiment rather than emphasizing an external event for its own sake.

Mask (or Masque): A formal, aristocratic entertainment combining poetry, music, song, and dance with masked players; often, in the sixteenth and seventeenth centuries in England, very lavish and expensive masks were produced.

Metaphor: A figure of speech in which one thing is likened to a different thing and spoken of as if it were that other.

Metaphysical conceit: An ingenious comparison between two dissimilar things (e.g., tears and coins), characteristic of the poetry of John Donne. We are asked to recognize and be aware of both aspects of the comparison, the point of likeness and that of unlikeness as well.

Meter: The number and pattern of accented and unaccented syllables in a verse, stanza or poem.

Metonymy: A figure of speech in which a word or phrase is substituted for some other term that is closely associated with it or that suggests it (e.g., "bones" for "body").

Mode: A particular variety or form of something, the form or manner of expression.

Modulation: A musical term indicative of a variation in pitch or in the intensity of the voice; hence, a variation or change in *tone* of a literary work.

Monody: A synonym for *Elegy.*

Motif: A theme, image, phrase or word which usually accompanies a situation, place, character, etc., and whose repeated use forms a kind of pattern in the literary work.

Occasional poem: A poem written to celebrate a specific event.

Ode: A long, formal poem with an elaborate stanza form; also any long serious poem on the arts, on friends or patrons.

Open quatrain: A four-line stanza rhyming *abab.*

Oxymoron: A figure of speech in which two contradictory terms are combined (e.g., "fiery ice" or "pleasant pain").

Paradox: A statement that seems contradictory, unbelievable, or absurd (e.g., "stone walls do not a prison make").

Paraphrase: A rewording of a thought or meaning expressed in a literary work, following the work closely, point by point.

Parody: A work imitating and exaggerating the characteristic style or substance of a work or author in order to ridicule some aspect or make fun of the work as a whole.

Pastoral poetry: Poetry portraying a stylized, idealized form of country life and usually concentrating on romance and the debate over the relative value of city or country. The term literally means "of shepherds," and pastoral figures often abound in such poetry.

Pun: The usually humorous use of words which are formed or sounded alike but have different meanings.

Pentameter: A line of any five metrical units (e.g., iambic pentameter).

Persona: The personality or voice assumed by the poet (e.g. outraged lover, deserted shepherd, deranged artist).

Quatrain: A stanza of four lines.

Rhyme: The regular recurrence of corresponding sounds, especially at the ends of lines. In the strict sense, rhyme exists when the last accented vowel and all succeeding sounds are identical in two or more words.

Romance: A verse or prose narrative, usually a love story, featuring high adventure, wonderful or supernatural events, etc.

Satire: A literary work in which the vices, follies, stupidities, abuses, etc., of men are held up to ridicule and contempt.

Scan: To analyze verse into its rhythmic components, scansion marks are ′ or ‾ for an accented syllable, ∪ or × for an unaccented syllable, / for a foot division, and ‖ for the *caesura.*

Spenserian stanza: A nine-line stanza, eight iambic pentameter lines followed by one line of iambic hexameter, rhyming *ababbcbcc* (named for Edmund Spenser, 1552–1599).

Stanza: Several verses, two or more, in a recurrent pattern with respect to their number, meter, and rhyme.

Stasis: A state of balance or equilibrium.

Symbol: Any concrete device used to represent something, especially something abstract.

Syntax: The way in which words are put together to form phrases and clauses.

Tercet: A stanza of three lines, with or without end rhyme.

Tetrameter: A line of four metrical units (e.g., iambic tetrameter).

Theme: The topic, or subject, of a literary work; or a succinct formulation expressing the subject (e.g., the theme of *Macbeth* may be said to be, "Ambition doth outrun the pauser Reason").

Tone: A manner of speaking or writing that reveals a certain attitude on the part of the speaker or writer to his subject, as admiration, contempt, amusement, etc.

Trimeter: A line of three metrical units (e.g., iambic trimeter).

Understatement: A figure of speech in which something is expressed by a negation of the contrary (e.g., "not a few were missing" meaning "many were lost"). Chaucer has numerous examples; about the fat Prioress he writes, "She was not undergrown."

Verse: A single line of poetry; also used generally as a synonym for metrical composition.

Biographical Sketches

WILLIAM SHAKESPEARE (1564–1616) was born and educated at Stratford-on-Avon, where he married Anne Hathaway, the daughter of a prosperous local farmer. Some time before 1592 he moved to London and began a successful career in the theater. His career as a sonneteer had begun by 1598, for a published reference was made to his sonnets by this date. Scholars have conjectured variously about the persons to whom the sonnets may have been addressed. (The sonnets divide themselves into two groups—1 to 126 addressed to a fair young man, and 127 to 154 addressed to a "dark lady" who casts a spell over both the young man and the poet.) Whether or not the persons addressed in the sonnets were a part of Shakespeare's life, this sequence of poems may be appreciated and admired as, perhaps, the supreme expression in this verse form.

BEN JONSON (1572–1637) was born at Westminster, where he received his education under Camden, immortalized in Jonson's poetic tribute. After a traditionally classical education at Westminster School and perhaps at Cambridge, Jonson did a variety of work before turning to a career in the theater. His plays, modestly successful in their time, are not so often performed today as Shakespeare's, but *Volpone*, a satire on sensuality and greed, is probably the most often revived. To many modern readers, Jonson's lyric genius equals his ability as a playwright; and his verse letters, addressed to the learned and the courtly, are a mirror of his society. Besides his plays, lyrics and verse letters, Jonson in his published work proved himself to be a critic and classical scholar of merit. The writers of his day looked upon Jonson as their poet laureate.

JOHN DONNE (1573–1631) was born into a prosperous London family, and was educated at Oxford and Cambridge. He began a career in public life before falling early into disfavor among the powerful. Born a Catholic, Donne switched his allegiance to the established faith, and after a long period of uncertainty, he took orders in the Anglican Church. Although he had already written his *Songs and Sonnets* and other poems, Donne published no poetry until 1611, and most of his great poems were not published until after his death. Like Jonson, he courted the great in verse letters. Under the sponsorship of King James, Donne turned away from a legal career and entered the Church in 1614. He was advanced to the Deanship of St. Paul's in 1621. Donne's sermons, which survive, were immensely popular. In his early career, Donne wrote verse of startling realism and passion, including the *Songs and Sonnets;* in his second period he wrote his verse letters; and in his third period, after his ordination, he wrote his *Holy Sonnets*. Donne's early poetry showed him to be very much of the world, and when he transferred his allegiance to God, his passion was not abated.

JOHN MILTON (1608-1674) was the son of a London scrivener and composer, who discovered his son's genius early. After attending St. Paul's School and Cambridge, Milton spent six years in study to prepare for the writing of poetry, a career to which he had early dedicated himself. His "L'Allegro" and "Il Penseroso" and his other apprentice work at Cambridge he considered preparation for his greater task in *Paradise Lost*. Milton concluded his systematic education with a trip to Italy in 1638-39, which was interrupted by a civil war in England. He settled in London as a tutor for his nephews, and for twenty years, except for occasional sonnets, he dedicated himself to public life, using his pen to support the Commonwealth. He rose to become the official apologist for the Commonwealth under Cromwell. Although he was blind after 1652, Milton continued in his government job until shortly before the Restoration. During his blindness he dictated his epic poem *Paradise Lost*, followed by his other long work, *Paradise Regained*.

ALEXANDER POPE (1688-1744) was born into a Catholic family of London. As a result of a childhood illness, he was deformed from the age of twelve. His religion limited his formal schooling, but he made up for the religious handicap on his education by independent reading. In London, at the beginning of his career, he was encouraged by a fashionable and witty group of writers, including Wycherley and Congreve. His first literary work was welcomed by powerful figures in society. Pope immersed himself in politics and literary vendettas; in his day political considerations colored everything in prominent society. Conservative in his views of society and politics, Pope satirized that which was faddish, new, or, by some, considered progressive. Through his satirical verse, Pope popularized some of the learning of his day and devastated sham and hypocrisy. Having attacked the great in his satire and having taken an active part in political quarreling, Pope in his old age was depressed by the abuse of his enemies, together with the ill health which had plagued him all his life.

WILLIAM BLAKE (1757-1827) was born in London, the son of a hosier. He was apprenticed to an engraver, and after studying at the Royal Academy, he produced water colors and engravings. His two volumes, *Songs of Innocence* (1789) and *Songs of Experience* (1794), are a blending of both the finest lyric poetry and of the illustrator's art. He designed, illustrated, and wrote a number of mystical volumes, which lack the universal appeal of his lyrics. Besides his book illustrations, Blake produced some widely admired paintings in tempera, but his most successful pictures were his religious illustrations for the Book of Job, published when he was nearly seventy. During his lifetime, Blake was not recognized by the public; only a small circle of admirers encouraged him in his work. Throughout his life, as in his writings, Blake was a mystic, and he believed himself visited and guided by forces from the spirit world.

WILLIAM WORDSWORTH (1770–1850) lost both parents at an early age and grew up in the Lake District, a formative period of his life described in his long autobiographical poem, *The Prelude*. He attended Cambridge where he fell under the influence of agnostic and revolutionary ideas. He visited France in 1790, enthusiastic about its revolution in the early stages; he was later to be disillusioned over the direction the revolution took. Wordsworth returned home in 1793 after England's declaration of war against France. With the collaboration of Coleridge, he discovered his vocation of writing poetry about humble folk living close to nature. The *Lyrical Ballads* (1798), published in collaboration with Coleridge, was a manifesto of the new poetry of the nineteenth century. Later Napoleon's despotism discouraged Wordsworth's revolutionary sympathies, and he wrote numerous patriotic and religious sonnets. He received recognition as England's poet laureate in 1843.

JOHN KEATS (1795–1821) was born the son of a London livery stable keeper. He was apprenticed to a surgeon in 1811, and later was a medical student in London hospitals. Although he did well as a medical student, he was more interested in the arts, and many of his friends were painters. After he was introduced to some prominent writers, including the poet Shelley, he published his first sonnets in 1816. Keats returned exhausted from a walking tour of Scotland in 1818, when family sorrows and an exasperating love affair made his life even more troublesome. By a supreme effort, despite his physical debility, he published in 1820 *Lamia and Other Poems*, a landmark in English poetry, which contained some of his greatest poetry. By the time he had prepared this volume for the press, he was seriously ill of tuberculosis, and he sailed for Italy to rest. He died in Rome at the age of twenty-six, having written in his few years some of the supreme poetry in our language.

ALFRED, LORD TENNYSON (1809–1892) was the son of the Rector of Lincolnshire. His elder brothers were both poets, and despite the early death of his father, Tennyson was somehow enabled to go to Trinity College, Cambridge. One of the men he met at Cambridge was Arthur Hallam, whose early death was mourned in the long elegiac poem, *In Memoriam*. His first public recognition came with his volume of poetry of 1833. In 1850 he succeeded Wordsworth as poet laureate, and thereafter experienced the homage of the English nation. His poetry flatteringly portrayed the England of Queen Victoria, and the morality of his day was imposed on his poetry, whether it dealt with his own time, ancient Greece, or legendary Camelot. He was buried in Westminster Abbey a fitting honor for a writer so dedicated to his country.

ROBERT BROWNING (1812–1889), son of a bank clerk, showed early his literary and artistic tastes; he was educated at University College and traveled abroad extensively. In 1833 he published a long dramatic poem, written at the age of nineteen. Although he won some recognition in literary circles with his poetry, he received little public attention until 1855 with his volume of poetry, *Men and Women*. In 1846 he married Elizabeth Barrett, a poet recognized more by the public than he was, and they lived in Florence. After the death of his wife in 1861, he settled in London and published his long epic poem, *The Ring and the Book*, in 1869. The realism, almost journalistic, which he incorporated in this long work is scattered throughout his poetry; it was welcomed in the poetry of his century. He, like his contemporary Tennyson, was buried in Westminster Abbey.

GERARD MANLY HOPKINS (1844–1889) was born in London and educated at Balliol College, Oxford, where he studied under some outstanding figures, including Jowett, Pater, and Pusey. He became a convert to Roman Catholicism in 1866, was later ordained, and in 1884 was appointed to the chair of Greek at Dublin University. None of his poems was published in his lifetime, and his friend and literary executor, Bridges, published in 1918 a full edition of Hopkins' work. Bridges in his introduction to Hopkins' poetry warned the reader against the oddity and obscurity in the poetry. In 1918 the reception of the poetry was mixed, but in 1930 with a new edition, the poems gained the approval of the foremost British critics and were praised as revolutionary writing. The publication of Hopkins' theory of poetry in his letters to Robert Bridges placed the poetry in a new and favorable light. Without doubt, Hopkins has had a substantial influence on modern poetry, but recent criticism tends to regard him not so much as a revolutionary writer, but a major poet, nonetheless.

WILLIAM BUTLER YEATS (1865–1939) was born near Dublin, the son of an artist. He was educated in Dublin and London as an art student, and developed an interest in occultism. In his early twenties, he turned from painting to writing. In 1893 he published an influential work, *The Celtic Twilight*, a title that labels a school of writing that attempted a renaissance of ancient Irish culture. He helped in the formation of an Irish National Theatre, and produced himself, several popular plays. His collected poems appeared in 1933. He was awarded the Nobel Prize in 1923. Yeats died in the south of France, but in 1948 he was re-interred in his native Ireland.

INDEX

This is my play's last scene; here heavens appoint, 41

This morning, timely rapt with holy fire, 29

This rich marble doth inter, 51

Thou art not, Penshurst, built to envious show, 21

Thou still unravished bride of quietness, 130

Thyrsis, the music of that murmuring spring, 69

'Tis the year's midnight, and it is the day's, 38

To mercy, pity, peace, and love, 98

To wake the soul by tender strokes of art, 90

Tonight, grave sir, both my poor house, and I, 26

Toussaint, the most unhappy man of men!, 126

Turning and turning in the widening gyre, 246

Two loves I have, of comfort and despair, 14

U

V

"Vallombrosa—I longed in thy shadiest wood, 117

Vane, young in years, but in sage counsel old, 64

Vanity, saith the preacher, vanity!, 207

Vex not thou the poet's mind, 160

W

We had a female passenger who came, 127

We have cried in our despair, 237

We sat together at one summer's end, 233

Weary with toil, I haste me to my bed, 11

Weep with me all you that read, 20

Were you but lying cold and dead, 245

What if this present were the world's last night?, 43

What needs my Shakespeare for his honored bones, 53

When daisies pied and violets blue, 9

When forty winters shall besiege thy brow, 2

When I consider everything that grows, 2

When I play on my fiddle in Dooney, 244

When I would know thee Goodyere, my thought looks, 28

When icicles hang by the wall, 9

When my mother died I was very young, 96

When the voices of children are heard on the green, 100, 100

When wise Ulysses, from his native coast, 86

Who shall doubt, Donne, where I a poet be, 28

Who will believe my verse in time to come, 4

Why didst thou promise such a beauteous day, 12